Is *Star Trek* Utopia?

# Is *Star Trek* Utopia?
## *Investigating a Perfect Future*

SEBASTIAN STOPPE

McFarland & Company, Inc., Publishers
*Jefferson, North Carolina*

*This book has undergone peer review.*

Originally published in Germany
as *Unterwegs zu neuen Welten: Star Trek als politische Utopie.*
Copyright © 2014 Büchner-Verlag eG, Darmstadt.

ISBN (print) 978-1-4766-8636-3
ISBN (ebook) 978-1-4766-4668-8

LIBRARY OF CONGRESS AND BRITISH LIBRARY
CATALOGUING DATA ARE AVAILABLE

Library of Congress Control Number 2022029087

© 2022 Sebastian Stoppe. All rights reserved

*No part of this book may be reproduced or transmitted in any form or by any means, electronic or mechanical, including photocopying or recording, or by any information storage and retrieval system, without permission in writing from the publisher.*

Front cover image by Victor Habbick Visions/Shutterstock

Printed in the United States of America

McFarland & Company, Inc., Publishers
Box 611, Jefferson, North Carolina 28640
*www.mcfarlandpub.com*

For my bridge crew
Katarina, Caspar, Jonathan, and Matteo

# Table of Contents

*Preface* 1

*Introduction: Why* Star Trek *Matters* 5

1. The Meaning of Utopia 11
2. How Technology Changes Society 41
3. Life in Space: Utopia on a Ship 57
4. Politics in *Star Trek* 73
5. Anti-Utopia: The Borg 125
6. Post-Utopia: Does *Star Trek* Become Darker? 141
7. How Utopian Is *Star Trek*? 158

*Chapter Notes* 165

*Works Cited* 175

*Index* 191

# Preface

I first became familiar with *Star Trek* as a teenager. Back then—in the early to middle 1990s—I saw *The Next Generation (TNG)* on TV for the first time. It was probably already a rerun because the first broadcast in Germany dates back to 1990. Of course, my first experience with this series was in German, because in Germany foreign TV series are typically always dubbed.

So, unlike the older generation, I did not grow up with *The Original Series (TOS)*, and for me, Captain Picard—and not Captain Kirk—was always the true hero of *Star Trek*. In the mid-nineties *Deep Space Nine (DS9)* and *Voyager (VOY)* were running on TV every weekday in the early afternoon, so for me, as a student, it was the perfect way to start the afternoon—coming home after school and watching the next episode. It happened that I gradually consumed all the episodes of *TNG* and most of *DS9* and *VOY*. Then the time slot changed, and the newest episodes were shown only on weekends. At this point, I became less involved with *Star Trek* for a while, but even later, in university, *Star Trek* never completely left me.

After finishing my studies in political science and media studies, I wanted to add a Ph.D. thesis, and while searching for a subject, I came across a hint on the website of a professor from my neighboring city Halle in Saxony-Anhalt, Germany, that he would supervise topics in the field of science fiction and utopia. It seemed like the ideal combination of my university majors and my passion for the franchise to investigate whether *Star Trek* might not be even more than science fiction, whether this franchise is not actually a large utopian narrative. In 2014, my Ph.D. thesis was eventually accepted at the Martin Luther University Halle-Wittenberg and was also published in Germany in the same year.

This book is a completely revised and updated version of my original thesis. Therefore, the text not only considers the English-language literature on *Star Trek* but also refers to German-language authors, especially in the chapter on utopia and science fiction. For better readability, I have translated direct quotations from German sources in this text without indicating this each time. In the bibliography, however, the original sources are all listed. A few sections—especially on methodology—have been omitted or shortened, while several other sections have been rewritten to take into account, on the one hand, more recent literature on *Star Trek*, and, on the other hand, the new series. For example, the final chapter, in which I deal with the latest incarnations of the franchise, namely *Discovery (DIS)* and *Picard (PIC)*, has been newly added.

The fascinating thing about *Star Trek* is that this franchise has not only existed for more than fifty years but also is constantly reinventing itself in multiple variations. Just as die-hard *TOS* fans looked at *TNG* with a certain amount of skepticism, many probably felt the same way about these new series—especially since they are no longer written in the classic episodic structure, but rather are told horizontally with overarching story arcs, adapted to the streaming age. But *Star Trek* has lost nothing of its relevance. On the contrary. In autumn 2019, I was invited to give a lecture on *Star Trek* at Leipzig University, Germany, at the so-called *Kinderuniversität* or Children's University. It is a lecture series that takes place four times a semester, each time with a different topic aimed specifically at children between the ages of eight and twelve. I am accustomed to giving lectures in very different settings, but a lecture hall with about 400 kids gave me the same respect I would have had if I were taking a final exam. I discussed the *TNG* episode "The Measure of a Man" from 1989, and to my astonishment, an absolutely serious and productive discussion came about with the kids on the subject of whether an android should have the same human rights that we do. I had not expected at all that I would be able to discuss this with children who were not even born when the episode had its premiere. This is just another indication of the immanently important topics that *Star Trek* has addressed and continues to address today.

There are a few acknowledgments for the English edition that I would like to make. I thank Angelika Bold for the suggestion that I publish my work in an English version. I was even more pleased that McFarland agreed to accept it, and I would like to thank my editor, Layla Milholen, for her competent and friendly support throughout the publication process.

In my last two years at school, I had an English teacher who is also a Trekkie himself, and it was then that he first showed me *TNG* in its original version on VHS. Neither DVDs nor the Internet were so widespread back then that you could have done this in Germany without further ado. I still remember that I was taken with Patrick Stewart's British accent and the so-different-sounding American English and understood only about half of the plot at that time. Fortunately, that has since changed, and that was probably due, at least in part, to Ralf Knackstedt's teaching. Many thanks for that! Thanks also to my dear friend Sascha Kummer for long conversations about *Star Trek* and in particular the recent installments *Discovery* and *Picard*. I would like to thank my parents Hella and Manfred Stoppe and my sister Franziska for enduring my obsession throughout all the years when I was still living at home and for even going to the movies with me back then.

My greatest thanks, however, go to Katarina and my sons Caspar, Jonathan, and Matteo. You are my support, my very true explorers of the universe, and my bridge crew I can rely on at all times. Or to say it with Data in *PIC* "Et in Arcadia Ego": "Knowing that you loved me formed a small, but statistically significant part of my memories."

# Introduction
## Why Star Trek Matters

*Star Trek* is a global phenomenon. It is not only a text that is known by people all over the world but also has been present for over 50 years, especially on television, but also in the movie theater. Because of this presence, *Star Trek* achieved a huge worldwide prominence in popular culture and a vast influence beyond television and cinema (Robb 2012, 271). "It has [...] become part of the identity of millions of people" (Robb 2012, 275).

The original television series, created by Gene Roddenberry, first aired in 1966 and initially ran for three seasons until 1969, before being cancelled due to poor ratings. This makes clear that *Star Trek*, despite its utopian view, was initially intended as an entertainment product. Herbert F. Solow, the head of the production company Desilu at that time, says: "Star Trek was not created or developed as a critical study of truth, life's fundamental principles, or concepts of reasoned doctrines. We just wanted a hit series" (Solow and Justman 1996, 431).

*Star Trek* is about the exploration and colonization of space by humankind, as is said at the beginning of every *The Original Series* episode: "Space: the final frontier. These are the voyages of the starship Enterprise. Its five-year mission: to explore strange new worlds, to seek out new life and new civilizations, to boldly go where no man has gone before." The first series, now known as *The Original Series (TOS)*, was followed, in 1973, by *Star Trek: The Animated Series (TAS)*—a short-lived animated series that was long considered noncanonical—and finally by the feature film *Star Trek: The Motion Picture* in 1979. This movie, in turn, was followed in 1982 by *Star Trek II: The Wrath of Khan*; in 1984 by *Star Trek III: The Search for Spock*; and in 1986 by *Star Trek IV: The Voyage Home*. After that, Gene Roddenberry conceived a new series for television, *Star Trek: The Next Generation (TNG)*, which was set after the time frame of *TOS*. *TNG* ran with a new cast from 1987 to 1994, significantly longer than its predecessor series, but was accompanied in parallel by two more films featuring the crew of the first series: *Star Trek V: The Final*

*Frontier* in 1989 and *Star Trek VI: The Undiscovered Country* in 1991. *TNG* also moved from television to cinema in 1994 with *Star Trek: Generations*. Another three movies with this cast have been produced, *Star Trek: First Contact* in 1996, *Star Trek: Insurrection* in 1998, and finally *Star Trek: Nemesis* in 2002.

The franchise remained present on television with three other spin-offs: *Star Trek: Deep Space Nine (DS9)* from 1993 to 1999, *Star Trek: Voyager (VOY)* from 1995 to 2001, and *Star Trek: Enterprise (ENT)* from 2001 to 2005. In 2009, the eleventh feature film, simply titled *Star Trek*, was released. This motion picture is again based on the characters of *TOS*, but it is set before the series and also in an alternate timeline. The sequels *Star Trek Into Darkness* and *Star Trek Beyond* were released in 2013 and 2016, respectively. In 2017, a new television series was launched for the first time with *Star Trek: Discovery (DIS)*. Also, the year 2018 saw the release of the short film anthology *Star Trek: Short Treks (ST)*, and 2020 saw the releases of the series *Star Trek: Picard (PIC)* and the second animated series called *Star Trek: Lower Decks (LD)*. With *DIS*, a wide-ranging expansion of the *Star Trek* universe was developed under executive producer Alex Kurtzman. The year 2021 saw the release of *Star Trek: Prodigy*, the third animated *Star Trek* series intended for a younger audience. In the same year, the fourth season of *DIS* and the second season of *LD* ran; a fifth and third season, respectively, are in production. In 2022, the second season of *PIC* ran (a third has already been shot) and *Star Trek: Strange New Worlds*, a spin-off of *DIS* starring Captain Pike and the *Enterprise*, was launched. Since work on this book was completed in the summer of 2021, these new episodes are not yet considered in the text.

*Star Trek* follows a fairly strict fictional chronology. The feature film *Star Trek: First Contact* takes place for the most part in the year 2063 (when the Earth's very first contact with another species happens). In *ENT* "Broken Bow," the year 2151 is established, so that the further seasons of *Enterprise* thus cover the years 2152 to 2155. *TOS* takes place about 100 years after *ENT*, while *TNG* again takes place about 100 years after *TOS*. Sternbach and Okuda state the date of commissioning of the *Enterprise*-D as October 4, 2363 (1991, 17). The events in *DS9* and *VOY* largely overlap in time with *TNG*, from 2369 to 2378. The table shows the timeline of the *Star Trek* universe (see pages 8–9).

This book endeavors to explore the fundamental question of whether the *Star Trek* franchise can be seen as a utopian text rather than "just" science fiction. If *Star Trek* is a utopia, it should represent a certain philosophy. But is there really such a philosophy that points beyond the *Star Trek* universe? Are we confronted with a possible future image of society in the *Star Trek* universe, even possibly a utopian blueprint for society?

## Introduction

To begin, my main assumptions are the following.

1. A utopia attempts to describe—always mirroring the present—an ideal form of power and society, in which difficulties that exist in the present are finally overcome. Science fiction, on the other hand, focuses on technical and scientific innovations that open up new possibilities for humanity in terms of research and the discovery of new worlds.
2. *Star Trek* is based on fundamental considerations and ideas that can already be found in the early utopias.
3. New technologies always have implications for the political and social system in which a society finds itself and cannot simply be reduced to technological progress.
4. Spaceships are the dominant structures within which political and social life is organized in *Star Trek*.
5. *Star Trek* formulates a new social order with the United Federation of Planets as the authoritative political institution and Starfleet as the authoritative executive. This social structure is organized hierarchically.
6. However, within *Star Trek*, there are other types of societies, like the Borg, that threaten the utopian idea of the Federation.
7. Finally, in the whole narrative, *Star Trek* always makes references to the present in which the series and films were created. This begins with the 1960s for *TOS* to the end of the Cold War (as in *TNG*) to the transformation period of the 1990s (*DS9*, *VOY* and *ENT*) and further extends to the post–2000 era in the newer films and series.

In the following chapter, I will first discuss what distinguishes a utopian text from science fiction by contrasting classical utopias and scifi. What meaningful conceptual distinction can be made? What ideas found in early modern utopias does *Star Trek* reference? Which ideal concepts are taken up again, and where can parallels be found?

Then, in subsequent chapters, I first discuss the representation of technology in *Star Trek* and its relevance for a utopian ideal. Second, I show how a utopian society manifests itself in *Star Trek* by using the starship as a model world. Third, I discuss the negotiation of political and social issues in *Star Trek*.

In the last two chapters, I look at certain elements within *Star Trek* as a possible anti-utopia: first, it is about the society of the Borg and how it differs from that of the Federation. Second, it is about *Star Trek* in the post–2000 era. With the reboot movies and the new series like *DIS* and *PIC*, is the image of a perfect utopia changing?

**Table 1: Timeline of *Star Trek***

|  |  |
|---|---|
| 2063 | *Star Trek: First Contact* |
| 2151 | *Star Trek: Enterprise* (ENT) |
| 2152 | |
| 2153 | |
| 2154 | |
| 2155 | |
| 2254 | TOS: The Cage |
| 2256 | *Star Trek: Discovery* (DIS) (seasons 1 and 2) |
| 2257 | |
| 2258 | |
| 2265 | *Star Trek: The Original Series* (TOS) |
| 2267 | |
| 2268 | |
| 2269 | *Star Trek: The Animated Series* (TAS) |
| 2270 | |
| 2271 | *Star Trek: The Motion Picture* |
| 2285 | *Star Trek II: The Wrath of Khan* / *Star Trek III: The Search for Spock* |
| 2286 | *Star Trek IV: The Voyage Home* |
| 2287 | *Star Trek V: The Final Frontier* |

## Introduction

|  | | | | |
|---|---|---|---|---|
| 2293 | *Star Trek VI: The Undiscovered Country* | *Star Trek: Generations (prologue)* | | |
| 2364 | | | | |
| 2365 | | | | |
| 2366 | | *Star Trek: The Next Generation (TNG)* | | |
| 2367 | | | | |
| 2368 | | | | |
| 2369 | | | | |
| 2370 | | | | |
| 2371 | | *Star Trek: Generations* | *Star Trek: Deep Space Nine (DS9)* | *Star Trek: Voyager (VOY)* |
| 2372 | | | | |
| 2373 | | *Star Trek: First Contact* | | |
| 2374 | | | | |
| 2375 | | *Star Trek: Insurrection* | | |
| 2376 | | | | |
| 2377 | | | | |
| 2378 | | | | |
| 2379 | | *Star Trek: Nemesis* | | |
| 2380 | | *Star Trek: Lower Decks (LD)* | | |
| 2399 | | *Star Trek: Picard (PIC)* | | |
| 3188 | | *Star Trek: Discovery (DIS) (season 3)* | | |
| 3189 | | | | |

# 1

# The Meaning of Utopia

## Utopia as a Literary Genre

*Star Trek* is generally regarded as a work of science fiction. Nichols and Brosnan, for example, classify *TOS* as a "phenomenon among sf tv series" (1993, 1156), which "rarely departed from sf stereotypes, though in its first 2 seasons it was certainly adequate and even quite strong relative to much televised sf" (1993, 1157). Nichols, however, interestingly limits his view of *Star Trek* with regard to *TNG*: "It could be said that *ST:TNG* is not really sf at all" (1993, 1159). Is *Star Trek*, if not science fiction, then possibly a utopia? What is it a utopian text and how can we distinguish utopian texts from that of science fiction?

The literary genre of utopia derives from Thomas More's *Utopia*, which gave its name to the whole genre. In his work, More reports on an ideal-typical society that is located in a distant, mostly inaccessible place. The term "utopia" is formed from the Greek "ou" and "topos," and can be roughly translated as "non-place" or "nowhere."[1] That means that Utopia exists "as specific place even though its reality or location may be uncertain" (Pintér 2010, 14). For example, islands are a preferred location on which utopian societies are placed (Biesterfeld 1982, 16).

However, there is hardly a general definition of what a utopia is. "It was only gradually that the concept of utopia broke away from the work of Thomas More and became, on the one hand, the designation of a literary genre, the utopian state novel, [...] on the other hand, even with the detachment from the unique literary work, such an expansion of the concept took place that a uniform definition became impossible" (Gnüg 1999, 9). Right at the beginning of her book, Levitas puts it straight, saying that "utopia is about how we would live and what kind of a world we would live in if we could just do that" (2011, 1). However, Freyer points out in his work that it "must seem almost impossible to find a universal concept of utopia or even to give a canon of characteristics that utopian thinking always fulfills" (1936, 22). Therefore, it is not a surprise at all that More's novel itself is frequently used as a template for a manageable definition of utopia. In this respect, I argue that the genre of utopia begins with More and is thus a modern genre—despite the fact that More himself repeatedly refers to Plato's *Politeia* in his work (Saage 1991, 15–6; Heyer 2005, 25–6).

But what makes novels like *Utopia*, and also Campanella's *City of the Sun* and Bacon's *New Atlantis,* so utopian? Freyer argues that there are "some formal characteristics common to all utopias [...]" (1936, 22). Utopian thinking is commonly thought of as being far from reality, an escape to another, faraway world, because one cannot or does not want to cope with the present. Or—at the opposite extreme—utopia is seen as a failed attempt to change the world. Frequently, utopias are rejected "as an impossible quest for perfection whose political consequences are almost necessarily totalitarian" (Levitas 2013, 7). But a utopia is neither necessarily an unrealistic fantasy nor an abstruse fairy tale. Neither is it a real or existing attempt to create a better society; nor must it necessarily become totalitarian.

In my understanding of utopia, I concur with Saage "that political utopias are fictions of inner-world societies that condense into either a wish or a fear image. Their projection is characterized by a precise critique of existing institutions and socio-political conditions, which they contrast with a well thought-out and rationally comprehensible alternative" (1991, 2–3). This is to some extent consistent with Levitas' approach, which views utopias as a method of "speculative sociology" (2013, 153).

Levitas identifies three modes of utopian method. First, it is a piecing together the images of a good society in an archaeological manner. Second, it is an ontological method that addresses the question of what kind of people societies develop. Third, it is the imagination of potential alternative scenarios for the future in a kind of architectural mode (Levitas 2013, 153). Yorke also argues with the double function of utopias, assigning them a constructive-imaginative and a critical-satirical one (2004, 2). It is important that the utopia does not describe the society that can already be experienced: "For us, utopia, no matter in what kind of text it appears, is always understood from the point where the description of a society, which is not the experienced one, begins. This may manifest itself as an independent, self-contained fiction of a community, this may result as a pointwise composition of the image of a society in the course of a text, this may be embedded in a frame of any size" (Biesterfeld 1982, 11).

Utopias are therefore nothing more than imagined political societies—either drawn as an ideal image or, in the case of dystopia, as the negation of an ideal image. "A 'dystopia' is a narrative construct of a false utopia—not simply a bad or evil society, but one that is evil in spite of, or specifically because of, its utopian claims" (Wagner and Lundeen 1998, 119).

However, I strongly want to point out that these utopian texts are always *fictional*, i.e., not designs that have been realized or are becoming reality. Against the background of a real, existing society, utopia thus wants to present a better alternative of a social model; dystopia, on the other hand, wants to warn against a worse alternative. And although "utopias are, to a large extent, reactive products of their environments, they are also capable of transcending the boundaries of time, space, and culture" (Yorke 2004, 8). Contemporary society is the very frame of reference for utopia, so utopias are not devoid of any realities. Nor are they fantastic because they refer to the present even though they are located in a distant future. This is why "criticism of existing conditions and the desire to create a better future distinguish utopias from the mere daydreaming fantasy which, as it were, is 'without a timetable'" (Gnüg 1999, 12). Saage points out that this juxtaposition of present and future is essential for the "emancipatory impetus" of a utopia (1991, 5). Freyer calls this "a future in the present, a future that admonishes, demands, and acts upon" (1936, 14). However, it is a future that is at the same time so well rooted in the present "that it begins around every corner and that it has its own well-founded reality" (Freyer 1936, 12). Utopia is thus different from paradise.

Instead, it is a coherent and convincing world, which—if it is not reality—could at least become reality (Freyer 1936, 22–3). There is always a certain *possibility of realization* that is immanent in a utopia. However, that possibility is limited. Consider: these texts are still fictional, drafts of reality that are possible in principle but do not have to be realized.

The utopia is therefore not so different that the reader could not recognize the world outlined. It consists of familiar elements of the present, but arranged differently, namely in a way that the author considers ideal. However, this requires that the utopia must be a system *closed to the outside world*. Only then the ideal order may remain; only then one can design a social system from the ground up and let it grow according to a precise plan. "If unpredictable winds that come in from outside bring the things of my 'world' out of their own motion [...], the calculation becomes invalid and the balance is disturbed" (Freyer 1936, 24). One can only achieve this by removing utopia from the immediate access of the present—for example, by placing it on an island (Freyer 1936, 25). However, a secluded city in the middle of a jungle or a desert would fulfill the island position just as well. Pintér explicitly points out that the distance from the author's present can also be achieved by placing the utopia in a different time (e.g., the future), although this is a later development within the genre (2010, 15).

Utopia is also a *self-contained* system. Planned from the ground up, utopia can and must only function if each of its components is highly integrated. It is thus, so to speak, "a closed system of causes and effects between these elements" (Freyer 1936, 28). The idea of such a self-contained system is a meticulous planning of individual areas of society; thus, a world is created "in which everything individual is necessary as a member of the whole" (Freyer 1936, 32).

According to Freyer, the consequence of these characteristics of a utopia is that, once established, it must be *unchangeable and preserved against change* (1936, 35). This is because, on the one hand, the created order is ideal (otherwise it would not be a utopian world) and no longer needs any improvement, and on the other hand, the utopia must be stable, because otherwise it could fall apart. Diverging opinions lead to a discourse in the utopian world that—if no agreement can be reached—results at best in a compromise, at worst in a split within the utopia. But in a utopia, a compromise cannot be the best choice, so that in a static utopia, the aim must be to make possible disturbances impossible from the start (Freyer 1936, 36). If this succeeds, the citizens of a utopia are inseparably linked to it; they are, as it were, a necessary, not just sufficient, part of a stable system. "Utopias do indeed take absolute possession of their people" (Freyer 1936, 36). This leaves no space for individual freedom in the utopia. Instead, utopias require a dense network of surveillance and control. Only in this way can it be ensured that the ideal state, the realization of the utopian idea and thus the utopian society, itself is maintained.

But what makes a utopia political? Utopias—as I will show in the following examples—always describe the everyday life of a certain population. This is done by an account of the geographical conditions, such as the country or the city. Then the daily routine of the people living there is described—their trades, their social associations, their economic system, and even their diet and modes of reproduction. Furthermore, utopias also describe the exercise of power in these societies and their interactions with the outside. The utopia is thus by no means a space free of politics: it is about power, about a certain territory, about a defined order, about a population; in short, even in the complete absence of the concept of politics, a utopia is always political because it wants to regulate the affairs of precisely these people in precisely this place and establish an order. "They are therefore political utopias in the precise sense that they are based on the desires and fears of communities" (Saage 1991, 4). In this respect, the actual form of government is not important. Utopias are, therefore, not limited to a particular type of state; they can be hierarchical, democratic and even repressive (Wagner and Lundeen 1998, 117).

## More's *Utopia*

In Thomas More's *Utopia*, the author reports on his meeting with the traveler Raphael Hythloday, in the course of which a discussion of the present constitution of the English state unfolds. Hythloday warns against placing oneself in the dependence of a king: "I do not mean that you should be in servitude to any king, only in his service" (More 2002, 13). Instead, Hythloday lives as he wants to live (More 2002, 13). Man must, therefore, be allowed to continue to exist and develop as an individual, but must nevertheless serve and thus be useful to a superior state system without being an incorporated part of it. "In his very modern argumentation he proves that the economic practices of the big landowners [...] have made a large number of tenants without bread" (Gnüg 1999, 33). More's criticism here is explicitly directed against the oligopoly of a few who can set the prices in the capitalist economy—both for the goods produced and for the value of the work of the lower, non-possessing class.

"Hythloday [...] embarks on a radical criticism of the political and social circumstances in England" (Pintér 2010, 78), and "More deliberately uses a fictitious person to develop his views on the best state" (Jenkis 1992, 106) and takes this image of his contemporary political system to build a positive counter-image in the second book of his work. In this work, Hythloday reports on his encounter with the people of Utopia and their ideal state constitution.

## *The Geography of Utopia*

More begins the second part with a precise geographical description of the state of Utopia. In the middle, the island is 200 miles wide, with the width decreasing towards the ends so that it appears in its topography like a waxing moon. This landscape forms a bay that serves as a natural harbor and, due to the rocks and shoals, can only be navigated safely with the exclusive knowledge of the Utopians.

Interestingly, More mentions the state founder Utopus rather casually in this passage. It was Utopus who gave the island its name, then he "brought its rude, uncouth inhabitants to such a high level of culture and humanity that they now surpass almost every other people" (More 2002, 42).[2] Why Utopus did this remains unknown—his person is not further described by More. Just like its founder, Utopia appears suddenly and as if from nowhere—artificially created in every respect (Pintér 2010, 93). Originally, Utopia was not an island, but a peninsula. When the state was created, 15 miles of land were removed to separate the peninsula from the mainland (More 2002, 42). So, Utopia deliberately sealed itself off from the rest of the world.

Utopia has 54 cities (including the capital Amaurotum) in which the inhabitants reside if they do not live in one of the farms that are systematically distributed over the island to cultivate the land. These rural inhabitants are always temporary, and there is a regular movement of rural people to the city and *vice versa* (More 2002, 43). The cities are all the same in their appearance—"if you know one of their cities you know them all, for they're exactly alike […]" (More 2002, 44)—and they are built according to a specific plan. Within walls, watchtowers, and ditches, all houses are lined up along exactly defined streets (More 2002, 45–6). Each city is built in a square (More 2002, 45) and divided into four equally sized units. More calls them quarters.

This classification has a direct relation to our reality. Especially medieval towns have often been divided into four districts, which were formed by the crossing of two main streets, which were also trade routes. This resulted in four city entrances and a central market square in the middle. More takes up this city plan, but goes one step further in his vision. Each individual district has markets for the purchase of work products from the population and one common building per row of houses, where the residents of the adjacent houses eat their meals together (More 2002, 55–6). More's design of the housing blocks within the districts suggests an equally square layout, and "the housefronts along each block are separated by a street twenty feet wide" (More 2002, 46).

What More anticipates here is a planned city, as it exists today in many variations. A square arrangement of blocks of houses with streets running at right angles to each other results in a checkerboard pattern that found its way into many urban planning projects in Europe and the world, especially in the 19th century. The most prominent example is certainly New York's Manhattan district, which was planned and built according to this pattern, consisting of avenues in a north-south direction and intersecting streets in a west-east direction. So, there is a rational-functional idea behind More's urban development. Due to the square layout, houses and streets can be built in a standardized way. With More, equality is realized and even illustrated in this city order. Finally, More mentions that there are public hospitals in every city (More 2002, 56).

## *The Social and Economic Structure of Utopia*

Utopia's society is organized in a hierarchic way. More understands family as the smallest unit of society. These family associations consist of 10 to 16 adults, and each city has 6,000 such associations (More 2002, 54). So, Utopia's cities are not only planned in their geography, but also in their population structure. More even provides for family members to be exchanged between associations and cities in order to maintain a constant population of between 60,000 and 100,000 inhabitants per city (More 2002, 54). This consistent population planning corresponds to urban planning.

Only in this way is it possible to plan a city with residential buildings and social facilities in a well-defined way. Any uncontrolled population growth would result in an adaptation of the geographical urban planning—a city could therefore no longer be planned from the outset but would grow naturally and sometimes chaotically beyond its original boundaries. We are familiar with this kind of urban development, which can only be planned to a limited extent, from our world; More, however, achieves an effective control mechanism with the interaction between precise urban planning and population growth. Such a society—as it is framed within the city walls—is controllable and manageable. However, More in principle expects a growing population; Utopia is by definition an expanding state (Saage 2006b, 41). For this reason, More explicitly provides for the founding of colonies, although the Utopians do not see colonies as an element of a policy of conquest. Colonies are only founded where the natives allow it and where there is enough space (Saage 2006b, 41).[3]

In More's utopia, each year 30 family associations elect a leader, which More calls a phylarch. The political system of Utopia is thus firmly based on the families (Saage 2001, 87). For every ten phylarchs there is a head phylarch as superior, and he is also elected annually. So, there are 200 phylarchs and 20 head phylarchs per city. The entirety of the phylarchs elect a governor who is the head of the city and, together with the senate, which is made up of the head phylarchs, conducts all affairs of government (More 2002, 47–8). According to the text, there must be several governors, one per city, since More indicates an inner-city hierarchy. Aside from the city administration, there seems to be no other permanent authority. Although More mentions an annual citizen meeting in the capital, this is apparently only an informal forum: More mentions only three experienced inhabitants per city who may discuss common matters (More 2002, 43). Obviously, this does not necessarily refer to the phylarchs or the governors—otherwise this would have been explicitly stated.[4] Also, the capital has no special administrative powers over the other cities and has a merely honorary title, because it is the oldest of the cities. More leaves us in the dark about who ultimately decides on the affairs of the state as a whole. It is also not clear which form of government Utopia actually possesses. Saage points out that the entire construction of utopias is opposed to an autonomous society, in which citizens are individual subjects, and calls the form of government a "representative democracy without the model of the responsible citizen" (Saage 2001, 88). However, the question is, what is actually left of a democracy then? In fact, Utopia is more of a "strictly regimented society" (Pintér 2010, 90), which, as we understand it, has little to do with democracy—apart from the so-called elections mentioned above. Instead, the citizens of Utopia experience some sort of intensive surveillance and control.

This kind of regulation is also represented by a uniform style of dress, with even the leading positions wearing the same clothes. "Their clothing—which is, except for the distinction between the sexes and between married and unmarried persons, the same throughout the whole island and throughout one's lifetime, and which is by no means unattractive, does not hinder bodily movement and serves for warm as well as cold weather [...]" (More 2002, 49). Clothing here is therefore an expression of belonging to a uniformly structured population. However, it should represent neither wealth nor status nor individual preferences of the individual. By the way, jewelry is also rejected by the Utopians and used in a contrary fashion. Criminals do wear gold jewelry as a sign of their contempt and dishonor (More 2002, 61).

All inhabitants of Utopia are adept in agriculture, men and women alike. In addition, every Utopian learns a certain trade. Among the trades that can be learned are clothmaking, weaving, masonry, metalwork, and carpentry (More 2002, 49). All these trades serve to satisfy the basic needs of the population. In addition to clothing and buildings, the focus is on ensuring adequate food supplies. Goods are collected in warehouses near the markets and distributed without payment (More 2002, 55). Surpluses are distributed between districts and even between towns (More 2002, 59).

Utopians have a distinctive work schedule. They work in their professions in two shifts of three hours a day with fixed meal and rest times (More 2002, 50). Their free time is also planned in advance. Thus, the Utopians organize their evening leisure times "in their gardens during the summer, or during winter in the common halls where they have their meals. There they either play music or amuse themselves with conversation" (More 2002, 50). During the day, the Utopians are formally free to engage in any activity between work and free time, but subject to a certain usefulness. "Generally, these intervals are devoted to intellectual activity" (More 2002, 50). A craftsman in Utopia is therefore not limited to his learned profession, but is required to develop himself intellectually. As an incentive for this intellectual pursuit, the phylarchs in Utopia regularly relieve citizens of their work so that they may begin full-time studies. If a citizen proves to be permanently capable in this, he is admitted to the class of the "literary educated"; otherwise, he works again in his learned profession (More 2002, 52). In Utopia, therefore, a second, upper class is recruited from the lower classes (from which, moreover, the government positions mentioned above are recruited). Thus, despite the fact that all of them have a profession, there is a "primacy of intellectual activity" (Gnüg 1999, 37) in which, according to the Utopians, "lies the happiness of life" (More 2002, 53).

The economic principle of Utopia is therefore not designed to maximize profits and growth, but to satisfy constant needs. The lack of private property goes hand in hand with the lack of need for luxury items. A lavish lifestyle is rejected as inappropriate. "In this respect, there are also no multifaceted professions in the Utopian state, since only a few skills are needed to satisfy the important, since reasonable, needs" (Gnüg 1999, 38). The result of this economic system does indeed appear utopian. In Utopia, one does not suffer from hunger, poverty or financial problems and therefore has "no worries about the future" (Pintér 2010, 90).

### *The Utopians at War*

Utopia resembles an ideal society; however, war still plays a role. Although the Utopians reject war as despicable in principle, all inhabitants continue to receive military training—men and women alike (More 2002, 85). In Utopia, however, war is only an option "to protect their own land, to drive invading armies from the territories of their friends, or to liberate an oppressed people, in the name of compassion and humanity, from tyranny and servitude" (More 2002, 85).

The Utopians therefore react to attacks on peoples allied with them and even to a supposed oppression of one people by someone else. More even explicitly mentions the possibility of pre-emptive strikes (More 2002, 85). This motive seems astonishing in view of the Utopians' high moral standards. For Utopia, a reason for war is thus already given when it is not their territory as such that is threatened, but their moral convictions and ideas, and this, even if outside their state, is within their sphere of influence. Utopia thus sees itself as a moral hegemon over its sphere of influence and considers its ideas and attitudes to be morally correct. In this way, the Utopians elevate their legal norms and their way of life to a norm of international law that must, if necessary, be enforced (Heyer 2005, 48).

## Campanella's *City of the Sun*

Another classical utopia I like to discuss is Campanella's *City of the Sun*. Campanella might have been familiar with More's text (Gnüg 1999, 68) and so it is probably no coincidence that Campanella puts his utopia on the island of Ceylon,[5] exactly where Hythloday—More's fictional eye witness of Utopia—stopped during one of his journeys (More 2002, 10). Similar to More, Campanella's text also takes also the form of a dialogue between a traveler (whom Campanella calls the Genoese) and his interlocutor, an unspecified Grand Master. The person of the Grand Master is essentially limited to giving keywords, for which Campanella, in the form of the Genoese, describes and explains the City of the Sun in more detail.

## The Geography of the City of the Sun

The City of the Sun is two miles in diameter and divided into seven concentric rings. There are four gated access routes into the city, which routes point to the cardinal directions. The seven circles of the city form independent strong fortifications with towers and ditches, "so that who wishes to capture that city must, as it were, storm it seven times" (Campanella 2009, 5). Located at the center of the circles and thus of the entire city is a temple, which is also circular in shape (Campanella 2009, 7). Campanella gives no further information about the rest of the city. Although he mentions "large palaces, all joined to the wall of the second circuit in such a manner as to appear all one palace" (Campanella 2009, 6), as well as houses and dormitories, which are repeatedly reinhabited in a rotation principle according to the orders of the authorities (Campanella 2009, 25). The exact nature of these buildings remains unclear. Campanella—unlike More—does not provide any information about other community facilities, either. For example, he reports on the treatment of diseases (Campanella 2009, 54–5), but does not refer to whether specially built hospitals, like the ones in Utopia, exist.

Like More, however, Campanella deliberately settles his utopian state on an island. Thus, the City of the Sun is sufficiently detached from the rest of the world so that an ideal society can be created and maintained there. The secludedness of this society is astonishing. Although More also goes into great detail about the fortification efforts of the cities of Utopia, Campanella surpasses More's visions by far. The City of the Sun appears to be a veritable fortress. In this way, it does not merely separate itself from the outside: it seems as if Campanella sees in the outside world such a constant threat to utopian conditions that his utopia must literally wall itself in in order to survive. The constant surveillance confirms this fact. "There are guards in the city by day and by night, and they are placed at the four gates, and outside the walls of the seventh ring, above the breastworks and towers and inside mounds" (Campanella 2009, 45).

The geometrical layout of the city is also striking. In More's work, the cities are arranged nearly squared, but Campanella's City of the Sun is circular. This has an additional meaning because such a shape emphasizes the center. The distance from the edge of the shape to the center is the same in every location, and this is exactly what is not the case with the square. Campanella will, therefore, not have chosen the circular shape by accident. All life in the city is aligned to its center and thus to the temple.

Thus, in his utopia, Campanella introduces an essential aspect that More is missing: within the City of the Sun religion literally has a central significance. Besides, Campanella uses special numbers as symbols. There are four access routes, aligned according to the cardinal points. Furthermore, the city is divided into seven concentric rings. Four and seven are numbers with religious meaning.

The circular layout reflects the core idea of Campanella's utopian state much more extremely than with More. In a circular city, there is literally no corner behind which the individual inhabitant could "hide," not even a single house, when they all seem to form a unit. In this respect, this city complex guarantees maximum control over its citizens. The massive fortification of the city can also be understood in this respect in that no one can escape control. A totalitarian regime is being formed here (Saage 2001, 111–2).

## *The Social and Economic Structure of the City of the Sun*

The society of the City of the Sun is far more hierarchical and tightly organized than in Utopia. The supreme ruler is Hoh, or the Metaphysic, who "is head over all, in temporal and spiritual matters, and all business and lawsuits are settled by him, as the supreme authority" (Campanella 2009, 9). The Metaphysic is assisted by three dignitaries with the names Pon, Sin, and Mor[6]—or Power, Wisdom, and Love—each of whom presides over a certain area of competence. Pon is the commander-in-chief of the military and is responsible for all military matters (Campanella 2009, 9). Sin is in charge of all the arts and sciences as well as the relevant authorities and schools (Campanella 2009, 10). Mor is responsible for the supervision of the reproduction of the Solarians (as Campanella calls the citizens), as well as for medicine and nutrition (Campanella 2009, 14–5). Campanella is not clear in the relationship of these three offices to the Metaphysic. On the one hand, he stresses that the Metaphysic acts only in agreement with the three other offices, so that the Metaphysic appears as a *primus inter pares*. On the other hand, the Metaphysic seems to have a kind of authority to give guidelines, because "in whatever Metaphysic inclines to the rest are sure to agree" (Campanella 2009, 15).

No distinction is made between secular and spiritual power in the City of the Sun. The Metaphysic is the highest priest besides his position as head of city and state. All other magistrates are also priests. Although More's Utopians also know religion, it plays only a subordinate role in the constitution of their state. There are even different religions—although a monotheistic religion makes up the majority of followers (More 2002,

93)—and More also makes clear "that everyone may cultivate the religion of his choice" (More 2002, 94). Unlike More's Utopia, the City of the Sun is clearly founded on religion. There is no freedom of religion; every citizen is obliged to belong to a religion without exception. The extent of this connection between religion, state and society is exemplified by the fact that human sacrifices are regularly offered (even if only symbolically and not with fatal outcome) and that always one Solarian prays uninterruptedly in the temple in front of the altar until he is replaced by the next, so religion is always a central element in the life of the Solarians (Campanella 2009, 65).

What is remarkable about this utopian construction is the high degree of autocracy. The office of the Metaphysic is usually conferred on a priest for life (Campanella 2009, 22, 64), and the three assigned offices can also relinquish their offices only of their own accord; there is no provision for deselection. "In this manner they assemble daily, Hoh and his three princes, and they correct, confirm, and execute the matters passing to them [...]" (Campanella 2009, 57). Apart from the Metaphysic as the distinguished leader, the three other offices cover exactly those essential systems that are necessary for the preservation of a utopia: military, science and the people. Below each of these three offices there are additional subordinate authorities. The heads of these authorities, the Metaphysic, and the other three officers meet every eight days to discuss state affairs in general. The heads of these authorities are also elected by the assembly. All leading positions that exist in the City of the Sun are assigned to one of the three officers. There is also a general assembly of all citizens, but this is apparently of only an advisory nature (Campanella 2009, 56). The City of the Sun is thus far more bureaucratically organized than More's Utopia because there is a separate authority for each area of life (Jenkis 1992, 134).

As Campanella explains in the last chapter of his treatise, everything that exists is based on what he calls Entity (2009, 70). Entity is equal to God, and "all things are therefore in various degrees godly" (Freyer 1936, 106). From the Metaphysic, "a range of levels of reality goes down to the individual citizen, and each one has his reality only by virtue of the function he exercises to the best of his ability for the state as a whole" (Freyer 1936, 107). Thus, for Campanella, the pursuit of divinity is the true ideal of the society. Each individual, in his or her function, serves the society in order to approach this striving for divine equality. However, this also means that the singular person is worthless as an individual; only life as a whole, as a great unity, can be considered valuable (Freyer 1936, 107). "It is true that Campanella's *solar state* functions according to a strictly military discipline and leaves no room for the development of subjectivity" (Saage 2001, 115).

## 1. The Meaning of Utopia

In Campanella's City, the individual is the smallest unit in the whole society; it is no longer the family, as it is in More's Utopia, where premarital sex is even punishable (More 2002, 79). Instead, a "community of wives" is considered as a common good of the entire society by Campanella (2009, 16). In the City of the Sun, the family as such does not exist; reproduction and thus the preservation of society are carried out under state supervision and with a certain selection process: "The race is managed for the good of the commonwealth, and not of private individuals, and the magistrates must be obeyed. [...] For they say that children are bred for the preservation of the species and not for individual pleasure [...]" (Campanella 2009, 31).

Apart from the community of women, Campanella, like More, does not know any other private property (Campanella 2009, 16), and men and women also wear the same kind of clothes (Campanella 2009, 19). The handicraft training is even less diversified than in More's Utopia. In the City of the Sun, all inhabitants learn the same activities and practice them collectively. While More still requires everyone to work six hours a day, Campanella reduces this time to just four hours. "The remaining hours are spent in learning joyously, in debating, in reading, in reciting, in writing, in walking, in exercising the mind and body, and with play" (Campanella 2009, 34–5). Also, as in More's Utopia, those who learn and practice several professions are generally considered to be more respected and are sometimes appointed as teachers in their respective subjects (Campanella 2009, 47). Campanella also mentions that the economic system of the City of the Sun, like that of Utopia, does not need money. However, money itself is not unknown: merchants from foreign countries come to the City of the Sun to buy its surpluses (Campanella 2009, 47).

### The City of the Sun at War

Campanella treats war in the City of the Sun quite extensively. There is a separate office, Pon, which is the supreme commander of the City's army: "The triumvir, Power, has under him all the magistrates of arms, of artillery, of cavalry, of footsoldiers, of architects, and of strategists; and the masters and many of the most excellent workmen obey the magistrates, the men of each art paying allegiance to their respective chiefs" (Campanella 2009, 37). The army is recruited from all citizens, and women receive the same military training as men (Campanella 2009, 37–8).

Campanella mentions that there are four other empires on the same island, and they envy the City for its achievements (Campanella 2009, 39). Campanella's City of the Sun is thus a utopia that is always threatened in its existence and that not only has to separate itself from other empires but also apparently has to actively defend its ideals. Obviously, to the outside world, the utopia of the City is by no means static but must literally fight for its continued existence anew.

Campanella describes the practice of war of the City in detail. First, diplomacy is used to settle a dispute between the City of the Sun and an aggressor. Only when diplomatic means are exhausted, when the aggressor does not meet the demands of the Solarians, are military options are considered (Campanella 2009, 40). Defeated cities are assimilated. They must submit to the laws of the City of the Sun; they are assigned officials from the City; and the entire social system is adapted to that of the City (Campanella 2009, 44). Although there are no reports of pre-emptive strikes, there is something aggressive about this behavior of the City people. So, the utopia of the City is to install its own system of rule on aggressors after a victory. In this way, the City of the Sun not only consolidates its supremacy but also simultaneously eliminates hostile tendencies in its interior. By assimilating its enemies, they are rendered meaningless and the utopian system triumphs.

## Bacon's *New Atlantis*

Sir Francis Bacon's *New Atlantis* has a special position in the utopian texts of the early modern period because his narrative is only a fragment. However, similar to Campanella and More, Bacon begins with a travelogue. The author is on the high seas in the Southern Ocean, and the ship is off course. When the crew spots land, they set course for it and arrive at a fortified port (Bacon 2009, 7). The local population initially refuses the newcomers entry into their country and asks them to continue their journey. "Land ye not, none of you; and provide to be gone from this coast, within sixteen days, except you have further time given you" (Bacon 2009, 8). As there are some sick people among the crew, the author asks the strangers for permission, and after they have affirmed under oath "that ye are no pirates, nor have shed blood, lawfully, nor unlawfully within forty days past" (Bacon 2009, 10), the crew is granted permission to debark. The strangers are accommodated to a so-called Foreigner's House, and they are granted a six-week stay on the island (Bacon 2009, 16). We then learn that the inhabitants "of this island of Bensalem [...] have this; that by means of our solitary situation; and of the laws of secrecy, which we have for our travellers, and our rare admission of strangers; we know well most part of the habitable world, and are ourselves unknown" (Bacon 2009, 18).

Here Bacon's narrative resembles the other two utopian texts. Once again, a society is established on a remote island that is and should remain hidden from the remaining world. Here, too, the inhabitants of Bensalem know of the rest of the world; unlike Campanella and More, however, with Bacon the inhabitants are forbidden to speak of their world. Bensalem is to remain hidden and thus invisible to the outside.

The envoy of Bensalem further reports about a former king named Solamona, "and we esteem him as the lawgiver of our nation. This king had a large heart, inscrutable for good; and was wholly bent to make his kingdom and people happy" (Bacon 2009, 30). Bacon thus also introduces a founder of the state to whom the utopian society of New Atlantis goes back. The story is similar to that of More and his King Utopus. King Solamona appears as a benevolent and wise ruler whose goal was "to give perpetuity to that which was in his time so happily established" (Bacon 2009, 31). At the same time, however, we are once again left in the dark about the origin and motives of the king. In order to preserve his utopia, Bacon continues, this king imposed a ban on immigration and also drastically restricted the population's own travel. If people entered the island, they were either allowed to leave or to stay at the expense of the state. With these decrees the ruler pursued two things: On the one hand he was "doubting novelties, and commixture of manners" (Bacon 2009, 31). On the other hand, he wanted to achieve "preserving the good which cometh by communicating with strangers, and avoiding the hurt" (Bacon 2009, 32–3). Bacon's text, like More's and Campanella's, is thus also a criticism of the political conditions of his time. But unlike the other two, Bacon hardly criticizes the contrasts between poverty and wealth, nor private property, but above all the insignificance of marriage (Saage 2001, 152). It also seems that a monetary economic system still exists in New Atlantis. Civil servants are paid (Bacon 2009, 14). The foreign house, where the shipwrecked people are accommodated, has plenty of cash, "for it hath laid up revenue these thirty-seven years" (Bacon 2009, 16). The goods brought with them could be sold at a reasonable price, and there seem to be merchants on the island who make a living from their trade. For example, Bacon speaks of a merchant named Joabin (2009, 42). "The existence of such an activity suggests that the distribution of the goods is done by private individuals for profit" (Saage 2001, 154). Bacon's utopian concept is fundamentally different from that of More and Campanella in this respect, even though a capitalist economy seems to have its limits in Bacon's creation (Saage 2001, 154–5).

Bacon's utopia is a less material-based than knowledge-based economic concept. In fact, Bacon reports the founding of a society called "the House of Solamona," a scientific organization commissioned by the king to study nature. One of the members of the House of Solamona is described in more detail in Bacon's writing, and this description stands in striking contrast to More's and Campanella's characterizations. The "Father"—as Bacon calls him—is splendidly dressed in a toga and a robe of fine cloth, wears gloves adorned with precious stones and velvet shoes. He first meets the stranger in a kind of sedan chair, which Bacon describes as both splendid and decorated. After a few days he receives the author for a private audience in a throne room, which is again described as richly decorated (Bacon 2009, 48–50). This detailed description is striking and cannot be accidental. Bacon emphasizes the special position of this "Father": he obviously stands out from the rest of the population of Bensalem, and at the same time, with his striking appearance, he points out the importance of the House of Solamona. In comparison with More, a different, changed understanding of luxury and materialism is revealed here (Gnüg 1999, 80). With More, precious stones and splendid robes have no meaning, and even with Campanella there is no mention of special furnishings for the dignitaries (although one might most likely expect it here). With Bacon, on the other hand, the uninhibited striving for prosperity seems to be the maxim of utopia.

Subsequently, we learn more about the purpose of the House of Solamona from the "Father." "The end of our foundation is the knowledge of causes, and secret motions of things; and the enlarging of the bounds of human empire, to the effecting of all things possible" (Bacon 2009, 51). This statement is central to Bacon's utopia. Although the utopias of More and Campanella are also about new scientific knowledge and the new possibilities of making use of this knowledge, Bacon places this at the absolute center of his society. The inhabitants of Bensalem are concerned with the maximum controllability of nature through science. Bacon explains how this can be achieved. There are deep caves to harden or cool substances, to preserve bodies, to artificially manufacture minerals and metals, and finally to produce ceramic bodies and store fertilizers. There are "high towers" (Bacon 2009, 52) for weather observations; there are also so-called "Chambers of Health" and large baths for curing diseases and preserving the human organism (Bacon 2009, 53–4). Fruit plantations are used for the cultivation of fruit, wildlife enclosures for keeping and examining various animal species in order to gain knowledge about the functioning of the human body, and animal experiments are also carried out here (Bacon 2009, 55–6). In the further course of the text, Bacon reports on food companies, pharmacies, the clothing industry, and possibilities for heat production (Bacon 2009, 56–9). There are houses for optics, for acoustics, for smells; there are engine houses, a house for mathematics, and finally a house for sensory illusions, in which experiments and research are carried out in the respective fields (Bacon 2009, 60–2). It is striking how faithfully and meticulously Bacon describes these facilities. The intricacy of the descriptions goes far beyond the descriptions in *Utopia* or the *City of the Sun*—and it is also striking that Bacon is not concerned with simplifying the method of production, but rather with improving goods already available. It is not the spiritual striving for a better humanity that seems to be at the forefront of Bacon's concept, but the subjugation of the surrounding nature. "Throughout, the tendency can be observed to imitate nature and at the same time surpass it in charm and abundance" (Gnüg 1999, 82).

In order to gain scientific knowledge, a strict division of labor is applied in the House of Solamona. There are different professions that are supposed to generate new knowledge and to investigate its applicability. In detail these are:

1. the "Merchants of Light," who travel to foreign countries under a foreign identity to obtain books and samples of inventions;
2. the "Depredators," who compile the experiments described in the books;
3. the "Mystery-men," who collect material on experiments in the field of pure science, mechanical engineering and other practical applications of science;
4. the "Pioneers" or "Miners," who deal with new experiments that appear promising;
5. the "Compilers," who catalog test results and derive general rules;
6. the "Dowry-men" or "Benefactors," who review the experiments of their colleagues and evaluate them for practicability;
7. the "Lamps," which design new experiments on an abstract level based on previous experiments;
8. the "Inoculators," who carry out and document these tests; and
9. the "Interpreters of Nature," who expand the knowledge gained to larger complexes and derive general rules and principles from it [Bacon 2009, 63–5].

With Bacon, the production of knowledge and new findings has the character of a thoroughly structured workflow reminiscent of the industrial age. Here, knowledge is consistently checked for usefulness. Only after proven suitability for practical application is the knowledge gained reflected on a meta-level. The Bensalemans apparently do not shy away from consistently exploiting the knowledge of other peoples for their own purposes. Even more: the House of Solamona has such power that it may decide for itself whether to publish the knowledge. "We have consultations, which of the inventions and experiences which we have discovered shall be published, and which not: and take all an oath of secrecy, for the concealing of those which we think fit to keep secret: though some of those we do reveal sometimes to the state and some not" (Bacon 2009, 65).

Bacon, however, makes no statement about the relationship between the House of Solamona and the state of New Atlantis—which may be owed to the fragmentary nature of the work. Indeed, we learn little about the form of the state in *New Atlantis*. There is obviously a king and also a senate, but the tasks of these institutions remain unknown. Apparently, the House of Solamona has an essential part in maintaining the structure of society, as the exploration of nature is a central moment in *New Atlantis*.

Unlike the descriptions in *Utopia* or in *City of the Sun*, we learn little about daily life on the island of Bensalem. Bacon reports of a "Feast of the Family" which, on the basis of a law, must take place at the home of anyone "that shall live to see thirty persons descended of his body alive together, and all above three years old" (Bacon 2009, 36). But this is by no means a private family affair. The celebration is supported by the state, namely both monetarily and institutionally by the governor of the city. The head of the family presides over the celebration and all members of the family are invited to participate. During the festival, disputes are settled, the family members are questioned (and if necessary, helped out) to ensure that they have sufficient means of subsistence, and warnings are issued in the event of objectionable behavior. In case of opposition, the governor may enforce instructions on the head of the family (Bacon 2009, 37).

Bacon attaches particular importance to this event, as "indeed we have experience that those families that are partakers of the blessing of that feast do flourish and prosper ever after in an extraordinary manner" (Bacon 2009, 44). Marriage matters are also decided at these celebrations, with marriage being under the special protection of the family. In New Atlantis the parents' consent is required for a marriage to be valid; polygamy is forbidden. Bacon thus stands in contrast to Campanella's view of women being common property. However, men and women may not see each other naked before entering into marriage, which is an orientation very similar to that in More's *Utopia* (Bacon 2009, 47). Marriage is thus also, with Bacon, the nucleus of society, which is apparently patriarchally structured. The head of the family is male; the women are only required to be "leaning against the wall" (Bacon 2009, 40) at the family feast. Furthermore, Bacon makes no statement about a common education or activities performed by men and women. It even seems as if the well-organized scientific activity carried out in Bacon's utopia is maintained primarily by the male inhabitants.

## Science Fiction as a Genre of Its Own

In contrast to utopia, the term "science fiction" is often used in a pejorative way. Fuhse, for example, quotes the sociologist Pierre Bourdieu, who regards science fiction as a "lesser art form" and writes, "[I]n science fiction novels and -films, an escape from society would be made into the unreal. Adventure stories, space stories, magical world view and orgies of special effects would thus stand for pure entertainment and for a departure from the everyday world" (Fuhse 2003, 223).

So, I could actually stop discussing the differences between science fiction and utopia on the spot. If utopia wants to criticize contemporary society and propose a new social design, science fiction simply serves to escape from the reality to be criticized. And yet it is not quite so simple. In the further course of his essay, Fuhse develops the thesis, using examples from science fiction cinema, that science fiction should by no means be understood as an escape from, but rather as a critique of, society. "Society is understood as a simulation that makes it almost impossible to understand the structures of power. Reason therefore remains subjective and related to the individual situation, instead of referring to the big picture in an objective perspective" (Fuhse 2003, 236).

So, is science fiction a bottom-up criticism of society, inductively from the particular to the general?

"The term 'science fiction' resists easy definition. [...] [W]hen it comes down to specifying in what way SF is distinctive, and in what ways it is different from other imaginative and fantastic literature, there is disagreement" (Roberts 2000, 1).

A certain similarity to the utopian genre cannot be denied in science fiction, as both genres deal with advanced, future societies. Schwonke argues that there is a direct relationship between utopia and science fiction. For him, the design of a perfect ideal state is no longer credible enough today, for this contemporary world is subject to constant change (Schwonke 1957, 4). With Schwonke, however, the change is mainly of a technical nature. "The soberly predictive intention and the often very careful analysis of technical future possibilities and their consequences show how much today's utopian thinking is determined by science and technology" (Schwonke 1957, 5).

According to this, utopia as an outmoded concept would simply have been replaced by science fiction. Is Orwell's *1984*, therefore, already science fiction because the utopian genre no longer existed in Orwell's time? Or because science and technology take up a large part of Orwell's narrative? Fuhse at least mentions Orwell's work in the same breath as Mary Shelley's *Frankenstein* and Huxley's *Brave New World* (Fuhse 2008, 6), but

Schwonke expressly denies this and argues that Orwell as well as Huxley are utopian texts (Schwonke 1972, 67). This alone suggests that it is difficult to distinguish clearly between science fiction and utopia.

Nevertheless, one fact seems undisputed: Prolonged reference to technology and science is distinctive for the science fiction genre. Science fiction narratives are "texts—be they novels, comics, short stories, films or television series—[…] that work with technical innovations as stylistic devices" (Fuhse 2008, 7). Roberts, however, states that an essential structural feature in science fiction texts is a device that he calls "novum"—probably in reference to Ernst Bloch and Darko Suvin (Suvin 1972, 87). The novum is "the radically (though not purely) new, which by definition cannot be exhaustively or definitively mapped" (Freedman 2000, 74): "It seems that this 'point of difference,' the thing or things that differentiate the world portrayed in science fiction from the world we recognise around us, is the crucial separator between SF and other forms of imaginative or fantastic literature" (Roberts 2000, 6). Moylan points out that "the novum is the *formal* element that generates and validates all elements of the text, from the alternative world to plot, characters, and style" (2021, 91).

The novum has to feature a certain "fundamental compatibility of both worlds" (Becker and Hallenberger 1993, 144)—which means that it must be in some way rooted in our present reality although it is not limited to pure technology (Roberts 2000, 7). Spreen sees science fiction primarily as an adventure story that is related to a fictional technical-scientific novelty (Spreen 2008, 21). So, science fiction is about *technical-scientific progress*.

In addition to this idea of progress, other novums can also be subsumed under the term science fiction. If there is something that distinguishes the world of science fiction from ours so clearly that there is a difference, it must be something not discovered or invented by man himself. Instead, this novelty can also be something unknown, almost something different, which approaches or is approached from outside. Thus, science fiction novels are *confrontations with the other* that "provide a symbolic grammar for articulating the perspectives of normally marginalised discourses of race, of gender, of non-conformism and alternative ideologies" (Roberts 2000, 28). Thanks to its own technical progress, science fiction opens up new, different spaces. "Examples of this are the opening up of sea space, air space and outer space, the exploration and colonization of foreign planets or the construction of cyberspace" (Spreen 2008, 21). This inevitably leads to the fact that humanity goes on *journeys into the unknown*, on "voyages extraordinaires" (Schwonke 1957, 24), and encounters with the foreign take place in the process. In these three interrelated aspects, I see the basis for science fiction texts.[7]

## Technical and Scientific Progress

Seeßlen and Jung maintain that "when the 'Industrial Revolution' finally seemed to put technology into the state of unlimited future possibilities [...], it had become not only possible, but also necessary, to create a form of literature that was capable of aesthetically translating both the perspectives and the metaphysics of technology and disseminating them on a mass scale" (2003, 12). Science fiction thus manifests itself as a genre rooted in the emerging enthusiasm for new technologies and sciences in the late 19th and early 20th centuries. Nevertheless, it is difficult to identify a fixed starting point of the genre. Mary Shelley's *Frankenstein* from 1818 is sometimes regarded as the first science fiction story ever (Roberts 2000, 48; Freedman 2000, 91).[8] *Frankenstein* symbolizes the possibilities of new technology on the one hand, and the dangers of it on the other. A scientist creates an artificial human being, thereby elevating himself to the rulership of nature—and nature will immediately take revenge on its new creator by failing the experiment. However, "when Mary Shelley wrote *Frankenstein* (1818), SF had neither a name nor any recognition as an independent form of literature. After Mary Shelley, there was a prolonged gap" (Bhelkar 2009, 18)—and it will be another 80 years before H. G. Wells takes up science fiction again in *The Island of Dr. Moreau* (1896). Along with Jules Verne, Wells is considered one of the forefathers of the genre (Jameson 1982, 149).

In the book, Dr. Moreau is a formerly respected scientist who had to flee his home country, England, for conducting forbidden animal experiments. The first-person narrator—the shipwrecked Edward Prendick—is rescued by Moreau's assistant, Montgomery, and soon learns about Moreau's experiments on a remote island. Moreau has created human chimeras from animals—chimeras that live in a small colony on the island. Fearing his own creatures, Moreau has dictated a law to them: "Not to go on all Fours [...]. Not to suck up Drink [...]. Not to eat Flesh nor Fish [...]. Not to claw Bark of Trees [...]. Not to chase other Men; *that* is the Law. Are we not Men?" (Wells 1988, 59). Not only does a scientist rise above nature, but he is also even worshipped as a God by his creatures (Roberts 2000, 61): "*His* is the House of Pain. *His* is the hand that makes. *His* is the hand that wounds. *His* is the hand that heals" (Wells 1988, 59). The scientist is the absolute power here, the one who judges life and death.

Wells and Shelley are both precedents of Isaac Asimov's science fiction, in which man's mastery of nature *and* technology is portrayed in the ultimate creative process. By creating his own beings—artificial humans—man becomes God, and by means of technical progress, he no longer even needs biological material, but simple builds them. Hence robots are born.

Humans are thus becoming transcendent figures (Lem 1972, 170). It is interesting to see who can and may dominate whom here: man, nature (and thus also the machine) or nature, man. "The fear of becoming incapacitated and unfree through technology seems quite real, especially since the beginning of the Industrial Revolution" (Weber 2008, 37). However, this implies that the machine can turn against man if nature cannot be made a subject, and despite all progress, man cannot and will not dominate nature. In the end, the message would be one does not play God!

This consideration of technical and scientific progress brings us back to Fuhse's concept of science fiction as a "simulation of society" (Fuhse 2008, 6) or an "aesthetic experimental laboratory" (Fuhse 2003, 226). Scientific and technical progress can thus be seen as a constant crossing of boundaries. If progress is about the "optimization, efficiency, [and] increase" (Spreen 2008, 26) of technical achievements and scientific knowledge, this raises the question of how "reasonable" a creature or a machine must be. In this way, science fiction could move away from the purely technical-scientific notion of progress to the implications that this progress brings with it. In the case of both Shelley and Wells, this progress fails as both stories end in the death of the creators and the destruction of creatures.

We may say that as science fiction looks for other, ethically justifiable ways of progress, it "often takes on an experimental character, [and] conceivable possibilities of future existence are tested in thought experiments" (Jenkis 1992, 60). A dynamic process opens that tries to minimize failure by means of trial and error. Thus, normative limits are set to progress, such as Asimov's Robot Laws, according to which a robot may not harm any human being, must unconditionally follow orders from humans, and must protect its own existence (whereby the first laws take precedence over the next) (Roberts 2000, 158; Weber 2008, 38). Man—so powerful that he himself has become a creator—basically does not trust his own abilities and sets normative principles for his creatures (which has already been realized by Wells); in the case of robots, he programs them into better beings.

The progressive findings in science fiction can thus be understood as a model, "as a guiding vision of developments that points the way ahead and guides action. [...] In their guiding function they bundle intuitions and knowledge about feasible and desirable goals [...]" (Steinmüller 2010, 22). This also means, however, that it is inherent in technical-scientific progress that there is neither just *one* way nor *the best* way regarding what a future society could look like—nor is there already an end state, nor could there ever be one (Schwonke 1972, 65–6). In this sense, science fiction always has a dynamic moment.

## The Journey into the Unknown

"Space travel is *the* classic theme of science fiction. Visions of flights to other star systems have shaped this genre from the very beginning" (Steinmüller 2010, 22). So, there is again that dynamic moment when space travel is seen as a journey into the unknown. It was Jules Verne who first made use of the motif. Besides travelling to the moon in *De la terre à la lune* (1865) and *Autour de la lune* (1870), there are expeditions to the center of the earth in *Voyage au center de la terre* (1864) and to the depths of the sea in *Vingt mille lieues sous le mers* (1869). "Verne's heroes are the often-daring rulers and conquerors of the new world with its previously unimagined possibilities. They find their way with the new technology and use it for enormous adventures and discoveries" (Alpers 1972, 246).

When Captain Nemo succeeds in facing all kinds of dangers and passing adventures on his underwater voyages in *Vingt mille lieues sous le mers*, this is also a triumph of technology over nature—and at the same time a triumph of man who conquers the unknown with his technology. Thanks to his technology and scientific knowledge, man is no longer at the mercy not only of nature but also of the unknown.

In Wells' *The Time Machine* (1895), the aspect of time travel becomes interesting because Wells combines the motifs of travel with technical and scientific progress. "The time machine is a glittering metallic framework, scarcely larger than a small clock, and very delicately made" (Bhelkar 2009, 20). The time traveler not only visits an unknown place but also looks at how this place may have changed in the distant future. But time travel offers another interesting aspect in science fiction. Through travelling into the past, the traveler may alter the present through his actions or even his presence alone, and perhaps even improves it. In this respect, society is, in fact, a simulation (to speak with Fuhse) in which variables may be changed at will in the past with consequences for the present and the future. By means of trial and error, the effects of one's own actions can thus be checked almost in real time by traveling back and forth in time.

If one considers journeys into the unknown as the "obligation to go out into the world and conquer it in the name of reason" (Seeßlen and Jung 2003, 7), then a downright colonialist claim arises in science fiction. The traveler—equipped with a great lead in technological knowledge—uses his knowledge to travel into the unknown to finally use his technological superiority to subdue the unexplored and unknown world.

## The Encounter with the Different

But this means also that the traveler will inevitably encounter not only the abstract unknown but also, eventually, alien life forms. Therefore, the traveler experiences a "'First Contact,' the moment of encounter between human and aliens, a moment familiar to us from anthropological investigation and historical accounts; one which, consciously or not, re-enacts the encounters of European 'discovery' of the New World" (Fitting 2000, 125).

Of course, there is a certain problem: how shall we deal with the other ones? There are three possibilities: defeat the other (after all, one may consider oneself technologically more advanced in comparison to the other and can derive one's moral-ethical superiority from this); live in peaceful coexistence; or be defeated. In this respect, the encounters with other species are similar to the colonization movements of the past (Schwonke 1957, 141). The exploration of the world goes hand in hand with taking possession of it. "In fact, all this, freedom, encouragement, and support of any kind of research, served mainly the one purpose of reinforcing the British Empire's claim to power. [...] However, this system of research ultimately produced results that attacked ideological premises, for example Darwin's theory of descent, which challenged not only a religious but also a cultural, and ultimately a political, axiom: man's unconditional superiority over nature" (Seeßlen and Jung 2003, 72).

So, despite the belief in technical progress, man is not invincible, even if he thinks he can sufficiently control nature. In H. G. Wells' *The War of the Worlds* (1898), the population of the Earth is confronted with an invasion by extraterrestrials. Martians land with their spaceships on Earth—more precisely, in the United Kingdom—and begin a full-scale invasion of the planet. The Martian technology is far superior to human technology, and the aliens show no respect for human life. "His [Wells'] Martians are imperialists who use their superior technology to invade a nation, England, which had been accumulating its own Empire in part because of a superior technological sophistication" (Roberts 2000, 63). The technological superiority of humans thus finds its limits in the even greater technological superiority of another species. "This Darwinian fable, depicting an interplanetary struggle for survival, is the most influential of all alien contact stories" (Bhelkar 2009, 25). In Wells's work, the Martians are not simply the best adapted evolutionarily: their evolution has also brought about a physiological efficiency. Martians absorb nutrients directly (they inject the blood of other living beings directly into their veins). They do not eat; they do not sleep; they are not guided by emotions (Fitting 2000, 135). "[...] The Martians are lifted above all these organic fluctuations of mood and emotion. They are absolutely without sex, and therefore, without trumultous [sic] emotions that arise from the difference between men" (Bhelkar 2009, 26). That alone makes them stronger because they have optimized their way of life.

Wells' fictional account of humankind's first encounter with an alien race thus ends in death and destruction. Humanity is no longer the center of the cosmos; instead, humans finds themselves in competition with other species who, whether hostile or not, may be superior to it. Our universe has become one that "could be enlivened by intelligences that exceed man by as many dimensions as the universe exceeds the closed earthly world; to which man is nothing more than a pet, an atom, a nothing" (Schwonke 1957, 141). What can humanity do now? Perhaps it can unite and form a planetary unit to better face the dangers that lurk in the encounter with the other. Wells suggests that, at least (Bhelkar 2009, 28–9).

# Conclusion

The three utopias of More, Campanella and Bacon have in common that all place their ideal society on an island. These societies are separated from the rest of the "old" world; they are, however, placed in a real world, but without having a real place (Foucault 1998, 178). In all three texts, it is seafarers who report on the existence of the utopian society, i.e., who not only observe it from the outside, but have somewhat experienced it, even if not as full members of the society, but as strangers. Interaction with strangers is thus quite permitted in utopian society.

## Table 2: Comparison of Utopias

|  | *Utopia* | *City of the Sun* | *New Atlantis* |
|---|---|---|---|
| **Geography** | island, square-planned city with community facilities | island, circular-planned city with orientation towards the temple in the center, community facilities | island, no further information on urban structure |
| **Form of Rule** | oligarchy | autocracy | oligarchy |
| **Smallest Unit** | (extended) family | individual citizen | family |
| **Gender Equality** | women subordinate to men, but with equal education and activity | women are common property of men, equal education and activity | women are subordinate to men, no information on equal education or employment |
| **Religion** | several existing, but not part of the state structure, freedom of religion | state religion, obligatory for all inhabitants | Christianity as state religion |

What is striking about all three utopias is that the ideal form of government is obviously not quite a democracy. All three represent totalitarian systems to varying degrees, or science itself has the primacy of rule over state institutions. Elections and even pluralistic opinion making seems irrelevant.[9] The overall design is one that renders "a world without surprises, whose absolute transparency does not tolerate individual deviations" (Saage 1991, 27).

So, can there be a clear distinction between science fiction and these utopian texts? The relationship between both genres will probably always remain a controversial one (Saage 1997, 45), but it is possible to identify both similarities and differences that can help to differentiate between the two types.

Schwonke never tires of pointing out that utopia is "conceived with political and social categories and linked to political and social ideas" (1957, 91). From this, and from the enthusiasm for technical-scientific progress during the Industrial Revolution, he implies that science fiction has taken over from utopia. Science fiction is capable of "transcending all the practical and theoretical boundaries existing at the moment in thought experiments" (Schwonke 1957, 89)—starting from the natural sciences as a legitimate basis and not limited to the sketching of merely a political-social order.

However, Schwonke certainly reaches too far. During the Industrial Revolution, science fiction stepped alongside utopia and focused on science and technology as an additional genre. It is ultimately "an outgrowth of the science and technology optimism of the 19th century" (Saage 1997, 48). However, technical and scientific progress is not a feature exclusive to science fiction. On the contrary, Bacon shows in *New Atlantis* that science and progress can be the primacy of a utopia. Nevertheless, utopia is more interested in the specific role that technology can play within a society than in technology itself (Saage 1997, 49). "Science and technology are in a servant relationship to it, so to speak" (Saage 1997, 52).

We have shown that utopias are primarily social designs that radically change the lives of their inhabitants. The societies portrayed here were by no means created *ex nihilo*. Based on the realization that the previous way of life does not lead the society any further, the leaders of the respective societies decided to make an absolute reversal of the previous way of life. This is probably the most striking difference from science fiction. It explains social change—as we have seen—through technical-scientific progress, which, step by step, gives people the opportunity to expand their space and thus to explore. So, while utopia focuses on future social models and is socio-politically oriented, science fiction focuses on the relationship between man and technology or—more pointedly—between man and machine. "It is centrally concerned with the 'if and how of technical innovation'" (Saage 1997, 49).

More's *Utopia*, like the other utopias, shows a picture of a small, isolated ideal society, and in doing so, More himself claims to make this picture as comprehensive as possible. This completeness thus encompasses not only state structures or social conventions, but goes down to the details of the infrastructure, the economy, education, and the private, intimate life in this society. "As an outflow of secularized reason, it wants to project [political utopia, i.e.] models of society that should contribute to a humanization of human conditions: either in the form of wishful thinking or in the form of fearful images of future societies" (Saage 1997, 51).

So, in utopian narratives, the change from reality is far more total than in science fiction ones. Since the latter refers primarily to technology and science, the change described is only partial. Jules Verne's explanations about the deep-sea voyage of the *Nautilus*, therefore, say little about the state constitution and the future society on Earth, and the warp drive in *Star Trek* alone does not allow any conclusions about the economic system of Earth in the 24th century.

Science fiction, rather than utopia, therefore, attempts to establish continuity between the present and the fictional future by extrapolation (Suvin 1972, 95–6). In contrast, the utopia tends much more to create a break with reality. An ideal image is complete, the ideal world necessarily the best of all possible worlds. Science fiction, on the other hand, with its continuous extrapolation, pursues the goal of perpetual progress, which it can achieve by constantly researching and improving its technical abilities.

Science fiction is, therefore, much more dynamic in its flexibility and tells of ongoing changes, while utopia presents more of a static result of change. The *status quo* in science fiction is changeable and even strives for change. This dynamic is largely missing in utopia, because here one cannot travel very far—outside of utopia, utopia does not exist. So, while utopia is rather limited in space, in science fiction there is a tendency for space to expand. This finds expression not least in the journeys into the unknown, which are a recurring motif in science fiction. It is true that the travel motif is also present throughout the utopias depicted. These utopias are basically travelogues of sailors who discovered the respective utopian societies by chance. But this is exactly where the difference is understood. Here it is the inhabitants of the outside world who discover the utopias by chance and describe it in a way similar to how a newly discovered plant species is described by a botanist. The inhabitants of the utopias are the objects under investigation. They do not direct their activities outwards unless the utopia as such has its existence threatened. Only then do the inhabitants of the utopia go to war against the outside; only then do they subjugate other peoples and expand spatially. In principle, however, utopias are not expansive. In science fiction, on the other hand, the inhabitants of the science fiction worlds are the subjects who undertake the journeys, discover alien life forms, and expand their space of life and experience. This is not to say that in utopia the inhabitants would not expand their space of experience. They just do it in a different way. They study, they educate themselves, and they expand their immaterial knowledge. They are even required to do so by the social order. But this expansion of the space of experience literally and mainly takes place in their minds. In short: while utopia aims at a closed society, science fiction requires an open society in principle.

In *Utopia*, the picture of a better future is drawn from a view of contemporary society. The utopia does not necessarily have to be realized in the future.

However, the image of utopia changed towards the end of the 18th century with the publication of Merciers *L'an deux mille quatre cent quarante, rêve s'il en fut jamais* (1771). With this novel, the future was also discovered as a possible location of utopia (Orth 2008, 2). When the world was completely explored towards the end of the 18th century, "not only was space used, but with the temporalization of utopia a new, endless projection surface was created" (Orth 2008, 3) to maintain a distance from the recipient. In this way, utopia nevertheless remains attainable in principle by referring to the present in utopia. Thus, classical dystopias such as Orwell's *1984* are consciously located in the future.

However, Yorke rightly points out that utopia cannot be an attainable destination, because "(a) perfection itself is impossible to attain, or (b) [...] there exists no objective criterion for perfection that would let us know when it had been attained" (2004, 5). Utopia is thus more like an abstract target that must be continually striven for by improving and reforming our lives (Yorke 2004, 5).

Saage excludes the concept of science fiction from his definition of utopia (1991, 4), while Fuhse takes the view that science fiction certainly has a socio-political component and is socially critical, but again avoids utopia as a category (2003, 236). If we now look at the science fiction of Verne and Wells, it can be stated without doubt that these works are largely concerned with future, novel technology. But also, More, Campanella and Bacon do not ignore new technology and scientific progress in their utopias.

It just seems as if the terms *utopia* and *science fiction* resist a precise demarcation. Nevertheless, in the preceding discussion we have developed starting points that reveal the characteristics of the different genres. These characteristics can now be summarized to ideal types of the genres:

## Table 3: Classifications of Science Fiction and Utopia

|  | Science Fiction | Utopia |
|---|---|---|
| Reference | necessary | necessary |
| Time | present or future | present or future |
| Place | in reality | out of touch with reality |
| Extent | expansive, directed outwards | limited, directed inwards |
| Focus | technology and science | politics and society |
| Society | open | closed |
| Change | partial | total |
| Procedure | prognostic, extrapolated continuity of reality | normative, break with reality |
| Objective | progress | ideal state |
| Realization | evolutionary | hypothetical |

But we have also shown that this typology of both categories can only be the description of pure forms. The boundaries between science fiction and utopia can be and are crossed, so that a variety of hybrid forms appear. When Freedman argues that "utopias today are typically written within an explicitly science-fictional context" (Freedman 2000, 72), he expresses the ambiguity between the genres, but at the same time makes it clear that both genres still exist and that science fiction has not inherited utopia or even that utopia is to be seen as part of science fiction. Instead, a utopia can certainly occur in the context of a science fiction narrative, if the utopian content of a text is separated from the plot itself: then there are plot elements (such as new technologies), which, in turn, can be clearly assigned to science fiction. On the other hand, a narrated world, which can represent a utopian model of society, is transported through the plot (Orth 2008, 11). Thus, science fiction and utopia are by no means mutually exclusive, but can instead complement each other in a meaningful way. In this respect, Schröder goes too far when he reintroduces social fiction as a category, as "a subspecies of science fiction that focuses more on the social aspect of its stories" (Schröder 1998, 60).

Based on the classical utopias, I have now worked out three essential characteristics that I would like to examine in the further chapters in *Star Trek*:

First, a utopia is based on technology, but to different degrees. This element is most pronounced in Bacon's *New Atlantis*. Therefore, I now dedicate a chapter to the treatment of new technology in *Star Trek*.

Second, a utopia needs a defined space. In classical utopias, this is a remote, enclosed place. How this is reflected in *Star Trek*, I examine in another chapter.

Third, a utopia has an elaborated political-social system, in which the utopian society is embedded with rules and behaviors. I examine this in *Star Trek* in a third chapter.

# 2

# How Technology Changes Society

In the previous chapter, I showed that utopias and science fiction narratives can indeed be distinguished. Utopias are also based on technological progress—as Bacon shows us in *New Atlantis*—but take these new technologies as a basis to depict socio-political change based upon them. For Bacon, it is not only about scientific progress but also about the exploitation of knowledge and technology.

Therefore, let us have a look on how technology is being treated in *Star Trek*.[1] Picard says in *TNG* "The Neutral Zone" that "a lot has changed in the past 300 years," which also points to the fact that these social advances were made possible by technology.

Technology is ubiquitous in *Star Trek* and an essential part of the narrative. Gene Roddenberry repeatedly emphasized that technology has developed significantly in the future and therefore must look accordingly (Sternbach 1996, 3). At the same time, Roddenberry strongly believed that future technology had to be explained in a plausible way. "As far back as the writing of the original first pilot script, Roddenberry sought advice from the scientific community" (Solow and Justman 1996, 126). This is also why that there are so-called technical manuals for *TNG* (Sternbach and Okuda 1991) and *DS9* (Zimmerman, Sternbach, and Drexler 1998), which are considered canon and are based on the respective series bibles. Technology in *Star Trek* is therefore shown as a coherent part of the series reality, i.e., as consistent as possible in its appearance and use and not somehow arbitrarily invented.

Most of the series and films take place on spaceships—except for *DS9*, which is a space station. All of the crews are exploring unknown areas of the universe, a task of which the audience is reminded at each beginning of a *TOS* or *TNG* episode. The *Enterprise* is on its way many light years from Earth "to explore strange worlds, to seek out new life forms and new civilizations." Almost always, the advanced society of space travelers and researchers that humanity has become in the *Star Trek* future is compared with other species in space. "There is hardly an episode that is not about tracking down, establishing contact, or even dealing with a foreign culture [...]" (Hellmann 2000, 133). Although a vivid socio-cultural exchange takes place, these visits are always of short duration and are usually limited to an episode's length.[2] Life on Earth, however, has a minor role only.[3]

So, life in the *Star Trek* universe takes mainly place outside of a natural environment. Space has very low temperatures; there is no gravity; there is no water and no atmosphere. Technology is, therefore, required to live here and for the crew to fulfill its missions.

Early societies in human history were limited to the distances they could walk by foot. Inventions like wheels or ships then made it possible to extend the radii and explore unknown, more distant areas. This eventually led to railways and automobiles, and also to ever-larger ships, which, due to their mass and propulsion, could sail the open seas. Finally, the invention of the airplane led to the fact that, in principle, every point on Earth was accessible from then on.[4] Technological progress thus enabled societies to expand geographically and to establish contact with other cultures. With the advent of long-distance aircraft operating at high altitudes and the invention of submarines, humans were even able to advance into areas for the first time where they would not have survived due to unnatural conditions. However, for this to happen, the technology used had to serve not only for locomotion, but also for life support. Finally, in the 20th century, humans were able to leave their natural environment—which is Earth—completely for the first time by travelling into space.

In this respect, *Star Trek* consistently extrapolated the technological development of our present society. While Captain Kirk was still on a five-year mission in *TOS*, the *Enterprise*-D with Captain Picard in *TNG* is theoretically even capable of operating independently for about seven years without having to travel to a star base or even Earth (Sternbach and Okuda 1991, 2). So, in *Star Trek,* space has become increasingly unbounded for human society thanks to technology. However, life is at the same time strictly confined to a spaceship, the failure of which would result in the immediate deaths of all people therein. The crew of the spaceship is, therefore, completely dependent on hassle-free technology. "Safety is paramount: it [the spaceship] protects its crew from the horrors of outer space, with all manner of redundancies and back-up systems" (Braine 1994, 8).

It is an overall principle of all *Star Trek* series that technology is simply assumed to be there. In the everyday life shown in the series, technology usually does not play an important role. It was deliberately assumed by Roddenberry: "Tell your story about *people*, not about science and gadgetry" (1967, 5). Of course, there are some notable exceptions from this rule, exceptions that will be addressed later. However, generally, technology is seen merely as a device that enables the crew to carry out their duties.

Three technical systems are particularly important in *Star Trek*: Propulsion (especially the warp drive), sensors, and weapons. Without propulsion and sensors, it is obvious that the spaceship could not serve its purpose, the exploration of the unknown. The propulsion system is used to travel into the unknown and to move around in alien space, while sensors can be seen to a certain extent as the eyes and ears of the ship. Via sensors, the *Enterprise* crew literally look from their utopian place to the outside. Sensors provide images on the main bridge screen and data about approaching ships and stars and planets yet to be explored. Encountering unknown worlds also requires a minimum level of weaponry, even though the missions of the *Star Trek* crews are always described as peaceful.

Another technology which is commonly associated with *Star Trek* are the transporter systems with which the crew is able to be "beamed" within seconds from a spaceship in orbit to a planet or another spaceship.[5] "Extra-vehicular transport to and from the ship is accomplished by a number of transporter systems, which allow personnel or equipment to be transported at ranges up to 40,000 kilometers" (Sternbach and Okuda 1991, 102).

A number of other technical systems also support the crew. "Of all major ship's systems, life support and environmental control are among the most critical" (Sternbach and Okuda 1991, 142). These necessarily include atmospheric, water and power supplies, as well as a data network. Waste, for example, is transported to treatment plants for recycling (Sternbach and Okuda 1991, 81–3, 142–3, 145–6; Zimmerman, Sternbach, and Drexler 1998, 45, 51, 96).[6] Since there is a lack of gravity in space, gravity generators are installed on the ships to enable an Earth-like environment. These devices simulate the natural force of gravity within the structure of the spaceship and thus allow the crew to move around as they are used to doing (Sternbach and Okuda 1991, 144; Zimmerman, Sternbach, and Drexler 1998, 98).

Also, a technology frequently associated with *Star Trek* are the so-called replicators for food. "These devices permit replication of virtually any inanimate object with incredible fidelity and relatively low energy cost" (Sternbach and Okuda 1991, 90). This form of food supply is quite often shown as an everyday action within the series episodes, therefore the well-known catchphrase "Tea, Earl Grey, hot" by Picard. Replicators can be found in public rooms and in the crew quarters. The technology is not limited to Starfleet. Other civilizations in the *Star Trek* universe such as the Cardassians in *DS9* also use it (Zimmerman, Sternbach, and Drexler 1998, 108). Furthermore, each crewmember is also given personal access to the computer system for recreational purposes, such as using the *Enterprise*'s apparently very extensive music archive. In *Star Trek: First Contact*, for example, Picard listens to music by Berlioz in one scene; in *Star Trek: Insurrection* he instructs the computer to play music—not classical music, but a mambo.[7]

The holodeck enables its users to immerse themselves in simulated three-dimensional environments, i.e., virtual spaces. Controlled by a computer, the user is integrated into a completely virtual world that feels nevertheless astonishingly real. "[…] The holodeck permitted the simulation of virtually any environment or person with a degree of fidelity virtually indistinguishable from reality. The holodeck employed three-dimensional holographic projections as well as transporter-based replications of actual objects." (Okuda and Okuda 1999, 193).

All technical systems are supplemented by a ship-wide communication and computer system. This system enables easy verbal communication through personal communicator devices, which are attached to one's chest, and also serve to maintain connection during away missions, or through separate communication facilities located in the ship's rooms and corridors (Sternbach and Okuda 1991, 92–5; Zimmerman, Sternbach, and Drexler 1998, 64). A central computer core provides easy access to extensive information stored in the database via numerous input terminals (Sternbach and Okuda 1991, 49–51; Zimmerman, Sternbach, and Drexler 1998, 43).

The everyday technology shown in *Star Trek* can be understood as a reflection of the technology of our present. "Indeed, many of the purely fictional technologies of the original *Star Trek* series such as wireless communicators are now realities." (Ott and Aoki 2001, 395). *Star Trek* is somewhat unique, compared to most other television shows, in that the franchise extends over a long period of time—more than 50 years.

In contrast to science fiction such as Jules Verne's *De la terre à la lune* (1865), which dealt with human space travel at a time when it was not yet technically possible and thus seemed unimaginable, space travel was already established in the 1960s. In 1961, Yuri Gagarin was the first human being in space. The United States was initially taken by surprise by the Soviet Union's lead, but, after the Mercury and Gemini programs, the Apollo program was started, which led eventually to the first manned landing on the Moon. It is a coincidence that the first Apollo test missions took place in 1966, the same year that *TOS* was launched, and that the Apollo 11 mission eventually succeeded in the same year in which *TOS* was canceled, in 1969. *Star Trek* was thus aired at a time when the United States experienced an increasing interest in space travel. The possibility of leaving Earth and entering space was no longer impossible, but the exploration of outer space still was. So, Gene Roddenberry based his concept of *Star Trek* on the assumption that in the following centuries between the 1960s and the 23rd century, in which *TOS* is located, our solar system would be largely explored and mankind would be technologically capable of advancing beyond that into unknown expanses of outer space. In this, Roddenberry drew a comparison to the explorers who set out on their wagon treks towards the West: "The prologue contained in all 79 episodes of the *Original Series* [...] is reminiscent of the Frontier myth in the American Western" (Rauscher 2003, 25). This myth still has a strong influence on American national culture: "American 'civilization' poured into 'new' territory [...]" (Gregory 2000, 164). Consequently, Roddenberry described *Star Trek* as "Wagon Train in Space"—in clear reference to the television series *Wagon Train*, which took up this frontier theme (Rauscher 2003, 15).

In order to cover the vastness of outer space at an appropriate speed, a propulsion system is required that is far superior to the rocket engines of the Apollo missions.

According to Einstein's theory of relativity, however, exceeding the speed of light is not possible in our space-time continuum: "In general relativity, nothing can travel *locally* faster than the speed of light" (Alcubierre 1994, L73). However, if—according to Einstein's theories—space behind a spaceship is expanded and at the same time compressed in front of it, i.e., an artificial curvature of space is created, then super-light speeds are quite possible by carrying the spaceship within a kind of space bubble. "The traditional heuristic explanation of how the warp-drive spacetime works is that the space in front of a given region (the 'warp bubble') is contracted, whereas the space behind the same region is expanded. In response, the warp bubble moves forward with a speed determined by the contraction/expansion rate" (Natário 2002, 1157).[8]

With a so-called warp drive, the spaceship is able to cross great distances within the galaxy in a short time. The warp drive "is the latest version of the device that at last afforded humanity access to deep interstellar space, facilitated contact with other lifeforms, and profoundly changed all preeminent technological civilizations in the Milky Way" (Sternbach and Okuda 1991, 54). So, it is *the* key technology of the *Star Trek* universe. It is the prevalent indication of whether Starfleet will make first contact with other species. For example, in *TNG* "Who Watches the Watchers," Starfleet covertly observes a pre-warp population in order not to influence the technological development of the people. In *TNG* "First Contact" (not to be confused with the 2006 movie) the *Enterprise* crew encounters the Malcorians. This species has developed warp capability at an experimental stage and is also under covert observation by the Federation. In *Star Trek: Insurrection,* the Evora people are newly admitted to the Federation because they have recently acquired warp technology. Last but not least, it was Earth itself that had first contact with the Vulcans through the invention of the warp drive. In the film *Star Trek: First Contact,* the inventor of the warp drive, Zefram Cochrane, performs the first warp flight in history, at which point the Vulcans become interested in Humans: "Captain's Log, April 5, 2063. The voyage of the Phoenix was a success—again. The alien ship detected the warp signature, and is on its way to rendezvous with history" (Picard in *Star Trek: First Contact*).[9] The significance of warp drive as a key technology is questioned in this film in an interesting way. Cochrane is *the* hero of the Federation in the 24th century, and there is a statue of him at the launch site of the first warp spaceship. And yet the actual story seems to be quite different: "You look at me as if I am some kind of saint, or visionary or something. [...] You wanna know what my vision is? Dollar signs, money! I did not build this ship to usher in a new era for humanity" (Cochrane in *Star Trek: First Contact*).[10] Clearly, from the Cochrane contemporary view of 2063, the implications of this technological progress were not foreseeable during its development.

The core idea of the warp theory is an extreme curvature of space in the immediate vicinity of the spaceship by creating a warp field that completely surrounds the ship. By changing the curvature, it is possible to reach higher speeds than the speed of light.[11] Warp 1 corresponds exactly to the speed of light, Warp 2 ten times and Warp 6—which is the usual cruising speed for Starfleet ships—is 392 times the speed of light (Okuda and Okuda 1999, 556). An additional impulse drive is used for navigation in the area of planetary systems. "Aboard most Federation starships, impulse drive is powered by one or more fusion reactors that employ deuterium fuel to yield helium plasma and a lot of power" (Okuda and Okuda 1999, 204).[12] Phasers and photon torpedoes are used for defense. Photon torpedoes contain matter and antimatter, which react explosively with each other when hitting the target, releasing energy (Okuda and Okuda 1999, 357).

However, all of these systems require a high level of energy. In order to ensure a correspondingly powerful energy source for his spaceships, Roddenberry adopted the principle of nuclear fusion, which was still quite new in the 1960s, and used it to construct the warp core, in which matter and antimatter (a construct that was still theoretical in the 1960s) would react to create the energy needed to create a warp field.

This shows that *Star Trek* combines several theories and technologies of the present in order to create a fictitious technology which, due to its (seemingly logical) extrapolation from already existing knowledge, represents a plausible, possible extrapolation of today's technology. Roddenberry took a similar approach in other areas. In the 1960s, radio sets were still very large and difficult to handle. The communicators in *TOS*, on the other hand, are small, portable handheld devices that enabled wireless, computer-supported communication by simply opening the device.

However, reflections about our current technology and its future development in *Star Trek* are not one-way. As a cultural phenomenon, *Star Trek* has not only a huge impact within popular culture but also has led to a serious debate in science. Especially the technical possibilities that are shown in *Star Trek* have influenced our present. Thus, the current science does not rule out warp drive, at least theoretically (Hawking 2001, 160).[13] For example, Alcubierre's essay met with such a great response in scientific circles that five years later his theory was already improved to the effect that the energy requirement was reduced many times over (Van Den Broeck 1999; Natário 2002; Finazzi, Liberati, and Barceló 2009; McMonigal, Lewis, and O'Byrne 2012). In view of the fact that the warp drive is actually (still) a fictitious technology, the scientific debate on this topic is remarkable. In this respect, it shows that the technology of *Star Trek* is closer to our reality than one may initially think.

## Threat or Companion

Nevertheless, it must not be forgotten that in the 1960s most of the sophisticated technologies shown in *Star Trek* were not common at all in everyday life. Instead, "the 1960s and 1970s are characterized by a beginning and rapidly deepening and solidifying skepticism towards technical progress […]" (Weber 2008, 39). Computers, for example, were still huge machines used only by companies and the military. Home computers were not widespread until the late 1970s (Wagner and Lundeen 1998, 50). So, it is no surprise that especially in *TOS*, on the one hand the benefits of technology for a society are emphasized; however, on the other hand, these technologies are treated as potential threat (Booker 2018, 97). "The fear of a murderous, out-of-control technology as a counterpart to the comforts of a future with transporter systems and food replicators is a recurring theme in the *Original Series*" (Rauscher 2003, 71).

For example, in the *TOS* episode "The Return of the Archons," the *Enterprise* encounters an unknown species on planet Beta III that, as it turns out, is under total control of an alien power called Landru. Kirk discovers that Landru is, in fact, a highly sophisticated computer, designed thousands of years before by a scientist to care for the people and to protect them from danger. Over time, however, protection has inhibited progress and suppressed any individuality. Eventually, the crew manages to turn off the computer to free the people from its influence. In *TOS* "The Apple," the *Enterprise* crew meets a population on the planet Gamma Trianguli VI who call themselves the Feeders of Vaal. Again, it turns out that Vaal is, in fact, a computer that has enslaved the population of a planet in order to maintain its existence. The crew of the *Enterprise* destroys the computer in this episode, too—and the inhabitants are on their own from then on.[14]

The plots of both these episodes reflect the fear of curtailing or even destroying a free-minded society through technology. A computer begins to have a life of its own and behaves in a way similar to that of HAL in Stanley Kubrick's *2001: A Space Odyssey* (Weber 2008, 40). The computer suppresses an entire society that does not even recognize the computer as such, but virtually worships it as a godlike being. This is somehow reminiscent of dystopias such as George Orwell's *1984*, whereby total surveillance is not manifested by a totalitarian political system, but by a fully automatic, purely technical system. What is striking is that Landru in its origins was by no means intended as an instrument of surveillance, but was constructed for a supposedly good purpose. Thus, the advantages that a technologized society may have—the advantage of a more or less carefree life—also conceal the greatest dangers, namely, losing control over technology, no longer being able to control it, but instead being controlled by it.

In another *TOS* episode titled "A Taste of Armageddon," *Enterprise* reaches the planet Eminiar VII, which the crew learns is at war with the neighboring planet of Vendikar. However, as it turns out, the war is virtual. Two computers "play" war. They simulate it and eventually determine certain individuals of the respective peoples as victims of war. The individuals do not die in battle; however, they are executed in a specific ritual—now for real, not virtually.

In this episode, computers take on a social and political leadership role, too. In its technological development, the war is only taking place virtually, similar to a contemporary computer game. At the same time, however, real victims are being claimed despite all virtualization, and society is once again under the influence of corrupt technology, which has become uncontrollable.

*TOS* thus conveys an ambivalent image of a technologized society. On the one hand, technology stands out as a symbol for progress; on the other hand, it is a potential threat. Interestingly, the technological progress of the Federation society itself is rarely questioned in *TOS*. Whether the transporter poses health risks, whether phasers as disintegrating weapons could possibly be classified as cruel, and whether warp drive remains without effects on the space-time continuum despite the artificially induced curvature of space are generally not matters of debate. *Star Trek* often uses alien societies, instead, whose technological progress is evaluated from outside (Hellmann 2000, 138). Hence, *TOS* does not shy away from interfering with other cultures. Kirk does not query whether it is desirable to free the population of Beta III from Landru. The interference of the *Enterprise* crew could have more fatal consequences for the population than maintaining the current status. However, the further development of the population of Beta III is hardly considered.

In the understanding of *Star Trek*, technology can only be of benefit to a society if it can handle technology correctly. *Star Trek* thus wants to show that machines can never replace the human factor (Tyrrell 1979, 288). "Whether set against 'superior beings' or 'superior technology,' the value of the 'human factor' is constantly emphasized" (Gregory 2000, 34). For example, in *TOS* "The Ultimate Computer," Starfleet engineer Richard Daystrom develops the advanced computer unit M5, which is far more powerful than the *Enterprise*'s current on-board computer to an extent that it can be replace most crewmembers, including the captain, in the future. During a test, however, the computer gets out of control and severely damages the *Enterprise*'s sister ship, USS *Excalibu*r. Only with great effort does the crew succeed in getting the computer shut down and thus save the *Enterprise* and themselves.

In the course of *Star Trek*, well-known fictional technologies were further adapted in their appearance and functionality. With *Star Trek: The Next Generation,* the warp drive, computer systems, weapons and transporter systems retained their functions, but—*TNG* occurring roughly 100 years after *TOS*—they have advanced.

In the 1980s, technology became more prominent in everyday life. "In *The Next Generation*, technology moves to the fore, reflecting the advances in computers, telecommunications, medicine etc. that were altering daily life in the 1980s" (Braine 1994, 3). For example, computers in *TNG* are much more commonplace than in *TOS*, as computers already had a much greater significance in the 1980s than they had 20 years earlier (Wagner and Lundeen 1998, 51–2). Computer access terminals on the *TOS Enterprise* looked like bulky, dark boxes with several buttons in different colors, but the overall design on the *Enterprise*-D shows significant changes. Modern flat screens and touch screen keyboards indicate that—in the imagination of the *Star Trek* authors—computers are now a completely normal working device, ergonomically adapted to human needs. This is, however, a reflection of our own reality. While computers of the 1960s were still complicated to operate (just think of punch cards or tapes), computers of the 1980s—especially like the Commodore 64, the Amiga and the first personal computers—already had common keyboards and could be handled more easily. At the same time, *Star Trek* again anticipates the technological progress. Thirty years after *TNG*, touch screens are standard, and we have convenient tablets, convertibles, and laptops—but back in 1987 today's computer technology was not imaginable.

Everyone is able to use a computer in the future intuitively, of course. In both *TNG* and *DS9*, Starfleet officers are apparently familiar even with Klingon, Romulan or Cardassian terminals, and *vice versa*. It even seems possible to make the systems of the different species compatible with each other without much effort (Zimmerman, Sternbach, and Drexler 1998, 21).

Technological progress, *Star Trek* suggests to us, is developing in a linear way, making workflows easier and providing access to any knowledge database even in the remotest corner of the universe.

But it is not only with computers that *TNG* shows us the advantages of a highly technologized society. In the *TNG* episode "Samaritan Snare," Picard undergoes heart surgery. As it turns out, he was involved in an assault in his past, and his heart was severely injured by a knife. Thanks to advanced technology, in the 24th century it is no longer a problem to replace the organ with an artificial heart.

At the same time, *TNG*, like *TOS*, is also taking a stand on current technological debates. In the *TNG* episode "Up the Long Ladder," the *Enterprise* crew makes first contact with a society that reproduces itself exclusively through cloning. Due to the increasing instability of DNA caused by cloning, this technology is now reaching its limits, because no more perfect clones can be produced. In this way, this alien society is threatened in its very existence and wants to recover by reproducing genetic clones using new genetic material from the *Enterprise* crew. After the crew rejects the wish, the aliens obtain the genetic material by force, but can be dissuaded from their plan after an ethical and moral discussion. Instead, the *Enterprise* crew recommends that the society should deliberately abandon its cloning technology and rather starts reproducing in a more "traditional" way.

With this episode, *Star Trek* underlines its claim to describe a positively connotated, technicized society in which technologies that lead to ethical or technical problems are rejected and finally discarded. The danger that technology can always be misused is a recurring topic in *TNG*.

## Human Technology

In *TNG*, the android[15] Data takes on a central role when discussing advanced technology and artificial intelligence. One can say that in *Star Trek* Data could be seen as possibly the strongest integration of technology into a society and that the existence of an artificial life form is generally accepted in the future *TNG* society.

In the *TNG* episode "The Measure of a Man," Starfleet cyberneticist Bruce Maddox wants to explore Data's unique technology and dismantle him for this purpose.[16] He explains that Data, as an artificially created being, does not have any right to life and should not be considered a sentient being. "You are imparting human qualities to it because it looks human, but I assure you: it is not. If it were a box on wheels, I would not be facing this opposition" (Maddox in *TNG* "The Measure of a Man"). It is particularly striking that Maddox refers to Data as a thing ("it"). Implicitly, Data is denied the right to strive for more humanity by assuming that he is merely a machine. Picard concludes in his conversation with Guinan that if Data could be duplicated, it would lead to slavery. "Consider that in the history of many worlds there have always been disposable creatures. They do the dirty work. They do the work that no one else wants to do, because it is too difficult or too hazardous. And an army of Datas, all disposable? You do not have to think about their welfare, you do not think about how they feel. Whole generations of disposable people" (Guinan in *TNG* "The Measure of a Man").[17]

In the episode, it finally comes down to a court hearing, in which the judge finally passes a downright Solomonic judgment: "We have all been dancing around the basic issue: does Data have a soul? I do not know that he has. I do not know that I have! But I have got to give him the freedom to explore that question himself. It is the ruling of this court that Lieutenant Commander Data has the freedom to choose" (Judge Louvois in *TNG* "The Measure of a Man").

The court ultimately evades the question of whether Data is a sentient being and not just a machine, but gives Data the (human) right to continue to investigate this question himself. Data is thus granted freedom by society to be allowed to decide for himself as an individual. So, there is the point in the future *Star Trek* society that the mere fact that a being could feel is sufficient for it to be accepted as an artificial individual, even as a full member of society.[18]

Data is a detailed replica of a human in terms of shape, appearance, and behavior.[19] But Data is incapable of experiencing emotions. They are too complex to be part of his programming. This sometimes estranges Data from the rest of the crew. Technically, he is perfect, even physically and psychologically superior, but from his point of view, not in human terms.[20] Data would therefore renounce his technical perfection for becoming less perfect but more human.

In the *TNG* episode "Datalore," Data and the crew of the *Enterprise* discover Data's twin, an android named Lore. Lore had been endowed by creator Noonian Soong with the ability to experience emotion. However, as he was unable to control his emotions and became increasingly aggressive towards him, Soong deactivated Lore and then built Data—without the ability to experience emotions, as a safety measure.

As with Wells, there is a creator of androids, a scientist who plays God and brings creatures to life. The fact that Lore, like Frankenstein and the Animal Men, becomes a danger to the creator as well as to mankind expresses skepticism towards technical progress on a personified level. However, Lore is dangerous not because of a technical imperfection, but because his technology is not compatible with the irrationality of human emotions. So, with Lore, it is the human factor that makes him evil. Asimov's Robot Laws are clearly violated by Lore.

In *TNG* "Descent," Data finally receives an emotion chip, which Soong subsequently constructed for Data (*TNG* "Brothers"). However, Data only dares to install the chip in the feature film *Star Trek: Generations* and is suddenly confronted with a flood of emotional sensations, which cause his circuits to overload. "Part of having feelings is learning to integrate them into your life, Data. Learning to live with them. No matter what the circumstances" (Picard in *Star Trek: Generations*). The emotion chip will bring Data closer to his aim, "making him more human, but in fact also weaker, because he is now subject to passions, fears and anxieties. Data, as a proxy for technology, is becoming more humane through technology" (Weber 2008, 44).

## Virtual Worlds

The most striking new feature of *TNG*, *DS9* and *VOY*, in contrast to the *Original Series*, are the holodecks.[21] Basically, the holodeck is an empty space with a high ceiling and no furniture at all. A yellow grid covers the walls of the room. When not in use, the holodeck is like a dark TV screen or a blank page in a book. But once a program is started, the holodeck comes to life. Holodecks simulate life in its lushest form (Stoppe 2016, 3–4). Simply spoken, a holodeck uses computer technology to simulate a three-dimensional, realistic environment in which the user can fully integrate and with which it can interact. The computer automatically responds to the user's actions according to the design of the respective program. The holodeck is not limited to simulations related to the service on a spaceship, such as crew training, but specifically serves as a recreation facility for the crew in their spare time. In this respect, the holodeck is some sort of technological hybrid between film and computer game. With increasing computing power, the "holodeck adventures" have become more and more elaborate and are to a large extent provided with a well-constructed plot—similar to a film script. The user thus quickly has a more active role within the holodeck story, instead of being a more passive recipient in front of the television or cinema screen. Boundaries between reality and fiction become blurred and a new, virtual reality is being created (Stoppe 2016, 6).[22] McLuhan explains that the cinema was originally called Bioscope, because it presented the audience with real, seemingly alive sequences of movements (McLuhan 2010, 310). Motion pictures share many characteristics with books, and "the business of the writer or the film-maker is to transfer the reader or viewer from one world, his *own*, to another, the world created by typography and film" (McLuhan 2010, 311). At the same time, the holodeck demands an active role of the user in this virtual world—like a game that works according to strict rules (McLuhan 2010, 257). So, it is no coincidence that there is also a publishing business for holonovels in *Star Trek* (*VOY* "Author, Author").

The holodeck is featured in a variety of episodes throughout *Star Trek*. In the *TNG* episode "The Big Goodbye," Picard takes the role of the private detective Dixon Hill, a character whose program is based in San Francisco in the 1940s.[23] The program is based on a plot in which Picard is involved in a murder case, similar to a crime novel, and has to solve it. Meanwhile, in "reality," the *Enterprise* encounters an alien species and is attacked. As a result of the attack, the holodeck malfunctions, and the holodeck's virtual reality suddenly becomes a real threat to Picard when all security functions are suddenly disabled. These functions are a standard feature of the holodeck to prevent accidents or even deaths when running a program.

This example shows two things: On the one hand, *Star Trek* considers the fact that in our present society technology is also increasingly used in leisure time. Combined with the current generation of computer games, which provide an ever-growing impression of reality and create virtual realities that can react better with artificial intelligence to the player's input, there is only a modest step towards a perfect, three-dimensional reality left.[24] *Star Trek* thus expands on ideas that were already dealt with in the 1982 movie *Tron*, except that humans are not accidentally molecularized and drawn into the computer but rather consciously enter a virtual reality. Furthermore, on the holodeck the user can (normally) pause the program at any time, like a kind of in-game menu, by verbally requesting the computer to do so.

Although *Tron* introduced the idea of virtual worlds in which a human being can immerse himself in the realm of cinematic fiction (an idea that was given an elaborate, dystopian perspective in *The Matrix*), the approach to creating virtual realities has long been established in science fiction literature. As early as in 1932, Aldous Huxley invented "feelies" in his work *Brave New World*—an extrapolated version of the then-new "talkies" (sound motion pictures), which increased the immersion into the medium. However, "feelies" were still linear motion pictures with no possibility of real interaction. But when a fictional "reality" begins actively to adapt to the user's actions, the border between reality and fiction begins to dissolve. In this way, feedback is directly created between the user and the simulation, making it ultimately impossible to check whether one is in reality or still immersed in the fiction.[25]

*TNG* "Hollow Pursuits" shows that the technology of the holodeck can also be misused. In this episode, the character of shy and awkward Lieutenant Barclay is introduced. Barclay has huge problems dealing with his fellow crewmates in both his professional and private life. Instead, he prefers to retreat to the holodeck, for which he has designed his own personal program. Inspired by *The Three Musketeers*, he fights with his sword against his adversaries, who consist exclusively of the holoimages of the series protagonists—and thus are Barclay's superiors (Braine 1994, 12). Barclay escapes from reality into fiction to compensate for his social insecurity. It is only in the virtual world of the holodeck he can act equally with his superiors; it is only in the program when he feels no insecurity in dealing with them. So, *Star Trek* deals with the potential danger of this technology to create a form of a substitute world, a kind of "artificial paradise like Disneyland" (McLuhan 2010, 259) if one is no longer up to the actual reality. Here again, *Star Trek* reflects the present society. Excessive use of media and especially computer games may result in escaping to a substitute world to avoid reality as far as possible. However, with *Star Trek*, the technology itself is not questioned, since the technology itself is not the sole reason. So, it is obvious that, with the help of the remaining crew, Barclay builds up self-confidence and is being integrated into society again during the episode and thus does not have to continue using the holodeck in this form.

However, *Star Trek* does not assume that technology is flawless and admits that every form of technology is susceptible to disruptions even in the 24th century. In this context, however, it is interesting to note the technological flaw in *TNG* "Elementary, Dear Data." In this episode, Data plays through a fictional story of Sherlock Holmes on the holodeck. Data takes the role of the title character; his friend and chief engineer Geordi LaForge plays Holmes' companion Dr. Watson. Both meet Holmes' arch-enemy Professor Moriarty, but since Data as an android uses his immense logical abilities and, moreover, knows all the detective's cases anyway, the obstacles posed to him in the holodeck episode are all known, so that he solves the case immediately, much to the displeasure of LaForge. LaForge therefore instructs the computer to create a case (and thus vary the given plot) in which opponents appear who have the ability to beat Data, and which is designed in such a way that only Data can solve it. When they then encounter the newly generated Moriarty, they discover to their surprise that he is aware of the holodeck and the *Enterprise*—as a computer-generated holodeck character who only acts within a holo-episode, this should not actually happen. LaForge now notices his slip. He has instructed the computer to create a case that only *Data* can solve, not *Sherlock Holmes,* whom he impersonates. Through this error by LaForge, the computer has adapted Data's more advanced abilities and, unintentionally but understandably, has created a character that is more intelligent than all human crewmembers. It seems that, as in *TOS*, the great danger of a technologically advanced society lies in the fact that technology becomes too independent and begins to dominate humans. In the episode plot, Captain Picard is summoned when Moriarty feels the desire to leave the holodeck, and Picard has to assure him several times that technology does not allow this. As a proof, he throws a holographic book through the open holodeck door, which disappears, of course (Schröter 2009, 117). Picard emphasizes that despite LaForge's mistake, humans can still master the technology.[26]

The situation is similar to the *TNG* episode "A Fistful of Datas," in which the holodeck again plays an important role (Braine 1994, 12). This time it is Worf, who is in a Wild West holo-simulation, while at the same time LaForge is conducting an experiment with Data, in which the latter is supposed to connect with the ship's computer, so that he can be available as a backup system in case of an emergency. The experiment fails, and Data is erroneously inserted as a multiple hologram character into the running holoprogram, where he becomes a threat to Worf.

## Conclusion

*Star Trek* draws an ambivalent picture of a technologically advanced society. Technology allows us to explore new worlds and to get into contact with other species. At the same time, computer networks provide easy access to knowledge and, through communication even over long distances, make it possible to establish and maintain social contacts. Complicated diseases can be treated; even the replacement of organs with artificial ones does not pose a major problem. Increasingly, technology has also found its way into leisure time with the holodeck.

At the same time, social interaction on board of space ships seems to be essentially unchanged. Although much of the communication is handled by the computer, personal contacts are still important. Moreover, with the character of Data, an artificial sentient being has been created that both represents technical progress and the importance of humanity.

In a nutshell, technology has an important and central meaning in *Star Trek*. But it never replaces social interaction and always only serves to complement existing social structures.

# 3

# Life in Space

## *Utopia on a Ship*

We have already pointed out that utopia is usually placed in a faraway location.[1] Or as Foucault says "utopias are emplacements having no real place. They are emplacements that maintain a general relation of direct or inverse analogy with the real space of society" (1998, 178).

It seems necessary to separate an ideal form of society from the real existing society within which the utopia was created. Only in this way may the ideal world develop undisturbed from current influences.

So, it is not a surprise at all that a utopian text is frequently located in a fictitious city with a limited population (Biesterfeld 1982, 17). Because utopias are always descriptions of an imagined society and because these societies are strictly organized in their ideal state, this is also reflected in the city's architecture.

For the constitution of a utopia, therefore, the construction of its site has an important role. In their ideal state, these worlds do not tolerate individual deviations of their inhabitants (Saage 1991, 27). However, a utopia does not necessarily have to be a fixed place on a fictitious island, but could also move around as an enclosed space. Thus, the ship is an ideal space for a utopia for Foucault: "A placeless place, that lives by its own devices, that is self-enclosed and, at the same time, delivered over to the boundless expanse of the ocean, and that goes from port to port, from watch to watch, from brothel to brothel [...]" (1998, 184–5).

Even before mankind was seriously engaged in space travel, spaceships had a special fascination. Jules Verne was perhaps the first author to use the concept of a space vehicle in his book *De la terre à la lune* in 1865. With the advent of unmanned space flight, this concept, previously considered to be mere science fiction, suddenly became real. And since manned space flight, these vehicles have taken on a further, special significance in addition to their function as a means of transport: they do offer a place in which to survive—like a ship that offers protection from the hostile sea and the airplane that offers protection from the thin atmosphere. Both ship and airplane also open up distances that humans would not be able to reach without such technology.

The spaceship now enables journeys beyond Earth and, at the same time, offers protection from the hostile environment of the outer space. In addition to the lack of atmosphere in space, there are also high radiation and low temperatures. In a sense, a spaceship is therefore a nearly perfect utopian place. Almost everything in *Star Trek* takes place on spaceships, or, with *DS9*, on a space station. Rabitsch points out that, although *Star Trek* is commonly related to *Wagon Train*, it is instead "the mythologized British Golden Age of Sail [which] serves as the primary model for *Star Trek*'s worldbuilding" (2019, 8). For Rabitsch, the naval corpus of *Star Trek* contains a clear hierarchy of ranks and designations, space as a kind of oceanic paradigm, and an archetypal *Star Trek* captain character who is not only an experienced master and commander but also a scientist in his own right (2019, 8–10).[2]

It is no coincidence that Gene Roddenberry named his flagship *Enterprise*, as this name has a long history for naval vessels, past and present (Rabitsch 2019, 81). A symbolic reference to this past is clearly made in the opening sequence of *Star Trek: Generations*, in which Worf gets his promotion to Lieutenant Commander in historic costumes and must walk the plank (Rabitsch 2019, 82). After all, even a real spaceship bore the name *Enterprise*, the NASA space shuttle prototype (Worland 1994, 27).[3] The USS *Enterprise*—although the name applies to several ships—has a major role in all of the *Star Trek* movies (except for *Star Trek IV: The Voyage Home*); in the series *TOS*, *TNG*, *ENT*; and also in season 2 of *DIS*.[4]

In *Star Trek: Voyager*, the ship's name also has a special meaning. As a spacecraft, which is accidentally drawn into unknown and uncharted territory, a parallel is drawn to the NASA *Voyager* probes, which explored the outer planetary system and eventually entered interstellar space. Finally, in *Star Trek: Deep Space Nine*, the name of the space station also reflects its remoteness in space.

Probably no other organization is more often mentioned in the *Star Trek* universe than Starfleet. "Starfleet has long been charged with a broad spectrum of responsibilities to the citizens of the Federation and to the lifeforms of the galaxy at large" (Sternbach and Okuda 1991, 1). Starfleet is the space force of the United Federation of Planets and maintains a large number of starships and space stations to "explore new worlds, to seek out new life, and new civilizations, and to boldly go where no one has gone before" (Sternbach and Okuda 1991, 179). In addition, Starfleet also is the principal means for defense, peacekeeping, and diplomacy. A characteristic feature of Starfleet is that all ships and stations are hierarchically organized, even if civilians are allowed on board. They are "commanded by an elite caste of senior officers [...]. Other members of a starship's crew are often simply addressed as *crewman* [...]. The higher tiers of Starfleet are populated by flag officers of various ranks" (Rabitsch 2019, 71), such as admirals who commonly reside either at Starfleet Command or at certain star bases.

## A Flying Village: The USS *Enterprise*-D

In the *TNG* era, the Galaxy-class USS *Enterprise*-D is clearly the flagship of Starfleet with enough space to accommodate not only the crew but also their families. Supervising producer Robert H. Justman says, "Gene [Roddenberry] and I wanted to have a place that was conducive to as comfortable a life as one was able to have on a space mission of perhaps twenty years duration. [...] I said that it was unconscionable to expect people to go out into space for X number of years and leave everything they hold most dear behind them. Just because you're on a space exploration, it doesn't mean that you have to give up your life. If you have loved ones, you have family, you should be able to enjoy and live and make your lives together, even though you're out in space" (Sternbach 1996, 10–1). In total, the usual ship's complement is more than 1,000 persons, including family members. For short-term missions, there are accommodations for 6,500 individuals (Sternbach and Okuda 1991, 152). Therefore, one could say that the ship resembles a small village, and even in the *Star Trek* future, this size is somewhat unprecedented. "Meanwhile, I am becoming better acquainted with my new command, this galaxy-class USS *Enterprise*. I am still somewhat in awe of its size and complexity" (Picard in *TNG* "Encounter at Farpoint"). So, it is no surprise that common ship's life is quite diverse: "Besides the arrival of Ambassador T'Pel, other events occurring today include four birthdays, two personnel transfers, a celebration of the Hindu Festival of Lights, two chess tournaments, one secondary school play, and four promotions. Overall, an ordinary day" (Data in *TNG* "Data's Day").

From the outside, the *Enterprise* does not appear to be particularly adapted to interstellar space. In its curved, bird-like appearance, the ship is reminiscent of a swan proudly floating on water. A flattened saucer section dominates with a very large outer surface, which has plenty of room for windows and thus allows the crew a view into space. This section of the ship contains the majority of the crew's living quarters. On the secondary hull, laboratories and working spaces are located. It is noticeable that exterior views of the *Enterprise* are shown on screen in a fixed frame of reference. The *Enterprise* always moves upright, and top and bottom are clearly defined—although there is no top or bottom in three-dimensional space without reference (Rabitsch 2019, 76). The representation thus very clearly resembles a ship at sea—with the bridge on the top deck and the keel line below. If the *Enterprise* is in danger, for example during an attack, due to the gravitational pull of a star, or because a warp nacelle suddenly fails, the ship lurches like a ship that is difficult to maneuver in high seas.

In total, the *Enterprise* consists of 42 decks.[5] "The interior spaces validate the concept of the interstellar organism, with the level of complexity rising dramatically once inside the hull. The starship possesses structures akin to a central nervous system and circulatory apparatus, food storage areas, a heart, locomotor mechanisms, waste removal paths, and numerous other systems" (Sternbach and Okuda 1991, 6).

The bridge is located on deck 1. "[…] A Starfleet bridge retains a residual similitude with the quarterdecks of old. They are brightly lid, open spaces. […] They all face *for'rad* and tend to feature a section in the back of the room which is slightly raised and separated from the central command and steering section by a *railing*" (Rabitsch 2019, 79). Next to the bridge are a conference room and the Captain's Ready Room. Apart from these three, there are no other rooms on deck 1.[6] Main engineering is located in the lower propulsion section of the ship on deck 36. Sickbay is on deck 12 on port side of the saucer section and "consists of two medical intensive-care wards, an attached laboratory, the CMO's [Chief Medical Officer's] office, and a small nursery. The second facility, located on the starboard side of Deck 12, is similar to the primary sickbay but features two dedicated surgery suites, a physical therapy facility, a nursery, and a null-grav therapy ward. Adjacent to the second facility is a dental care office and a full biohazard isolation unit" (Sternbach and Okuda 1991, 148).

Transporter rooms and shuttle ramps are used for transfers from and to the ship. Shuttles and transporters are practically the only means of travel outside the ship.[7] An extensive network of turbolifts ensures mobility within the ship. Turbolifts are similar in design to contemporary lift cabins and can take their users quickly to their desired destinations via vertical, but also horizontal, shafts (Okuda and Okuda 1999, 527).

As noted, the holodeck was introduced in *TNG* as a new type of room, which has since been used as technology in all chronologically following series and films. "Within the USS *Enterprise*, crew members can visit four main Holodecks on Deck 11. In addition, a set of twenty smaller personal holographic simulator rooms are situated on Decks 12 and 33" (Sternbach and Okuda 1991, 157). A holodeck's main purpose is to provide relaxation for the crew; however, the holodeck is frequently used for simulating combat situations or conducting research.

A popular meeting place for the crew is Ten Forward, a bar that—the name suggests it—is located on deck 10 in the front part of the ship. At Ten Forward you can have drinks, play games or gaze at the breathtaking course of the stars during a voyage through the panorama window. The bar is the preferred place on the ship where people meet when they are off-duty.

There are also several gymnasiums on the ship,[8] a theater (*TNG* "The Nth Degree," *TNG* "Frame of Mind"), an arboretum[9] (*TNG* "Dark Page"), schools (*TNG* "Hero Worship," *TNG* "When the Bough Breaks"), day-care centers[10] (*TNG* "The Child"), a library *(Star Trek: Insurrection)* and a barbershop[11] (*TNG* "Ensign Ro")—but also a mortuary (*TNG* "Suspicions," *VOY* "Renaissance Man"). There is also a so-called replication center. Here, crewmembers and guests can have larger objects replicated—in a manner similar to food replicators (*TNG* "Data's Day").

Therefore, we can assume that—aside from duty shifts—the crew does have a "normal" social life with sports, hobbies, and family life. For example, in *TNG* "New Ground," Worf and his son have a parent-teacher talk, and in *TNG* "Disaster," the winners of a school competition have a tour of the ship with Captain Picard—the tour was the first prize in the competition. Even the barbershop, run by a Bolian civilian named Mot, plays a role (as in *TNG* "Data's Day," *TNG* "The Host," or *TNG* "Schisms").

Living on the ship is also an important feature, and the living quarters—at least those of the senior officers—are frequently shown. Living quarters are available on the *Enterprise* in various sizes and configurations, depending on one's rank and family status. In principle, "each person aboard the *Enterprise* is assigned approximately 110 square meters of personal living quarters space. The accommodations typically include a bedroom, living/work area, and a small bathroom" (Sternbach and Okuda 1991, 152). For junior or non-commissioned officers, these are quarters in the inner parts of the ships, which have no windows and are usually shared by two people (*TNG* "Lower Decks"). Senior officers are generally entitled to larger quarters on the outer parts, usually with a larger living area and with large windows. Families with children also have larger quarters at their disposal or two smaller quarters can be combined into one large living space (Sternbach and Okuda 1991, 152). Finally, the captain's quarters and VIP quarters for special guests on board, such as ambassadors, are the largest in terms of size and equipment. Instead of a kitchen, quarters are equipped with a personal food replication system, which has a similar technology to the transporter and can replicate almost any kind of food (Sternbach and Okuda 1991, 153–4).[12]

We can assume that the living conditions on other Starfleet ships are somewhat comparable to the *Enterprise*. There were also gymnasiums on the *Enterprise* NX-01 (*ENT* "The Forge") and the *Enterprise* NCC-1701

(*TOS* "Charlie X"). However, a major difference is that, up to *TNG*, families were not intended on board a ship. Therefore, the predecessor ships of *Enterprise* were much smaller.

*Voyager*, much smaller than the *Enterprise*, is described as "Intrepid class, sustainable cruise velocity of warp factor 9.975, fifteen decks, crew complement of 141 [...]" (Lieutenant Stadi in *VOY* "Caretaker"), and families are not allowed on board *Voyager*, either.[13] Instead of Ten Forward, *Voyager* has a mess hall (this is also the case in *TOS* and *ENT*), which is less sophisticated than Ten Forward in *TNG*. Nevertheless, there are also holodecks on *Voyager*, which can also be used for the crew's leisure time. The crew quarters on *Voyager* also resemble those of the *Enterprise* in *TNG* in equipment and comfort.

The USS *Defiant* in *DS9* has a special position among the spaceships. Introduced as a highly flexibly designed warship, it has only four decks and no comfort facilities for the crew. The ship has no holodecks and only "twenty-two main cabins, ten contingency main cabins, replicators and wardroom, and sickbay compartments. The crew cabins are equipped with a minimum of two bunks, and can be outfitted for as many as six, for a potential total crew of 192. The normal operational crew is forty" (Zimmerman, Sternbach, and Drexler 1998, 136).

## *Deep Space Nine* as an Interstellar Port

*Deep Space Nine* was originally built by the Cardassians during the occupation of Bajor and placed in its orbit to process mined ores from the planet. When the Cardassians ended the occupation and withdrew from the planet, the Federation and Starfleet stepped in as Bajor's protective force, taking over the space station and eventually moving it out of orbit near the newly discovered wormhole that leads to the Gamma Quadrant.

In the production bible of *DS9*, Berman and Piller state that "wormholes, simply put, are shortcuts through space. You go in one end and come out the other in seconds... but find yourself billions of kilometers away" (1992, 1–2).[14] Therefore, *Deep Space Nine* is essentially a guarding post set in the outermost area of Federation territory, a fact that will become more important in the course of the series. So, an essential difference between the *Enterprise* and *Deep Space Nine* is that, on the one hand, we are dealing with Cardassian technology mainly instead of a pure Federation-driven ship—and, on the other hand, that *Deep Space Nine* is stationary. However, this does not contradict the ocean paradigm.

The space station is much larger than even the *Enterprise*. *Deep Space Nine* consists of two concentrically arranged rings, an inner so-called habitat ring and an outer docking ring. These are arranged around a cylindrical core, the so-called Ops Area. "Emerging above and below the ring plane are three tall pylons with wide buttresses and inwardly sweeping curves" (Zimmerman, Sternbach, and Drexler 1998, 15). Larger ships can dock at these pylons without any problems, while docking locks for smaller ships are provided on the outer ring. "Since both the previous and current avatars of Deep Space 9 must accommodate a variety of commercial, scientific, and military space traffic, the berthing facilities have been designed to provide adaptable connections to many different personnel and cargo transfer tunnels" (Zimmerman, Sternbach, and Drexler 1998, 52).

Access between the docking points and the station is ensured by a large number of airlocks, and a total of 253 cargo holds can be used to handle freight (Zimmerman, Sternbach, and Drexler 1998, 55–6). The station has a total diameter of 1.45 kilometers and a total height of 969 meters (Zimmerman, Sternbach, and Drexler 1998, 16).

Just like a spaceship, the space station combines several emplacements in a single real location (Foucault 1998, 181). It is a cargo hub. Also, however, passengers come from one ship and transfer to another. They use the facilities of the station, or they may even reside and make their livings there. Yet this place, as public as it may seem at first glance, is not so publicly accessible at all. "Either one is constrained to enter […] or one has to submit to rituals and purifications. One can enter only with a certain permission and after a certain number of gestures have been performed" (Foucault 1998, 183). Ergo, one must let oneself be "purified" through the airlocks before entering the station and before getting a docking permit in the first place; finally, one submits to the order that prevails on the station. Ordinary passengers do not see the living areas of the people living there. They have a few hours' time to change ships and spend it in the shops on the promenade or stay in guest quarters until they reach their connecting transfer, but they are only guests by chance and not by invitation (Foucault 1998, 183). Thus, the space station is also a non-place and somehow different from spaceships—in fact, bearing a striking similarity to train stations and airports of our time. Rabitsch compares *Deep Space Nine* "to an exotic/colonial port whose commander has a small squadron of vessels at his disposal" (2019, 94), which is also a fitting description. *Deep Space Nine* is on the edge of Federation territory—a fact that will become important in the later episodes with regard to Federation influence on the periphery—becoming a "leading center of commerce and scientific exploration" (Berman and Piller 1992, 2) and something "between a free port and a flea market" (Berman and Piller 1992, 5).

Probably the most striking difference is the high fluctuation of visitors. A spaceship is relatively isolated from the outside world, and the number of transfers is quite manageable. On a station, however, a large number of passengers arrive, meet, and leave again. "On a given day, there might be anywhere from ten to three hundred visitors to *DS9* as ships come through… explorers, scientists, merchants, spies… [M]ost of the visitors stay on their ships but there are special quarters for some guests" (Berman and Piller 1992, 5).

Despite the functional differences and the fact that it was originally a Cardassian station, the equipment of *Deep Space Nine* is comparable to that of spaceships. There is also a command station on *Deep Space Nine*, which is called the Operations Center (Ops for short). Similar to its position on a ship, it is located in a central position right in the middle of the station. "The primary control of all station activities is handled by the Operations Center, or ops, which occupies all of Level 1 of Deep Space 9" (Zimmerman, Sternbach, and Drexler 1998, 29). Adjacent to Ops is the Station Commander's office (Zimmerman, Sternbach, and Drexler 1998, 31), the Ready Room, so to speak. Below Ops in the central area are the station's computer cores, and at the bottom of the central core are the power supplies (Zimmerman, Sternbach, and Drexler 1998, 38, 45–7). So, the central core could actually be seen as the "heart and brain" of the entire facility.

Levels 5 to 7 are the promenade, the main place for all commercial activities, with the actual shops on the lowest level 7, whereas on the higher levels there are some observation windows and especially offices and storage rooms. "The Level 7 concourse provides a wide range of shops, trading posts, services, entertainment, and food establishments, plus the Bajoran temple. Commercial space is controlled by the Deep Space 9 Merchants Association […]" (Zimmerman, Sternbach, and Drexler 1998, 112). There are a number of facilities and shops on the promenade that exist quasi-symbiotically among themselves, but everything is kept to a small scale. The promenade is actually like the shopping mall of an airport. Even a chapel is included. "It has been built and furnished in the style of the temples of Bajor, based on architectural forms dating back to the ancient city of B'hala. Bajoran residents and visitors use the Promenade temple for daily prayers and meditations, as part of their search for guidance from the Prophets" (Zimmerman, Sternbach, and Drexler 1998, 113). The fact that the shops are rented out is a peculiarity in the *Star Trek* universe, as money is largely abolished within the Federation. But since the shop areas are not rented by Starfleet and money continues to exist in the *Star Trek* universe—for example with the Ferengi—commercial use is not unusual, especially considering the fact that this is a faraway outpost of the Federation. The variety of shops reflects typical business areas: dealers for space ship parts and communication devices, repair shops, clothing stores, art dealers, a gift shop, an exchange office, a jeweler, a florist, a hairdresser, and a travel agency. A self-service restaurant, a Klingon restaurant, and the bar of Ferengi Quark (one of the main characters in *DS9*) complete the offer on the Promenade Deck. The holodeck is also found in a modified form as a paid holosuite on *Deep Space Nine* (Zimmerman, Sternbach, and Drexler 1998, 112–3).[15]

The Promenade Deck is also home to the infirmary (Zimmerman, Sternbach, and Drexler 1998, 101). The easy accessibility of this facility suggests that the infirmary is not primarily intended for the residents, but rather for the visitors to the station. However, "two large noncritical-care wards are located in the Mid-Core on Level 13" (Zimmerman, Sternbach, and Drexler 1998, 101), and there are further medical facilities in the habitat ring, including "physical therapy suites, [… a] dental care office" (Zimmerman, Sternbach, and Drexler 1998, 103), and various laboratories. The Head of Security, whose office is also located on the promenade deck, is responsible for security on this deck. "The department is concerned with the internal volume of the station, and so external defensive operations involving Deep Space 9 or allied spacecraft are not normally involved and are left to Starfleet officials" (Zimmerman, Sternbach, and Drexler 1998, 104). Here, too, the focus is on the function of the space station as a visitor and passenger platform.

The permanent residents of *Deep Space Nine* usually live in the so-called Habitat Ring. Originally there were about 450 large and 230 smaller residential quarters here (Zimmerman, Sternbach, and Drexler 1998, 106). The Habitat Ring extends around the central core and also consists of several levels. Although the station is many times larger than the *Enterprise*, only about 300 people live here permanently (*DS9* "Sanctuary"). At the beginning of the series, it was assumed that there were about 200 Bajoran inhabitants and 50 Starfleet personnel living on the station (Berman and Piller 1992, 4). "A total of 343 additional quarters are maintained in the Mid-Core for overflow transient ship crews, for some engineering and security support personnel, and as contingency accommodations for evacuees or refugees" (Zimmerman, Sternbach, and Drexler 1998, 106–7). This also shows that the station is more or less a transfer facility rather than a permanent residence.

"The typical Habitat Ring residential space set into the outboard structural area includes a few large transparent aluminum windows, room partitions, a replicator, wash facilities, and connections for EPS-powered devices, com systems, and computer terminals" (Zimmerman, Sternbach, and Drexler 1998, 107). There is a central living room and one or more bedrooms and bathrooms. Although there is both a school (*DS9* "A Man

Alone") and a sports hall,[16] life on *Deep Space Nine* seems less comfortable than on ships like the *Enterprise*.

## Society in the Microcosm

A spaceship or space station is not a natural habitat for humans. Rather, these places are precisely predetermined and artificially created. In the *Star Trek* universe, these places are described as a complex microcosm, which is defined by private as well as public spaces.

In order to be able to survive in space, the spaceship functions as a barrier. The architecture of the spaceship "creates living spaces on its inside, which it shields from environmental influences on the outside" (Pabst 2003, 92). Without this framework, survival in space would be impossible; and thus, the formation of a social structure would also be impossible. Socially, too, the spaceship structure sets boundaries and defines and limits a social space (Pabst 2003, 92).

In a way, the architecture of the spaceship is to be seen as a symbol of human culture and its utopian-looking way of life. "The species itself becomes form and receives its primary signature through its ship [...]" (Pabst 2003, 88). When encountering other ships, the outward appearance symbolizes this culture and is thus the first thing that the other person becomes aware of. From the outer design of the spaceship, one can already deduce its inhabitants. This is underlined in the series by the fundamentally different design of the so-called warbirds or Birds of Prey of the Klingons and Romulans. Here, the dark appearance—both exterior and interior—and the bird of prey architecture signal that these species are warriors. "Thus, [...] Klingon ships [...] do not have a smooth hull as the outermost layer, but are covered with outsourced functional parts. In a sense, they lack an aesthetic element that would put appearance before functionality" (Pabst 2003, 108).

This can also be seen in *DS9* regarding the design of the space station. "It must be pointed out that varying artistic and industrial engineering styles abound in the galaxy, and there is no doubt that the functionality of the hardware has been melded together with a stylistic sense that appears to govern the Cardassians as builders" (Zimmerman, Sternbach, and Drexler 1998, 15–6). The design of the station is characterized by curved forms. The outer appearance conveys a certain symmetry, and inside, dark colors dominate. In contrast, the *Enterprise* in *TNG*—and also the other ships in Starfleet that can be seen in the *Star Trek* series and movies—symbolizes peace and a certain pride in having created and preserved a utopian society by their bright, curved, and smooth appearance. The outward appearance of the *Enterprise* also signals a high degree of perfection. The smooth hull represents and protects the fragile utopian social structure inside. In this respect, the spaceship provides sufficient insulation to ensure and maintain the functioning of the utopian system on this ship. This isolation, or rather a minimization of the effects on the system from outside, is what Freyer demands for a utopia (1936, 24).

The description of the interiors of the spaceships and space stations shows striking parallels to the descriptions of the living structures in More's *Utopia*, Campanella's *City of the Sun*, and Bacon's *New Atlantis*. When More says that "if you know one of their cities you know them all, for they're exactly alike [...]" (2002, 44), this also applies to the typical spaceship in *Star Trek*. All ships in the series universe are similarly constructed. More also refrains from presenting all cities in his work, but implies them by means of the most prestigious one (More 2002, 45). It is no different in *Star Trek*. The *Enterprise* "is Starfleet's flagship and has already distinguished itself in an impressive number of significant missions of exploration, as well as in several crucial incidents defending the security of the Federation" (Sternbach and Okuda 1991, 4). Through its function as the flagship of the Federation, *Enterprise* rises to the status of an architectural paradigm within Starfleet (Pabst 2003, 101).

More's utopian city is laid out with a square ground plan and fortified with a city wall (More 2002, 45). The *Enterprise*, *Voyager*, and *Deep Space Nine* are also laid out according to a plan. Not only are they divided into decks, but also into sectors and departments: "Note the first and second group of the locator address (totaling six digits) are generally used as room designator numbers within the habitable volume of the spacecraft. By keeping in mind this general scheme of room and compartment numbering, it is possible for crew members to locate virtually any room on board the ship by use of the internal coordinate system" (Sternbach and Okuda 1991, 21). On each door on the respective spaceship there is a unique numbering, so you can easily determine on which deck and in which section you are.

Life on the starships of Starfleet is therefore similarly planned as in the cities of Utopia. In a way, the spaceship provides the regulatory framework within which social life in the serial universe takes place. At the same time, however, the spaceship allows you to move freely in space. So, compared to our contemporary society, it is accurate to say that "the *Enterprise* represents a social utopia because it is free from the fixed and mapped spaces of [our] society" (Ott and Aoki 2001, 397).

A corporate design, which ranges from door lettering to standard equipment for the quarters, signals membership in a large community. The structure is inhabited by a defined number of people who work on the ship. The closed nature of the spaceship makes it difficult to escape its daily routine. Because each crewmember was not transferred to the ship for service without purpose, the work of each member is required to maintain the functioning of this system. Consequently, it is simply necessary to maintain the technical functioning of the ship in order to enable it to survive in space.

The protagonists of the series are all senior officers, and so their jobs are clearly marked.[17] "There is no alienation from work; everyone is doing exactly what he or she loves to do" (Wagner and Lundeen 1998, 137). Decisions are made after prior discussion among the protagonists. Another regularly recurring element of the series is the general evaluation and discussion of a situation. In this case, the officers meet in the conference room. Private discussions—for example between the captain and the first officer—are often held in confidence, in the Captain's Ready Room. That individuality has to step back behind the military chain of command is shown by in dialogue between the First Officer Chakotay and Captain Kathryn Janeway in *VOY* "Scorpion," after he acted too arbitrarily in Janeway's absence. Chakotay states, "Seven of Nine said that we lacked the cohesion of a collective mind. That one day it would divide us and destroy us" because of the crew's individuality which leads to natural conflicts between each other. However, Janeway replies, "We do not have to stop being individuals to get through this. We just have to stop fighting each other."

Janeway makes it clear that although individuality has its place on the ship, the other officers and crewmembers must subordinate themselves to higher-ranking officers and their decisions in the event of disputed decisions. In contrast to Picard, who repeatedly tries to establish decisions by consensus in *TNG*, Janeway increasingly takes them against the opinions of her command in *VOY*. Especially the isolated situation of *Voyager*—as it were, as a mobile colony of the Federation in unexplored space—seems to justify this approach.

In contrast, the way junior officers work differs. In *TNG* "Lower Decks" and throughout *Star Trek: Lower Decks (LD)*, we see junior officers who are subject to a strict regime and are integrated into the chain of command on the spaceship. A notable exception is Ben, a waiter of Ten Forward in *TNG* "Lower Decks." He addresses First Officer William Riker in an informal way (not by "Sir" or "Commander"), and on the perplexity of one of the junior officers he declares that he is civilian and not a member of Starfleet. Nevertheless, the informal form of address constitutes a border crossing. The chain of command is suspended for a moment, and the order on the ship is disturbed.[18]

So, within Starfleet on the ships—apart from pure civilians—a double-track system is apparently assumed. On the one hand, we have the officers mostly with the rank of an ensign or lieutenant junior grade, who complete a four-year educational program at Starfleet Academy and then continue their training on ships or space stations (Okuda and Okuda 1999, 467). In *TNG* "The First Duty," we get to know the training at the academy better.[19] On the other hand, there is apparently also the possibility to serve as a non-commissioned officer on a Starfleet ship. Chief Miles O'Brien is an example for this, as he ranks as chief petty officer (*TNG* "Family"), a rank he retains even when he is Chief Operations Officer on *Deep Space Nine* later (and therefore presumably a senior officer). There is also a cadet in *DS9* "Valiant" who is briefly promoted to chief. In addition, as seen in *TNG* "The Drumhead," there are also lower crew ranks. In this episode, there is a medical technician named Simon Tarses, who is referred to as crewman. So, in addition to the officer career, there are also non-commissioned officers and crew ranks in Starfleet. In *VOY* "Good Shepherd" there are also three members of the crew with the rank crewman. Similar to *TNG* "Lower Decks," this episode also features a crew evaluation. The three crewmembers perform below average on the ship, so Captain Janeway feels responsible: "Three people have slipped through the cracks on my ship. That makes it my problem" (Janeway in *VOY* "Good Shepherd"). In order to integrate the three members more strongly into the crew of *Voyager*, Janeway carries out an external mission with them using a shuttle. When the shuttle gets into a critical situation, the three crewmembers finally see themselves as part of the crew and support Janeway in solving the problem.

This episode shows two things: On the one hand, it underlines the obligation of the individual to identify with the crew of the spaceship and thus with the society on the ship, as we have already described above. On the other hand, the episode shows that in the *Star Trek* society, competition and performance are a significant part. Only selected and proven officers rise further up in the hierarchy. "There are always a few who do not make it past their first year on a starship. Normally they are reassigned" (Chakotay in *VOY* "Good Shepherd"). Career is therefore an immanent part of this social system, a fact frequently pointed out in *LD*.[20]

It is, therefore, hardly possible to "leave" the company on the ship and escape this social structure. In the *VOY* episode "Learning Curve," the adaptation process of members of the Maquis on *Voyager* is described. The Maquis is a separatist organization of former Starfleet members. When their members get stranded in the unknown Delta Quadrant together with the *Voyager* crew, both groups are dependent on each other and have to work together. Thereby, Starfleet regulations continue to apply on *Voyager* and the Maquis members are subject to these regulations. However, some of the members oppose this forced integration. "We are used to playing with a different rule book. There is the Starfleet way, and there is the Maquis way" (Crewman Dalby in *VOY* "Learning Curve"). Thereupon, Head of Security Tuvok is assigned to conduct a kind of boot camp with them to restore the integrity of the ship's company.

The duty to work and thus submit to a more or less implicit subordination is a fundamental characteristic of utopian social images (Biesterfeld 1982, 19). This is accompanied by blurring the barrier between work and leisure time. The utopian society does not know this sharp separation (Biesterfeld 1982, 18). Although there are work-free periods, these are also spent in the community. After work "they devote an hour to recreation, in their gardens during the summer, or during the winter in the common halls where they have their meals. There they either play music or amuse themselves with conversation" (More 2002, 50). This is strongly reminiscent of Ten Forward, the officers' mess halls, sports facilities, or holodecks in *Star Trek*. The ship's crew in *Star Trek* usually wear their uniforms (often also off-duty)[21]; civilians, a less strict, but more or less uniform clothing cut.[22] This also resembles the classical utopias. The *TNG* episode "Conundrum" shows how much the inhabitants of the spaceship identify with their clothing. When the *Enterprise* is hit by an energy beam from an alien ship, all crew members suffer from memory loss. The first action, however, is to restore hierarchy, and this is done by means of the clothing. Riker, for example, unknowingly but correctly identifies Picard as the leader based on his rank insignia.

In the social system of *Star Trek*, deviations from the norm do occur, but they are only accepted to a limited extent in the context of the series. In the *TNG* episode "Hollow Pursuits," the shy and insecure Lieutenant Barclay is portrayed in his social behavior towards other crewmembers. Barclay is also often not on time and unreliable on duty. Barclay seems like a stranger in utopian space. His appearance and his non-conformity are even reminiscent of Bernard Marx in Huxley's *Brave New World*. As noted previously, in his spare time, Barclay likes to retreat and compensate for his social weaknesses with a self-written holodeck program. Barclay tries to escape the utopian perfect world of the *Enterprise* and does so on the holodeck. Significantly, he creates holocharacters of his work colleagues in his program; only here he can speak out against them and deal with them.[23] The "attraction of the episode [...] is that Barclay's holographic fantasies are not limited to the immediately recognizable cloak and dagger scenarios, but also include the everyday life of the Enterprise" (Rauscher 2003, 260). Barclay uses the holodeck to construct a perfect, beautiful world far away from the *Enterprise* to which he can escape. He's realistic enough to appreciate the *Enterprise* as an ideal place, but the ship and its inhabitants are not ideal enough for him, so he has to fictionally create an even more ideal *Enterprise* on the holodeck. By chance, the crew learns about this particular program and confronts Barclay with it. Barclay realizes that he has to learn how to deal with his colleagues in real life as well and that he must not take refuge in an alternative fantasy world. The *Star Trek* utopia does not allow deviators in their society because a utopian community must not be disturbed from within. "This concern especially the unpredictable subjectivity of people, their feelings, passions and moods" (Hellmann 1997, 95). By making it possible for Barclay, through his colleagues, to once again take his intended place on the *Enterprise* and to once again fulfill his function for the ship in a sovereign manner, the utopian structure on the starship is stabilized. Of course, there would be no other way to solve the problem, unless Barclay left the ship. The social structure of the *Enterprise*, this utopian place, does not tolerate such a disturbing deviation. For deviants, these places remain "inaccessible, unless someone commits himself to them completely" (Freyer 1936, 25).

The fact that individuality in the *Star Trek* universe fades into the background in favor of a utopian socialization becomes clear in the following dialogue. In the *VOY* episode "Prey," the former Borg drone Seven of Nine, who was assimilated by the Borg as a human child and later re-assimilated as a woman by the *Voyager* crew, has to cope with the missing Borg Collective and her newly conceived individuality. Turning to Janeway, she says, "You encouraged me to stop thinking like a member of the Collective, to cultivate my independence, my humanity. But when I try to assert that independence, I am punished." Janeway points out, however, that on a Starfleet ship, individuality has its limits. It is true that Seven of Nine should explore and live out her independence, but only within the narrow framework of the ship's protocol. Seven, nevertheless, stands by her point of view and accuses Janeway of suppressing her own opinion. "I believe that you are punishing me because I do not think the way that you do" (Seven in *VOY* "Prey").

Nevertheless, the holodeck symbolizes that *Star Trek* cannot be about a utopia of the socialist type, in which the community stands above everything. Individual interests are considered and can be acted out as long as they do not exceed certain limits, as in the case of Lieutenant Barclay. Although private property does not play a major role in the *Star Trek* universe anymore, it is not abolished as in More's *Utopia*. Nevertheless, every quarter on the *Enterprise*, every room, no matter how individual it may be, is always recognizable as part of a superior structure.

## Conclusion

Space ships and stations in the *Star Trek* universe are utopian spaces; they are "model worlds" (Steinmüller 1997, 81). However, unlike the classical utopias, they are not sealed off from the outside world. In almost every *TNG* episode, for example, the *Enterprise* visits alien worlds; visitors are transported to the *Enterprise* or an away team to an alien planet. The *Enterprise* acts as a mediator between different cultures, and this exchange also has an impact on the ship's society, of course. However, this contact is always limited to a few moments within the episodes or to individual crewmembers. In the end, the *Enterprise* leaves—ready for the next adventure, for the next encounter. However, since the *Enterprise* remains coherent as a system, it is—despite the interchangeability of its inhabitants and the diverse number of its cultural contacts—a static construct that represents an ideal living space.

In the series, the protagonists are individually and very differently characterized, and we have no reason to assume that the rest of the crew is not similarly heterogeneous and individually composed. On the other hand, the individuality of the inhabitants and crewmembers is offset by their specifically assigned functions. The roles on the ships are meticulously assigned down to the last crewmember, so that this society functions within the spaceship structure. Last but not least, hierarchy has an important role in daily life.

There is no doubt that we are dealing here with a construct that offers a virtually ideal place to live in the universe. Spaceships and stations provide everything necessary for life. They are the place—the model world—in which a utopian society can be established. The spaceship is sufficiently far away from our world. Yet *Star Trek* does not want to be a socialist utopia. With all corporate design and functionality, the ship creates enough space for individuality. The escape route from utopia for the individual is the holodeck: Here, worlds far away from utopia open up to him—worlds in which he can move freely from the limited reality of the spaceship and in which he can get lost. Ultimately, however, the individual crewmember also remains a part of the larger organism, the ship, to which he must contribute his own in order to keep it functioning and to preserve his habitat in space.

# 4

# Politics in *Star Trek*

*Star Trek* is a huge narrative text, which means that stories are being told in contrast to the more descriptive texts of More's *Utopia,* Campanella's *City of the Sun,* or Bacon's *New Atlantis.* Therefore, it is difficult to extract a pure description of the political system in the *Star Trek* universe. However, in this chapter I will look more deeply into the text to examine "which different basic concepts of politics, for example interest and power, are implicitly or explicitly shown in Star Trek" (Göll 1997, 35).

It is also Göll who claims that in *Star Trek* "no ideas are developed and no drafts are sketched for the area of human coexistence, especially for political structures and processes" (1997, 43). Moore fills in that *Star Trek* is indeed not a political text, but not free of political opinions at all (1997–99, ron020.txt).

Anyway, it can be observed at various points in the text that a political system is built up in *Star Trek* and that politics does play a major role in *Star Trek*. "In other words, *Star Trek* teaches how important political involvement is to society" (Manuel 1997, 183).

I look at the political system in *Star Trek* from three different positions:

First, I like to examine the question of what kind of political institutions do exist in the *Star Trek* universe (polity). Is there a constitution? Are there laws and regulations?

Second, it is important to have a look at policymaking in *Star Trek*. Which policy areas are discussed in *Star Trek*? Which—possibly controversial—topics are dealt with and what positions does *Star Trek* take?

Finally, which actual political processes can be observed in *Star Trek* (politics)? According to the opening speech of *TOS* and *TNG*, it is always about discovering "strange new worlds, [...] new life and new civilizations." So, *Star Trek* is about contact-making with other cultures. But how does this contact take place? Which politics play a role here? And how are these processes represented?

## Political Institutions in *Star Trek*

Political institutions form the foundation of any state that permanently binds a certain number of persons (people) within a geographically delimited area (territory) and subjects them to its own power for the purpose of achieving certain national objectives. These constitutive elements are also found in all the utopias I have described above.

In *Star Trek*, we see a kind of supraplanetary "state" system in which our galaxy is populated by many different civilizations. This is in contrast to, for example, Wells' *War of the Worlds*, which is only about a battle between different species—a story that ends with the extinction of one of the species (Buzan 2010, 176). In the *Star Trek* universe, our galaxy is divided into four equally sized quadrants named Alpha, Beta, Gamma, and Delta Quadrants. However, the Federation has mapped only eleven percent of this galaxy so far, as stated in the *TNG* episode "Where No One Has Gone Before." So, our galaxy is still largely unexplored even in the future *Star Trek* age.

The United Federation of Planets is mainly located in the Alpha Quadrant; the Cardassians and the Ferengi also have their territories there. The Romulans and the Klingons are located mostly in the Beta Quadrant,[1] the Dominion has power over large areas of the Gamma Quadrant, and the Borg populate large areas of the Delta Quadrant (Zimmerman, Sternbach, and Drexler 1998, 2–3). The quadrants are further divided into so-called sectors, "a volume of space approximately twenty light-years across. A typical sector in Federation space will contain about 6 to 10 star systems [...]" (Okuda and Okuda 1999, 434). A sector that became somewhat famous within *Star Trek* is sector 001, which contains our solar system and Earth and was the main target of the Borg in *TNG* "The Best of Both Worlds."

### *The United Federation of Planets*

The United Federation of Planets is "an intersellar [sic] alliance of planetary governments and colonies, united for mutual trade, exploratory, scientific, cultural, diplomatic, and defensive endeavors" (Okuda and Okuda 1999, 536). Earth is the capital planet of the Federation, as it was founded in the year 2161 in San Francisco with the signing of the Charter of the United Federation of Planets by representatives from Andoria, Tellar, United Earth, and Vulcan (*ENT* "These Are the Voyages..."). In the *TOS* episode "Journey to Babel," it is said that the Federation consists of 30 member planets. At the time of *TNG*, *DS9*, and *VOY*, however, the Federation is "made up of over a hundred planets who have allied themselves for mutual scientific, cultural and defensive benefits" (Benjamin Sisko in *DS9* "Battle Lines").[2] In *Star Trek: First Contact*, Jean-Luc Picard speaks of over 150 members and more than 1,000 colonies of the Federation spread over a distance of about 8,000 light years. Thus, the Federation has grown considerably in the course of *Star Trek* history. The exact population size of the Federation is not known. In the *DS9* episode "Inquisition," a population of some billions is hinted at without giving a specific number.

There is only sparse information about the institutions of the Federation in the *Star Trek* text.

At any rate, the Federation is a presidential republic. Regarding the executive branch, the Federation president is both head of state and head of government as well as commander-in-chief of Starfleet (*DS9* "Paradise Lost," *Star Trek VI: The Undiscovered Country*). His office is located in Paris (*DS9* "Homefront," *Star Trek IV: The Voyage Home*). The Federation Cabinet supports the president with his duties (*DS9* "Extreme Measures"). However, it is neither specified exactly who are members of the cabinet nor which exact powers the cabinet has.[3] The *Star Trek* text further only mentions *that* the president is elected, but not *how*. A number of executive agencies are mentioned throughout the text. For example, in *TNG* "The Ensigns of Command," a Bureau of Planetary Treaties, is mentioned. In *TOS* "A Taste of Armageddon," a report is filed to Federation Central, and Picard was a speaker on a conference of the Federation Archaeology Council (*TNG* "Qpid"). Last but not least, Starfleet is the best known agency in the Federation.

In *Star Trek*, the legislature is represented by the Federation Council. The Council has its seat in San Francisco and consists of representatives of the Federation members *(Star Trek IV: The Voyage Home)*. However, the text remains essentially vague. The members of the Council seem to be elected as well—at least the planet Bajor prepares for such an election in the course of its membership application (*DS9* "Rapture")—but it is neither said how many representatives are in the Council nor what the exact powers of the Council are. In *Star Trek IV: The Voyage Home*, the Council seems to be a kind of court martial or at least a committee of inquiry when Admiral Kirk is accused of disobeying orders and stealing and then destroying the *Enterprise*. On the other hand, the Council appears to have actual legislative powers. In *TNG* "The Defector," the Council deals with a possible invasion of the Romulans, in *TNG* "Force of Nature" it passes a law that limits the maximum speed of starships in Federation territory, and in *TNG* "Journey's End," it eventually debates the upcoming ratification of a treaty between the Federation and the Cardassians. In *Star Trek: Insurrection*, the Council finally promises an investigation and the halting of the resettlement of a species from their home planet.

Manuel sees in the United Federation of Planets, or at least in United Earth, which is a member of the Federation, a democracy (1997, 185). Given that the modes of election of the executive and legislative branches are not clear, this classification seems rather speculative. For example, there is United Earth, which seems to have a parliamentary government[4] and consists of several member states. The chief engineer of the *Enterprise*, Geordi LaForge, for example, was born in the African Confederation (*TNG* "Cause and Effect"). There is also the European Alliance[5] (*TNG* "The Price") and probably still the United States of America (*VOY* "Imperfection"). However, "the exact details of the emergence of global democracy are not clear" (Manuel 1997, 185). Captain Kirk says in *TOS* "The Omega Glory" that "liberty and freedom have to be more than just words" and mentions that there are many democratic worlds in the Federation (Manuel 1997, 186)—but this says nothing about whether the Federation itself is to be considered a democracy. For example, Gregory even sees a kind of "'socialist paradise' which might even be characterised as 'pure communism'" (2000, 161) in the future society of the Federation, and Buzan also goes this way: "Money, capitalism and greed have disappeared in a way that might almost strike one (say it softly) as communist, though it is actually more an optimistic way of a post-materialist society" (Buzan 2010, 176–7).

The judiciary of the Federation consists of several courts with the Federation Supreme Court as the highest court that also has authority over civilians. For example, in the *DS9* episode "Doctor Bashir, I Presume," Julian Bashir's father is sentenced to two years imprisonment for genetic manipulation and wants to take his case to the Supreme Court for appeal.

The *Star Trek* text also mentions a Federation Grand Jury (*DS9* "The Ascent") and a Federation Special Jury (*DS9* "Waltz"), both of which are apparently based on the grand jury system of the United States. According to Okuda and Okuda the jury is a "panel of citizens who evaluated judicial cases to determine if evidence warranted an indictment" (1999, 149). Besides that, there are courts-martial within Starfleet. For example, Captain Kirk has to stand trial in *TOS* "Court Martial" because he is said to have caused the death of a comrade by negligence. Jean-Luc Picard had to answer in a court-martial for his actions in the loss of the USS *Stargazer*, too (*TNG* "The Measure of a Man").

In addition, there are also law enforcement agencies in the *Star Trek* universe. In *TNG* "Ensign Ro," the Bajoran ensign Ro Laren is released on parole from prison after being sentenced for disobeying orders. Also released on parole is Lieutenant Tom Paris, who is taken from the Federation Penal Settlement in New Zealand by Captain Kathryn Janeway in the *VOY* episode "Caretaker." However, the *Star Trek* text remains unclear about any details. While there are courts and correctional facilities, any lawyers or full-time judges are hardly mentioned. Nor is there a differentiated separation of powers between prosecuting authorities such as the public prosecutor's office, the police, and legal advisors (Joseph and Catton 2003, 35).

The economic-political system of *Star Trek* is a fundamentally different than our present one. Moore says that "by the time I joined *TNG*, Gene [Roddenberry] had decreed that money most emphatically did *not* exist in the Federation [...]" (1997–99, ron009.txt). This also corresponds to Captain Kirk's statement in *Star Trek IV: The Voyage Home*, when he explains that in the future *Star Trek* society, you do not pay with money anymore. Picard echoes this statement: "The economics of the future are somewhat different. You see, money does not exist in the 24th century. [...] The acquisition of wealth is no longer the driving force of our lives. We work to better ourselves and the rest of humanity" (Picard in *Star Trek: First Contact*).[6] Even if there seems to be a generally accepted currency with gold-pressed latinum in different units like pieces, strips, or bars, it does not have an important role in the Federation anymore. However, *DS9* takes a special position here continuing to use currency—probably because the space station is located in the outermost area of the Federation and other species in the *Star Trek* universe still continue to use money (Moore 1997–99, ron009.txt). This is also evident to More's *Utopia*. Here also, money no longer has a meaning in the Utopian state.

It is never specified exactly how the new political system in *Star Trek* was established. The Federation is apparently a society "without political decision making, without production or reproduction, without exchange, without property—indeed, almost without economic consumption" (Wagner and Lundeen 1998, 137). In fact, it seems that political decisions are mainly made within Starfleet instead of the Federation itself.

## *The Federation and Starfleet*

It is noticeable in the entire *Star Trek* text that there is not always a clear distinction between the United Federation of Planets and Starfleet. Starfleet is by definition the "deep-space exploratory, scientific, diplomatic, and defensive agency of the United Federation of Planets" (Okuda and Okuda 1999, 468) and bears a clear resemblance to the military structure of the U.S. Navy (Gregory 2000, 162; Sarantakes 2005, 78). Starfleet also seems to be a rather complex institution with the Federation as it consists of several departments.

As is shown, for example, in *TNG* "The Measure of a Man," military jurisdiction seems to play a major role. Here, a Judge Advocate General's

Office is mentioned, but at the same time, there are also hearings like the one in *VOY* "Author, Author," which take place in civil arbitration but deal with Starfleet matters.[7]

Furthermore, there is Starfleet Academy as the central training and educational department for personnel (*TNG* "The First Duty"). Passing an entrance examination is required for admission (*TNG* "Coming of Age"). As in the case of the Ferengi Nog in *DS9* "Heart of Stone," non–Federation members may also be accepted, provided they submit a letter of reference from a commanding officer. Starfleet is therefore explicitly not limited to Federation citizens. Academy training is obviously comparable to a university degree and offers several majors. In addition, there seem to be other educational institutions within Starfleet, like Starfleet Command School (*VOY* "Parallax"), and Starfleet Medical Academy (*DS9* "Explorers").[8]

Another Starfleet department is Starfleet Intelligence, which has been in existence since the beginnings of Starfleet in the 22nd century (*ENT* "Terra Prime"). The intelligence service plays an increasingly important role in *TNG* ("The Pegasus") and especially in *DS9*—especially with the appearance of the terrorist resistance group, the Maquis (*DS9* "Tribunal," *DS9* "For the Cause"), as well as in the Dominion War (*DS9* "Behind the Lines"). In fact, there is an even more secret organization within Starfleet Intelligence, Section 31. The existence of Section 31 is not officially confirmed by Starfleet, and its actions are carried out completely autonomously (*DS9* "Inquisition"). "We deal with threats to the Federation that jeopardize its very survival. If you knew how many lives we have saved, I think you would agree that the ends do justify the means. I am not afraid of bending the rules every once in a while, if the situation warrants it" (Section 31 agent Sloan in *DS9* "Inquisition"). It is not clearly stated in *DS9* whether Section 31 is, in fact, a department within Starfleet Intelligence or an independent agency. Sloan's statement suggests that it is more the latter; however, it is noticeable that Sloan wears a standard uniform and called himself Deputy Director of Internal Affairs at Starfleet Intelligence. Apparently, this is only a cover. Section 31 is prominently featured in the second season of *DIS* where personnel are seen with their own uniform style and black badges. Despite its existence back in the 23rd century, Section 31 must have maintained high secrecy, as its existence is unknown even to *DS9*'s senior staff (*DS9* "Inquisition").

The Federation must, therefore, be protected by Starfleet at all costs, and this obviously includes illegal measures. *Star Trek* mirrors here the development of present politics. While intelligence was initially only responsible for spying on other powers (like the Romulans in *TOS* "The Enterprise Incident" or *TNG* "The Pegasus"), the focus shifts more to the detection and destruction of internal dangers like the Maquis.

Furthermore, Starfleet seems to take over political functions, at least in part. "Their highest representatives, the admirals, seem to make political decisions in many cases, which would not be unproblematic from a democratic theory perspective" (Heinecke 2009, 161).

This function becomes clearly evident in so-called "diplomatic missions." Captain Picard, for example, regularly acts as official representative of the United Federation of Planets—for example, in *Star Trek: Nemesis* and *Star Trek: Insurrection*. In the former, Picard receives orders from the former *Voyager* captain and now-admiral Kathryn Janeway to travel to Romulus. A new head of government had been elected there, and the *Enterprise* is the closest ship. Also, in an official procedure in *Star Trek: Insurrection,* Picard welcomes the Evora people, who have been accepted as new members of the Federation. In both cases, therefore, these are political responsibilities that should not primarily have to do with Starfleet alone. Neither the welcoming of a new government nor the admission of a new people into the Federation are responsibilities of a military organization, yet Starfleet does exactly that. It would be understandable if ships of Starfleet were to carry political representatives to the respective events. At least in the case of the admission of the Evora in *Star Trek: Insurrection*, this would be an event planned well ahead of time. Nevertheless, there is no hint that a political representative of the Federation would be present at the reception—on the contrary. Only Starfleet officers in dress uniforms attend the ceremony. Even when the Federation becomes the new protective power over Bajor in *DS9*, this occurs only in the presence of Starfleet officers, not in the presence of political representatives. On the other hand, there is a dedicated diplomatic corps of the Federation, which participated in the Khitomer conference in *Star Trek VI: The Undiscovered Country* and thus negotiated the Khitomer Accords, for example.[9] The *Enterprise* sometimes also officially carried diplomatic representatives, as she did in *TNG* "The Host."

Based on these descriptions, it is unlikely that these are mistakes within the text's narrative. Rather, it can probably be assumed that Starfleet is somehow strongly integrated into the institutional structure of the United Federation and that there is no distinct separation between political and military structures. Starfleet is, therefore, not only a military organization of the Federation. It also has political and scientific (and thus genuinely civil) tasks. The exact distinction between them is not clear, so I do think that the close cooperation between the political body of the United Federation of Planets and its agency Starfleet is of a systematic nature.

How strongly Starfleet is anchored in everyday life on *Voyager* is made clear in *VOY* "Equinox." In this episode, the Voyager crew meets another Federation ship, the USS *Equinox*, which is also stranded in the Delta Quadrant. On board the *Equinox*, apparently lax regulations apply, as the *Voyager* crew is surprised to find out, for example that the commanding officer of the Equinox, Captain Ransom, is addressed by his first name. Ransom explains that the ship is far away from Federation territory. Thus, this strict protocol is no longer necessary. "When you have been in the trenches as long as we have, rank and protocol are luxuries" (Ransom in *VOY* "Equinox"). Janeway is able to sympathize with this position to a certain degree, but she refuses to completely discard customs that are mandated by Starfleet. "We have been known to let our hair down from time to time. But I find that maintaining protocol reminds us of where we came from, and hopefully where we are going" (Janeway in *VOY* "Equinox").

So, Starfleet has not only issued regulations, but these regulations embody a whole philosophy of life for the *Voyager* crew (and for the crews in the other series as well). The ethos, to which this philosophy is held, is rather of a conservative nature and thus (at least apparently) contradicts the social developments in the Federation (Gregory 2000, 161). The non-observance of these rules would therefore mean betrayal of Starfleet and thus of the entire system.

## *Federation Laws*

Within the *Star Trek* text, different Federation laws are repeatedly mentioned. "A legal system is not wholly separate from the general culture. It grows and changes in response to growth and change within the society that creates and uses it" (Joseph and Catton 2003, 28). As stated above, with the founding of the Federation, a so-called Charter of the United Federation of Planets was signed. An excerpt from the Charter—probably the preamble—is read in the *VOY* episode "The Void": "We the lifeforms of the United Federation of Planets determined to save succeeding generations from the scourge of war, and to reaffirm faith in the fundamental rights of sentient beings, in the dignity and worth of all lifeforms, in the equal rights of members of planetary systems large and small, and to establish conditions under which justice and respect for the obligations arising from treaties and other sources of interstellar law can be maintained, and to promote social progress and better standards of living on all worlds…"

The entire text of the Charter is unknown. However, at least one article of the Charter seems to deal with a general prohibition of discrimination. In the *DS9* episode "Accession," Sisko says, in any case, "caste-based discrimination goes against the Federation Charter." There is also a Constitution of the United Federation of Planets. Only two sections are mentioned once in *Star Trek*. In *TNG* "The Drumhead," the Seventh Guarantee of the Constitution states that no citizen of the Federation has to incriminate himself with his testimony in a court case. And in *VOY* "Author, Author" the Twelfth Guarantee is mentioned, which defines when a person is considered an artist. Okuda and Okuda suggest that the Charter and the Constitution of the United Federation of Planets are the same text (1999, 85).

Other laws are also mentioned in *Star Trek*. For example, a Federation Uniform Code of Justice is mentioned by Picard in *TNG* "The Drumhead," while in *DS9* "The Maquis," a group of Maquis terrorists is supposed to be charged under this code. There also seems to be a proper trial code, as it can be seen on a screen in *VOY* "Tinker, Tenor, Doctor, Spy."

Furthermore, there are directives specific to Starfleet. The Prime Directive has a special meaning within *Star Trek*. The origins of the Directive are discussed in *ENT* "Dear Doctor," when the crew of the *Enterprise* develops moral concerns after providing medical assistance to a people not yet warp-capable. The people ask the *Enterprise* to provide them with warp technology, and Captain Archer eventually refuses. He realizes that this could have a lasting and serious impact on development. "Someday my people are going to come up with some sort of a doctrine. Something that tells us what we can and cannot do out here, should and should not do. But until somebody tells me that they have drafted that directive, I am going to have to remind myself every day that we did not come out here to play God" (Archer in *ENT* "Dear Doctor").

The Prime Directive is a law that is most often quoted throughout all series and movies. Interestingly, its exact text is never mentioned. The main idea of the Prime Directive is a non-interference policy of Starfleet in the affairs of other species, especially if these are less developed than those of the Federation. However, the Prime Directive does not apply to civilian Federation citizens (*TNG* "Angel One"). It should be emphasized that the Prime Directive prohibits Starfleet from coercing any influence on the autonomous development of a society (Gregory 2000, 166). Picard says in *TNG* "Symbiosis," "the Prime Directive is not just a set of rules; it is a philosophy." In addition to the strict rule of non-interference, the Prime Directive also regulates first contact with other species. When the respective society is warp-capable, i.e., has invented warp drive and is therefore capable of interstellar travel, first contact is regarded as reasonable. Thus, *Star Trek: Insurrection* mentions the Evora people, who were admitted to the Federation because they recently had invented warp drive. First contact and the subsequent admission of a species into the Federation is in the

Federation's own interests, because, in this way, the Federation forms alliances and can secure its supremacy.

There are a number of exceptions in which the Prime Directive has been violated. In the *TNG* episode "Justice," the *Enterprise* visits a planet inhabited by the Edo. The Edo declare that their planet is free of crime, and they have only the death penalty for every crime, without exception. When Wesley Crusher accidentally destroys a greenhouse while on the planet, he is to be executed on the spot. Picard tells the Edo that the Federation have long since abolished the death penalty. However, since the Edo have not changed their minds, Picard takes Wesley back to the *Enterprise*. By doing so, he is violating the Prime Directive, which demands non-interference in the affairs of other peoples, and declares in his defense, "there can be no justice so long as laws are absolute" (*TNG* "Justice").[10] However, unlike Kirk's, Picard's action is preceded by a careful consideration of the event. "In a situation where Kirk would have barely hesitated at all before acting, Picard agonises over whether to intervene" (Gregory 2000, 169). This episode is also one of the few in *TNG* that echoes several *TOS* episodes like "The Apple," because, in fact, it is the Edo God—a higher developed entity of lifeforms worshipped by the Edo people—who has actual authority on the Edo people instead of the people itself.

The comparison with *TOS*, in particular, shows that contact with other species has changed over the course of the different series. As already described above, the *TOS* episode "The Apple" is about a very similar topic, but ends in the destruction of the dominant element by the *Enterprise* crew. The *Enterprise* crew meets a group of humanoids on a planet, people who seemingly live in a kind of paradise and support a religious cult, worshipping an entity called Vaal. Captain Kirk discovers that Vaal is indeed merely a computer, aware of itself. Kirk destroys Vaal because he believes the population of the planet was enslaved by Vaal and that they should be given freedom to develop themselves. When Spock points out the violation of the Prime Directive, Kirk argues: "These people are not robots. They should have freedom of choice. We owe it to them to interfere" (Lagon 1997, 238). From here on, they have to manage on their own, and Kirk is sure that they will learn to do so (Lagon 1997, 246). Kirk says that the people need freedom; however, "they're now free to live only the kind of life Kirk approves—which will primarily involve trying to figure out, from scratch, how to survive" (Johnson 2016, 49). Whether this forced change in society was intended is not questioned. "Sure, they had to feed Vaal, but does that really amount to *slavery*? [...] Furthermore, it's not clear at all that the Feeders of Vaal—or at least their ancestors—didn't *choose* to live under Vaal's rules" (Johnson 2016, 55).

In *TNG*, on the other hand, painstaking care is taken not to act destructively. Instead, Picard tries to convince the Edo God of the injustice of its law by argument. Picard thus makes it clear that the Prime Directive is to be observed as a matter of principle when dealing with other peoples, so that the consequences for society remain minimal. This clearly distinguishes *TNG* from the treatment of the Prime Directive in *TOS*. Kirk regarded the directive as an optional rather than a directly binding provision.[11]

The *TNG* episode "Who Watches the Watchers" deals with a similar topic. The *Enterprise* visits the planet Mintaka III, where a covert Federation observation post is located. The Mintakans are a so-called pre-warp society (i.e., a society that has not yet developed warp drive capabilities) and thus the object of observation of a group of Federation anthropologists. In order not to influence this society by the presence of alien observers, the observation is done in disguise. However, when a Mintakan is accidentally injured by a malfunction of the observation post camouflage, the crew transports him to the *Enterprise* to save his life and thus violates the Prime Directive. Although a memory wipe is performed on him in sickbay, he nevertheless remembers everything on board and tells his people about "the Picard" as a god-like being who miraculously saved his life. "Here the morality and limitations of the Prime Directive are questioned, throwing into focus the issue of the impact of technologically advanced cultures on 'primitive' races" (Gregory 2000, 170).

To prevent further harm, Picard convinces the Mintakan that he is not a god by having him wounded with a bow and arrow to show him that he is mortal. This episode shows than an unwanted cultural influence on a people by violating the Prime Directive may lead even to the formation of a new religion in a less developed civilization.

In *Star Trek: Insurrection,* Picard's application of the Prime Directive is once again the subject of discussion. At the beginning of the film, a similar observation post is depicted as in *TNG* "Who Watches the Watchers," and in parallel to the series' episode, this post is also accidentally exposed. In the film, the Federation observes the Ba'ku people. As it turns out, the people are to be resettled by force and without their knowledge, because another people, the Son'a, wants to use an essential resource of the planet for themselves with the support of the Federation. The planet of the Ba'ku is surrounded by rings of so-called metaphasic particles, which prevent the aging process in organic life. Therefore, the Ba'ku do not age.

More or less by chance, the crew of the *Enterprise* uncovers this plan. Picard believes it is incompatible with the Prime Directive because "some of the darkest chapters in the history of my world involve the forced relocation of a small group of people to satisfy the demands of a large one. I had hoped we had learned from our mistakes, but it seems that some of us have not" (Picard in *Star Trek: Insurrection*).

When Starfleet Admiral Dougherty, who is in charge of this case, counters that there are only 600 people involved, Picard replies, "[H]ow many people does it take, Admiral, before it becomes wrong? A thousand? Fifty thousand? A million? How many people does it take, Admiral?" (Picard in *Star Trek: Insurrection*).

Once again, Picard makes it clear that the Prime Directive is not just a system of rules but that there is also a moral philosophy behind it. The Federation presents itself as a highly developed political entity, which has learned from its history. But the Federation is also in danger of betraying these very ideals. The fact that the Federation Council approved the resettlement of the Ba'ku shows that, on the periphery of Federation territory, apparently different moral principles apply than at its center.

On the other hand, the Federation remains much more reserved in comparable cases. When the Bajorans are introduced into *TNG* "Ensign Ro," their planet has been occupied by the Cardassians for 40 years, and the activities of Bajoran resistance fighters are classified as terrorism. Bajorans and Cardassians share a close common past in the *Star Trek* universe, which is in part due to the relative proximity of both home planets (Zimmerman, Sternbach, and Drexler 1998, 3, 12). "The Bajorans, who were enslaved for decades by the fierce Chadassians [sic] and forced to live a life of the most primitive, unworthy level, see the Federation's non-interference as a cruel, neglected act of assistance" (Becker 2000, 63). Nevertheless, the Federation does not feel compelled to act, as these are internal affairs of the Cardassians. "And the Federation is pledged not to interfere with the internal affairs of others. How convenient that must be for you. To turn a deaf ear to those who suffer behind a line on a map" (Keeve in *TNG* "Ensign Ro"). The prohibition to interfere in the affairs of non–Federation members thus sometimes goes so far that their extinction may not be prevented by the Federation (Becker 2000, 63). This attitude, however, forms the basis for the later emergence of the Maquis, a resistance movement within the Federation.

When, in *VOY* "Equinox," Captain Ransom admits to having deliberately violated the Prime Directive more than once, the crew of *Voyager* is appalled. "[...] If we turn our backs on our principles, we stop being human" (Janeway in *VOY* "Equinox").

So, the Prime Directive has been deliberately ignored again and again in *Star Trek*. Further on, I noted that Captain Kirk broke the Prime Directive in *TOS* "The Return of the Archons" and in *TOS* "The Apple" with his interference in the affairs of other species. Kirk justifies this both times with the fact that the respective cultures were in a state of slavery and the

Federation could not accept this. Furthermore, these societies are fake because they are static. In this respect, Kirk is correcting a static (and thus, in his opinion, dystopian) society. "Utopias, according to these classic *Star Trek* narratives, are not only stagnant but tyrannical as well" (Wagner and Lundeen 1998, 127). Booker states that, "however devoted it might be to the idea of building a *better* society, *TOS* (especially in the early going) is actually quite skeptical of the notion of building a *perfect* society" (Booker 2018, 85). It is notable that this skepticism changes little with *TNG*, *DS9*, and *VOY* in the *Star Trek* universe. In *TNG* "The Masterpiece Society," for example, there is a static, perfect society, which does not want to allow outside help even in the face of the threat of a comet fragment approaching the planet. The society is so perfect that a small disturbance from outside upsets its balance (Wagner and Lundeen 1998, 133). Again, it is the static nature of a utopia that is criticized by *Star Trek*, but Picard, unlike Kirk, tries not to actively intervene. "He even wonders whether the intervention of the *Enterprise*-D might ultimately have been as destructive to the life of the colony as the core fragment would otherwise have been" (Booker 2018, 92). This, however, shows that *Star Trek* presents a different way in dealing with the Prime Directive than it did in the days of *TOS*.

## *Other Powers in the* Star Trek *Universe*

Besides the Federation, there are a number of other species in the galaxy (see following page).

Besides a multitude of smaller species that have joined the Federation (e.g., the Vulcans, whose most famous representative Spock might be in *TOS*), there are several major powers in the *Star Trek* universe that compete with the Federation for areas of influence. Among them are, for example, the Klingons, the Romulans, the Cardassians and the Ferengi in the Alpha Quadrant, the so-called Dominion in the Gamma Quadrant, and the Borg in the Delta Quadrant.

The Klingon Empire traces its origins to the mythical figure of Kahless, a former Klingon emperor, "who first united the Klingon people by killing the tyrant, Molor" (Okuda and Okuda 1999, 244). The symbolic head of state is the Emperor (*TNG* "Rightful Heir"), while the executive power lies with the Chancellor. The Chancellor is also the head of the legislative body, the Klingon High Council, which consists of representatives of the so-called Houses that make up Klingon society. These representatives are usually only males, even if there are exceptions to this rule, as in the case of Chancellor Azetbur in *Star Trek VI: The Undiscovered Country*. The main planet is called Qo'nos *(Star Trek VI: The Undiscovered Country)*.

Table 4: Other Powers in the Star Trek Universe

| | United Federation of Planets | Klingon Empire | Romulan Star Empire | Cardassian Union | Ferengi Alliance | Dominion | Borg Collective |
|---|---|---|---|---|---|---|---|
| **Form of Government** | Federal Republic | Oligarchy | Oligarchy | Military Dictatorship | Dictatorship | — | — |
| **Head of State** | Federation president | Emperor | Emperor | — | Grand Nagus | *de facto* Founder | *de facto* Borg Queen |
| **Executive** | Federation president | Chancellor | Praetor | *de facto* Cardassian Central Command | Ferengi Trade Authority | *de facto* Vorta | — |
| **Legislative** | Federation Council | Klingon High Council | Romulan Senate | *de iure* Detapa Council / *de facto* Cardassian Central Command and Obsidian Order | Congress of Economic Advisers | *de facto* Founder | — |
| **Judiciary** | Supreme Court of Justice the Federation | — | — | Cardassian Tribunal | — | — | — |
| **Military** | *de facto* Starfleet | Klingon Defense Force | Romulan Military | Cardassian Military | *de facto* Ferengi Military | Jem'Hadar | — |
| **Secret Service** | *de facto* Section 31 | Klingon Secret Service | Tal Shiar | Obsidian Order | — | — | — |

## 4. Politics in Star Trek

The Klingon Empire is, in contrast to the Federation, not a federal republic, but "a ruthless society, governed by a strict adherence to military discipline" (Manuel 1997, 188). However, as the Emperor is only a symbolic head of state and has no political power, it is not a monarchy. The structure, which has patriarchal houses meeting in a council and electing a supreme leader, is reminiscent of More's oligarchic concept of governance in *Utopia*, one in which family is an important element of society.

Military and warrior rites are very important to the Klingons; for example, warriors who have died in war are given special importance (Okuda and Okuda 1999, 247). However, Klingon society is technologically advanced and relies on an honor code that has been developed over 1,500 years (Grech 2016, 72–3).

The Romulans descended from the Vulcans centuries ago (Okuda and Okuda 1999, 418; *TNG* "Gambit," *VOY* "Death Wish"). Their home worlds are the twin planets Romulus and Remus (*TOS* "Balance of Terror," *Star Trek: Nemesis*). The Romulan Senate as governing body consists of senators, who are elected in individual constituencies of the empire and represent them (*TNG* "Unification"). The Senate is chaired by the Praetor (*Star Trek: Nemesis*), who is followed in importance by the Proconsul and Vice Proconsul (*TNG* "Unification"). One can assume that the Romulan system of government is a kind of oligarchy similar to that of the Klingons and that the Praetor—at least that is what the events in *Star Trek: Nemesis* suggest—practically acts as dictator. As Manuel states, "the Romulan leader, the 'Praetor,' has absolute power, and relies upon the military for his support" (1997, 188).

The Romulan military has an important place in society. With the Tal Shiar, there is a well-trained intelligence service (*TNG* "Face of the Enemy"), which, in turn, has great influence on the military.

The Cardassian people are first introduced in *TNG* "The Wounded," so they do not appear in *TOS*. The Cardassians' territory is also located in the Alpha Quadrant. Due to the lack of resources on their home planet, Cardassian society developed into a military dictatorship (*TNG* "Chain of Command") with the Cardassian Central Command as *de facto* executive branch and the Obsidian Order as the supporting intelligence service (*DS9* "Defiant"). The Detapa Council is the civilian main governing body; however, in reality it has no real power as the "Cardassian citizens have been systematically excluded from governmental policy questions" (Manuel 1997, 189). The Supreme Tribunal (*DS9* "Tribunal") is the highest court in the Union.

The Ferengi Alliance appears as another major power in the Alpha Quadrant since *TNG*. Manuel classifies the Ferengi as "inclusive hegemony"

(1997, 187), whereby the Ferengi Alliance is based on unconditional capitalism as an essential pillar of their society and represents a strictly contractualist society. The Ferengi are mainly traders and do not maintain military units in the strict sense. The Grand Nagus can be considered as head of state of the Alliance as "the Nagus has the greatest business mind in the entire Ferengi Alliance" (Quark in *DS9* "Prophet Motive"). The executive is mainly held by the Ferengi Commerce Authority (*DS9* "Body Parts"). The Nagus, however, has an absolute veto right on all decisions of the Authority (*DS9* "Ferengi Love Songs"). In return, the Commerce Authority—represented by its top management—is the body that elects the Grand Nagus (*DS9* "Profit and Lace"). Trade is the top priority for the Ferengi, which is also reflected in their supreme law, the Rules of Acquisition (Okuda and Okuda 1999, 151). Compliance with these rules and the subordinate Trade By-Laws is monitored by the Commerce Authority (*DS9* "Profit and Lace").

The Dominion is introduced in *DS9* as a major power in the *Star Trek* universe. It consists of a multitude of different species that are native to the Gamma Quadrant (*DS9* "The Search"). The Dominion was built by the Founders, a species of Changelings to which Odo also belongs, who have absolute rule. A large part of the executive is delegated to the Vorta species that are humanoids specifically genetically engineered by the Founders. The Vorta worship the Founders as gods (*DS9* "Treachery, Faith and the Great River").

In the military, the Dominion is represented by the Jem'Hadar. These are also a genetically modified humanoid species specially engineered for their tasks (*DS9* "To the Death"). The Jem'Hadar are subordinate to the Vorta. Other species in the Dominion include the Karemma species, for example, who are focused mainly on economic issues (*DS9* "Rules of Acquisition"). Thus, the Dominion resembles an absolute state in which key functions of society are performed by individual species.

The Borg are introduced in *TNG* and have a prominent role in *VOY*. As a major power in the *Star Trek* universe, they have their origins in the Delta Quadrant. Manuel sees the Borg Collective as "a closed, machine-dominated hegemony" (1997, 190). The question arises, however, whether the Borg can be regarded as a political society. In any case, there are no recognizable political entities in the Borg as there are among the other major powers in the *Star Trek* universe. Accordingly, there is no dedicated executive, legislative or judicial branch in the Borg Collective. Instead, within Borg society the individual is meaningless and all Borg people form a hive mind. Nevertheless, there is a so-called Borg Queen as a kind of representative of the Collective.

## Political Issues in *Star Trek*

*Star Trek* frequently comments on certain current political issues. Heinecke, for example, mentions the fields of technology and environmental policy, while he points out that social and family policy, as well as economic and financial policy, are hardly mentioned in *Star Trek* (2009, 162). However, most of these comments are more general and do not address specific issues in detail. In fact, comments on political issues are obviously less pronounced in the *TOS* era of *Star Trek* than in later times. There is one prominent exception, which I have already described: *TOS* deals extensively with new technologies and their potentially dangerous impact on society.

In *TOS* "The Conscience of the King," Kirk meets a former governor of the colony Tarsus IV. Twenty-two years earlier, this governor, named Kodos, executed half of the population in order to ward off a possible famine (the young Kirk was one of the survivors of the colony at that time). Kodos decided who was executed and who was allowed to survive according to his own eugenic theories. Kirk finally confronts Kodos with his actions, and Kodos justifies them. Considering that this episode dates back to the 1960s, it is reasonable to assume that *Star Trek* is commenting about the mass genocides of World War II. Kirk, as a representative of the younger generation, stands for justice; Kodos, as an older perpetrator, does not want to know about his past actions anymore.

A similar theme is found in *TOS* "The Cloud Minders." Here the *Enterprise* visits the planet Ardana to take an important mineral aboard, a mineral that is needed to stop an epidemic on another planet and that can only be mined on Ardana. The crew is irritated that they are ordered to navigate to a cloud city, as they had originally assumed that the mines are on the planet's surface and the mineral could be picked up there. It turns out that the society on Ardana is dominated by a higher class that lives in the cloud city, far away from their world, and trade with the mineral. In turn, the lower class has to live on the planet's surface and mine the poisonous mineral. As Spock aptly remarks in this episode, this planet is "a place of the most violent contrasts. Those who receive the rewards are totally separated from those who shoulder the burdens. It is not a wise leadership." *Star Trek* here criticizes apartheid, which is characterized by white supremacy. This social criticism is remarkably clear for a U.S.-American series, considering that racial segregation was not formally abolished in the USA until 1964 with the Civil Rights Act, barely five years before this episode was first broadcast.

With the introduction of *TNG*, comments on political issues increased. Interestingly, apartheid policy remains a topic of discussion. In *TNG* "Angel One," the *Enterprise* crew, while searching for survivors of a lost freighter, encounters a world ruled by women and in which men represent a lower class that is openly discriminated against. When the shipwrecked men arrive on the planet, they quickly notice the discrimination and fight against it. The leader of Angel One sees no other option than to execute the rebels in order to preserve their social structure. The *Enterprise* crew is able to convince her that by doing so she will only create martyrs. Eventually, the rebels avoid execution but are exiled. In times of *TOS*, Kirk would probably have pushed for a change in social conditions. However, *TNG* shows that the Federation only interferes very cautiously in the affairs of this planet.

Like *TOS*, *TNG* also frequently comments on new technologies. In *TNG* "The Arsenal of Freedom" the *Enterprise* is attacked by an automated weapons system. The system analyses the opponent's behavior and continuously adapts to the enemy until the enemy is defeated. As it turns out, the civilization that invented this system has been wiped out by its own invention—only the system as such (and a holographic salesman to advertise the product) is still active. Another example is addressed is the *TNG* episode "Force of Nature." While the *Enterprise* is investigating the disappearance of a research ship, it encounters two alien scientists who claim to have discovered that the warp drive creates subspace rifts that threaten the existence of their home planet. The scientists would have reported this to the Federation Science Council but would not have been heard. The crew of the *Enterprise* reviews the scientists' findings and confirms their fears. In the end, after receiving the *Enterprise*'s report, the Federation Council decides to introduce a general speed limit for all starships in Federation territory in order to minimize the environmental impact of using warp drive.

In addition, *Star Trek* repeatedly addresses socio-political topics. The dangers of genetic engineering are one of the recurring themes. In *TOS* "Space Seed," Kirk and his crew encounter an apparently disabled ship on which they encounter about 70 people in so-called sleeping chambers. It turns out that the humans began their journey at the time of the Eugenic Wars. This fictitious conflict arose when genetically manipulated humans, the Augments, attempted to take control of Earth by force. Their leader is Khan Noonien Singh: "From 1992 to 1996, absolute ruler of more than a quarter of your world, from Asia through the Middle East" (Spock in *TOS* "Space Seed"). When the *Enterprise* crew awakens Khan, he tries to start a new conflict by means of the *Enterprise*.[12] Considering that genetic engineering was hardly advanced at all in the 1960s, this episode turns out to be particularly forward-looking. *Star Trek* takes a clear position on the possible dangers of genetic manipulation and the creation of superhumans. Consequently, all genetic manipulations of humans on Earth and in the later Federation are forbidden and outlawed.

In the late 1980s, when genetic engineering also took up a broader space in politics, *Star Trek* takes up the topic again. *TNG* "Unnatural Selection," for example, is about a group of genetically manipulated children whose immune systems are so advanced that their antibodies not only counteract viruses but also change the genetic structure of humans. As a result, these children must remain in quarantine because they pose a danger to other people.[13] In *TNG* "Up the Long Ladder," the crew comes into conflict with a species that reproduces exclusively through cloning. As more and more genetic defects occur due to the large number of clone generations, the aliens try to obtain new DNA material from the *Enterprise* crew—even against their will, if necessary—in order to keep their society alive. Picard clearly rejects this request, pointing out that the Federation has long since banned cloning technology. In *TNG* "The Masterpiece Society," the *Enterprise* visits the planet Moab IV, on which a group of humans has created a "perfect society" through genetic modification. All the inhabitants have been genetically optimized, but as Picard rightly points out, "many of the qualities that they breed out, the uncertainty, self-discovery, the unknown; these are many of the qualities that make life worth living." The colony's existence is threatened by a comet fragment, and ironically, Geordi LaForge is the one who can save the colony—albeit because of his blindness he would have been someone not worthy to live in this very society.

In *DS9* "Doctor Bashir, I Presume," genetic engineering is discussed once again. It turns out that Doctor Bashir was genetically engineered as a child by his parents because he was delayed in his development compared to his peers.[14] Since genetic engineering is punishable in the Federation, his father is subsequently tried. *DS9* explicitly refers to Khan from *TOS* and *Star Trek II: The Wrath of Khan*: "Two hundred years ago, we tried to improve the species through DNA resequencing. And what did we get for our troubles? The Eugenics Wars. For every Julian Bashir that can be created, there is a Khan Singh waiting in the wings, a superhuman, whose ambition and thirst for power have been enhanced along with his intellect. The law against genetic engineering provided a firewall against such men. And it is my job to keep that firewall intact" (Admiral Bennett in *DS9* "Doctor Bashir, I Presume"). However, the episode shows that there is obviously still competition in the future highly developed society of the Federation. "Even in this utopian society there are 'children who fall behind at school.' Whatever it merits, it must be a society, like any, of winners and losers" (Gregory 2000, 191).

Finally, *Star Trek* discusses medical ethics in the *TNG* episode "Ethics." When Worf is paraplegic after an accident, Beverly Crusher finds herself in a dilemma. According to Klingon ethics, paralyzed people are allowed to commit ritual suicide and, if necessary, demand assistance in doing so (Grech 2016, 74). Crusher is seeking advice from neuroscientist Toby Russell, who wants to apply a new, previously untested therapy to Worf by replacing Worf's spine with a healthy, genetically replicated one. In the same episode, in a second storyline, the *Enterprise* helps injured people on a sister ship that has been hit by a mine. Toby Russell provides an injured person with a self-developed drug that she wants to test instead of the standard therapy. When the injured man dies, Russell is suspended. She is nevertheless allowed to carry out her experiment with Worf—because he would rather die than remain paralyzed.

Another political issue that is repeatedly addressed in *TNG* is terrorism. In *TNG* "The High Ground," the *Enterprise* crew gets into a conflict on planet Rutia IV. When the crew is on the planet, an explosive device explodes in a cafe. When Beverly Crusher comes to the aid of the victims, she is kidnapped by a terrorist. It turns out that the government of the planet has been in conflict with a separatist organization for some time. This episode refers to the Northern Ireland conflict, which was an unresolved conflict at that time in the 1990s. Once again it shows that *Star Trek*, as it were, takes up and discusses contemporary conflicts in its universe like in a mirror. Resurgent nationalism and religious fanaticism are problems that came to the fore with the end of the Cold War (Gregory 2000, 168–9).[15]

## Wars and Conflicts

With some breaks, the *Star Trek* franchise has been in existence since 1966. In politics, many things have happened since then, which makes *Star Trek* an ideal text for examining how different political issues have evolved over time. *Star Trek* features a more or less coherent time lime, which means that all series and movies take place on a well-defined date.[16] *TNG*, *DS9*, and *VOY* take all place between 2364 and 2379, following *TOS* and the movies up to *The Undiscovered Country*. On the other hand, *ENT* and *DIS* were produced after *VOY* but their narration takes place ahead of the events in *TOS* (with the exception of *DIS* Season 3 which is placed well ahead in the future). However, *LD* and *PIC* occur after *VOY*. So, with *Star Trek* we have a rather unique situation with a time line that is linear for the most part. When looking at political processes and how they are dealt with in all of the series and movies, a kind of future history emerges.

I have discussed the major powers in the *Star Trek* universe above and compared them with the United Federation of Planets. As I will show in the following, there are multiple contacts and developments between the major powers in the course of the series and movies.

With regard to whether *Star Trek* represents a political utopia, the depiction of conflicts and warlike confrontations in *Star Trek* seems to be problematic. I have shown further ahead that classical utopias basically assume a state of peace, even if wars are not completely excluded. Therefore, Wellmann questions the utopian claim of *Star Trek*. He attests "an (intended) lack of relationship between the *Star Trek* companies" (Wellmann 1999, 174). Richards states that the Federation "is surrounded by societies calling themselves empires and acting out of all the standard motives for imperial expansion" (1997, 24). He points out that the *Enterprise* rarely leaves the territory of the Federation because it is apparently surrounded by hostile cultures (Richards 1997, 25). It is, therefore, interesting to find out if the depiction of conflicts in *Star Trek* can be reconciled with the ideal image of a utopia.

## *First Contacts and the Beginnings of the Federation on* Enterprise

In *Star Trek: Enterprise* the United Federation of Planets is not yet founded. Starfleet (here still referred to as United Starfleet) is the military organization of the United Earth, a planetary state that was created in the 22nd century. After first contact with the Vulcans in 2063 (*Star Trek: First Contact*), United Earth has eventually established diplomatic relations with the species (*ENT* "The Forge"). *Enterprise* also deals with several other first contacts, such as the Ferengi (*ENT* "Acquisition")[17] and the Romulans (*ENT* "Minefield"). In the course of the *Enterprise* series, conflicts, and connections between the (later) Federation and the other species in the universe are foreshadowed, although not further deepened. For example, Earth successfully mediates in a conflict between the Andorians and Vulcans (*ENT* "Cease Fire"), which finally leads to a rapprochement of the two hostile species. Eventually, the Andorians become founding members of the Federation.[18] In *ENT* "Judgment," Captain Archer is accused of treason by a Klingon court. In the end, the convicted Archer can be freed by the diplomatic efforts of the Vulcans, even if this causes lasting damage to the relationship with the Klingons. The Borg also come into contact with humans for the first time in *ENT* "Regeneration."

In *ENT*, terrorism plays a strong role as an instrument of politics. In a larger story arc the Temporal Cold War is being told, a conflict in which different forces from the future are involved. This Temporal Cold War is carried out by several proxy conflicts in the 22nd century—that is, at the time when *ENT* is occurring. In *ENT* "Broken Bow," the United Earth has first contact with the Klingons, a species hardly known until then, when a Klingon messenger crashes with his ship on Earth. As it turns out, the Klingon had information about a people called Suliban, who tried to destabilize the Klingon Empire through targeted terrorist attacks. *Star Trek* refers here to the instrumentalization of terrorism by political powers and draws parallels to the Cold War in our reality. There, too, proxy wars were conducted. Another example of this conflict is the attack of the Xindi on Earth in *ENT* "The Expanse." A Xindi probe cuts a swath of destruction between Florida and Venezuela. "This unsubtle echo of real-world contemporary events—the attack on 9/11, the invasions of Afghanistan and Iraq—was a return to the kind of direct political comment that had fueled so many of the original *Star Trek* episodes of the 1960s and featured in many of *Deep Space Nine*'s best episodes [...]." (Robb 2012, 215).

The political world of *ENT* is fragile and imperfect. When the *Enterprise* mediates a peace treaty between the Andorians and the Tellarites (*ENT* "Babel One"), the ship is attacked by the Romulans. The Romulans try to prevent the peace talks between the two peoples and the resulting rapprochement to Vulcan and United Earth. "This mission was supposed to cause dissension in the region. The Andorians and Tellarites have formed an alliance. They are working together for the first time in history" (Romulan Senator Vrax in *ENT* "The Aenar"). The attacked, however, react with a close alliance and found the Coalition of Planets, a loose alliance between the four powers. "From what I have heard about these Romulans they mean business. If they are behind these attacks, we have to find some way to stop them, or next time they might come back with a thousand of those ships" (Archer in *ENT* "United"). Archer's prediction was to come true in the Earth-Romulan war, which is mentioned in *TOS* "Balance of Terror."

In response to the formation of the Coalition of Planets, some humans have formed a xenophobic terrorist group called Terra Prime (*ENT* "Demons"). When the terrorists threaten a conference on Earth, Andorians and Vulcans withdrew from the negotiations on the belief that the humans were not fully convinced that they could take a step towards an interplanetary organization. Archer succeeds in storming the terrorists' headquarters and arresting the leader. With a speech, Archer can eventually persuade the peoples to a successful conclusion of the conference and makes clear that the coalition is of enormous importance for the political development of the United Earth (*ENT* "Terra Prime"). Finally, in 2161, the United Federation of Planets is founded (*ENT* "These Are the Voyages..."). Although Wellmann disagrees (1999, 173), both the foundation of the Coalition and the United Federation of Planets show very well

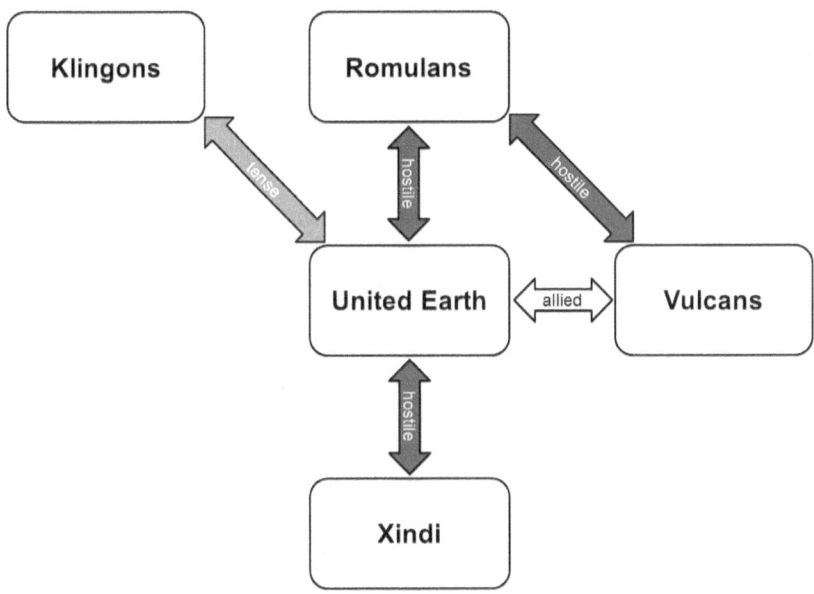

Political Relations during *Star Trek: Enterprise* (2151–2160).

that continuous diplomatic relations do exist in the *Star Trek* universe. The diplomatic relations between Vulcan and United Earth also speak for this—for example, Sarek, the Vulcan ambassador to the Federation (*TOS* "Journey to Babel," *TNG* "Sarek") or the Betazed ambassador Lwaxana Troi (*TNG* "Manhunt").

The political processes in *Enterprise* are reminiscent in their depiction of the formation of (quasi-)state structures in our reality. For example, United Earth may stand in for the United States of America. However, a closer parallel can be found in comparison to the European Union. If one considers that European states were at war with one another until the 20th century, a process of rethinking began after the Second World War, which led to an initially loose, then increasingly integrated, cooperation between the European states. This is roughly comparable to the Coalition of Planets. Realizing that an interplanetary cooperation is eminently important for the preservation of peace, the Coalition is founded and develops over time into a strongly integrated United Federation of Planets within the *Star Trek* universe.

## *War and Peace in* The Original Series

In *TOS* there are mainly two major powers besides the Federation, the Klingons and the Romulans. Although Gene Roddenberry had a great influence on the scripts, the political conflicts between the different species were largely developed by other scriptwriters, for example writer Gene L. Coon (Solow and Justman 1996, 136). "Under Coon's influence the latter episodes of the first season developed much of the political background and ideology of the Federation and the social customs and traditions of alien races" (Gregory 2000, 29).

The Romulans are introduced into the *Star Trek* universe for the first time in *TOS* "Balance of Terror." They were at war with Earth between 2156 and 2160 (when the Federation as such did not yet exist). At the end of the war, there was a ceasefire that established a neutral zone between the Romulan Empire and the Federation, a zone that must not be entered by either side.

The Klingons make their first appearance in *TOS* "Errand of Mercy." In this episode, in the year 2267, the Klingons try to occupy the planet Organia, and the *Enterprise* has been charged with preventing the occupation. Both parties are on the brink of open war, and Organia would be a strategically advantageous position for the Klingons. Eventually, the inhabitants of the planet themselves force both parties to a ceasefire in the Treaty of Organia, which establishes a neutral zone between these two empires, too. This has a clear parallel to the relationship between the USA and the Soviet Union in the 1960s (Sarantakes 2005, 80). The conflict was preceded by a long period of Cold War between the two powers, with the Battle of Donatu V in 2245 (*TOS* "The Trouble with Tribbles") as a major event. Worland compares the Treaty of Organia to the nuclear balance in the 1960s: "*Pax Organia* would seem to substitute for *pax atomica*, the fear of mutual annihilation that has produced an edgy peace between the superpowers since World War II" (1988, 113). In the course of *TOS*, the ceasefire between the Klingons and the Federation proves to be fragile. "Disputes remain, but the two interstellar powers would challenge one another only through indirect means" (Sarantakes 2005, 81). Again, and again, hostile disputes between the parties occur, for example over raw materials (*TOS* "Friday's Child"), accusations of conspiracy (*TOS* "The Trouble with Tribbles," *DS9* "Trials and Tribble-ations"), or interference in the affairs of third parties (*TOS* "A Private Little War"). Wellmann sees the neutral zone between the Federation and the Klingons as a central reason for the continuing conflict: "It is precisely the establishment of buffer zones to prevent contact that makes every contact a danger and the danger a cause for the use of violence up to and including war" (Wellmann 1999, 174).

In the *TOS* episode "A Private Little War," the *Enterprise* conducts scientific research on the planet Neural. This planet is home to a pre-warp civilization that Kirk had observed on a previous mission. However, given the level of development, the *Enterprise* crew is surprised that one group of the planet's inhabitants suddenly possesses modern firearms and threatens another group with them. It turns out that the Klingons have supplied the inhabitants with weapons, and Kirk now has to restore the balance of power. While doing so, he violates the Prime Directive; however, he argues that the Klingons already have had enough influence on the development of this civilization by their interference anyway. *TOS* "A Private Little War" probably shows one of the most direct parallels to our reality. As Franklin notes, this episode is an allegory of the Vietnam War: "The villagers, who represent the official U.S. view of the North Vietnamese, have been attacking and attempting to conquer the peaceful 'hill people,' who represent the official U.S. view of the South Vietnamese" (1994, 40).

The Klingons represent "the Soviet Union and/or Communist China" (Franklin 1994, 40). These parallels are by no means accidental. The authors of *Star Trek* had a vital interest in integrating current topics into their series. Screenwriter D.C. Fontana explains, "Gene Roddenberry and the *Star Trek* writers were more interested in stories that reflected the issues and problems of our times. We were the only show on the air that managed not just one but several episodes the examined aspects of the Vietnam War during a time when networks had decreed the subject absolutely taboo for anyone else" (2006, 38–9). From the writers' point of view, it was therefore a conscious effort to critically reflect contemporary conflicts in the series.

This can also be seen in the film *Star Trek VI: The Undiscovered Country*, in which a final peace treaty between the two powers is reached through the so-called Khitomer Accords. The events in this film have distinct parallels to the end of the Cold War. "Beginning with a tremendous explosion on a Klingon moon devoted to the Empire's energy production—transparent allusion to the 1987 Chernobyl nuclear power plant disaster [...]" (Worland 1994, 30), the film tells the beginning of final peace talks between the Klingons and the Federation. The Klingons' economic system is ailing because they have used their resources mainly to acquire military material, and, finally, the rather moderate Chancellor Gorkon is assassinated by Klingon hardliners (Gregory 2000, 162).

The characterization of the Klingons and Romulans in *TOS* is so interesting because they provide a direct reference to our reality. *TOS*, in fact, addresses the Cold War in a very direct way (Booker 2018, 68). In the reflection of the series, the two species are more or less analogous to the antagonistic major powers of Soviet Union and China (Worland 1988, 112; Sarantakes 2005, 78; Gregory 2000, 162).[19] This opinion is shared by Bernardi: "The Klingons, positioned as the Soviets, are stereotypically evil,

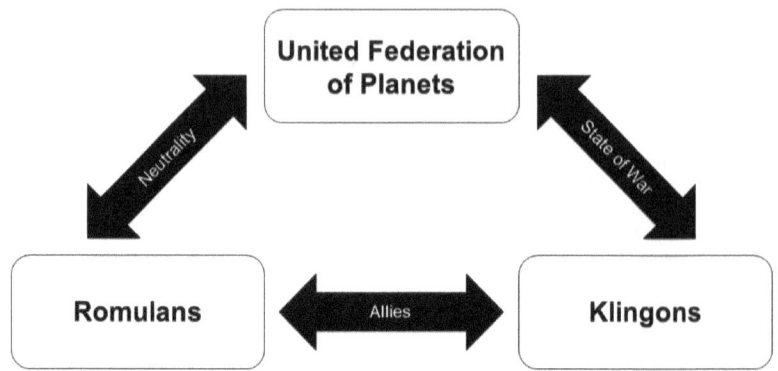

**Relations between the Federation, Romulans, and Klingons during *Star Trek: The Original Series*.**

dark and underhanded. They are a totalitarian, imperialistic regime who deem battle glorious. The Romulans, positioned as the Chinese, are stereotypically mysterious and ruthless. They rarely involve themselves in skirmishes with the Federation, but when they do they are cunning and vicious" (1994, 64).

It is interesting to note that Bernardi considers both characterizations as stereotypical and then compares them with the—in his opinion—democratic federation. However, there is no real statement about the constitution of the Federation in the *Star Trek* text, especially not in *TOS*. Also, the characterization of Klingons and Romulans as alter egos of the Soviet Union and China does not hold up, at least when viewed over the whole series. As Gregory correctly remarks, both species hardly appear in *TOS* and moreover are not exactly drawn as communist powers (2000, 162–3).

In *TOS*, therefore, we see a first approach for a political-utopian text. "Against a backdrop of science fiction, we talked about racial discrimination, determining one's own future, defending personal and national freedoms, compassion, love and friendship that held against all odds. *Star Trek* told stories of how Man [sic] could be far better than he was, how there could be a better future if we could only reach for it and build it" (Fontana 2006, 39).

Nevertheless, Hark limits that most stories in *TOS* are not utopian. "To be sure, imaging that Earth's various nations would band together to form a space fleet, after averting a nuclear holocaust and solving many social problems, did look wildly utopian from the vantage point of the late 1960s. Yet once humans move out into space, the same problems reappear. Instead of nations competing with each other on one planet, Earth becomes one planet with other planetary allies and adversaries trying to avert the same sorts of cataclysmic conflicts on a galactic scale" (2008, 33).

Hark's assessment is confirmed by the fact that *Star Trek* as an entertainment product should also definitely appeal to a mass audience. However, as we have already mentioned above, this was not the case at all. *TOS* was cancelled after three seasons and only attained cult status with the audience through numerous repetitions. But exactly this cult status led to the perception of *Star Trek* as a utopian narrative, as Hark has to admit (2008, 33). In view of the heyday of the Cold War with the threatening possibility of a nuclear world war, *TOS* gave the audience a structure in which a positive future was reflected—even more so in comparison to the political and social systems of the present, which were considered primitive (Gregory 2000, 107–8). Thus, *Star Trek* may not have been intentionally created as a utopia, but it was interpreted to be one by the audience.

## *Political Change in* The Next Generation

After *TOS*, almost 20 years passed before *TNG* was first aired on television—during which time politics in our reality underwent fundamental changes. A rethinking of foreign and domestic policy took place in the Soviet Union from the mid–1980s onwards. *TNG* premiered in 1987 just before the Iron Curtain came down. It is, therefore, interesting to observe to what extent the different politics are reflected in the narrative of *TNG*.

Gene Roddenberry used this as a starting point for his newly developed series. "[…] Roddenberry felt that he had a responsibility to all those fans who read utopian hopes into the original series to show those hopes coming to fruition. Second, the late 80s and early 90s were a time when it briefly looked possible that the world was entering a new era of peace and cooperation. Reagan and Gorbachev signed arms reduction treaties in the year *TNG* debuted" (Hark 2008, 65–6). Roddenberry took up those elements that were present in *TOS* and interpreted by the audience as utopian, in order to continue a utopian fiction with *Star Trek*. So even if Roddenberry did not necessarily want to create a utopian narrative at the beginning of *Star Trek* (after all, *TOS* was an entertainment product at first), this premise eventually changed with *TNG* (Richards 1997, 5), even if Roddenberry still understood the series as entertainment. "We now have more freedom and story latitude, because our series by-passes the networks and is made directly for television stations. As before, without neglecting entertainment values, we invite writers to consider premises involving the challenges facing humanity today (the 1980s and '90s), particularly those which interest the writer personally. The new *Star Trek* episodes will continue the tradition of vivid imagination, intelligence, and a sense of fun, while still assessing where we humans presently are, where we're going, and what our existence is really about" (Roddenberry 1987, 4).

In the beginning, Roddenberry relied mostly on veteran writers who had already helped shape *TOS*. "The initial impetus and creative ideas behind the new series came largely from members of the original series' production team. Roddenberry had a number of meetings with original *Trek* co-producers and writers Bob Justman, David Gerrold, Eddie Milkis and D.C. Fontana" (Gregory 2000, 43).

The *Enterprise* crew in *TOS* under Captain Kirk was composed of diverse people, including the Vulcan Spock, and this was similar in *TNG*. With Lieutenant Worf, for the first time a Klingon was a senior officer of the *Enterprise*. This is remarkable because although the Klingons and the Federation are no longer in a state of war in *TNG*, the Klingons (unlike the Vulcans) are not members of the Federation.[20]

In general, relations with the Klingons take on a much stronger and more differentiated role in the course of *TNG* than was ever the case with *TOS*. It is right away, in the first season, that Worf's inner conflict between his Klingon roots and Starfleet is put to the test. Worf constantly strives to retain his Klingon heritage and suffers from being regarded as an outcast from Klingon society (Grech 2016, 78). In the *TNG* episode "Heart of Glory," the *Enterprise* discovers a damaged space freighter carrying three Klingons. As it turns out, they have captured the freighter, which is why a Klingon ship is searching for them. When the *Enterprise* and the Klingon ship meet, the Klingons try to seize the *Enterprise*, whereupon Worf kills them. So, the Klingons are portrayed as a war species, a depiction that seems increasingly anachronistic (Gregory 2000, 178). While this episode is initially a character story, it introduces two important pieces of information that become vital for further politics between the Klingons and the Federation. First, the episode explains Lieutenant Worf's affiliation with Starfleet. As a child, he survived the Khitomer Massacre, an attack by the Romulans on a Klingon colony on the planet Khitomer, and was found and adopted by a Starfleet member. Klingon by birth, but raised in Starfleet, he experiences an inner conflict between two cultures (Weber 1997, 111). "Worf must constantly assimilate to Federation values, entailing a process of *acculturation* [...]" (Grech 2016, 79). At the same time, the episode suggests an unresolved conflict between the Klingons and Romulans. Although both species appeared in *TOS*, there was no mention of a conflict between the two.

In the same season, the Romulans appear for the first time in *TNG* in the episode "The Neutral Zone." Here, too, politics remains vague at first. At Starfleet's behest, the *Enterprise* approaches the neutral zone between the Romulan Star Empire and the Federation. Several Federation outposts along the zone have broken off contact and Starfleet Command suspects the Romulans. When the *Enterprise* reaches the outposts, they appear completely destroyed, confirming the crew's suspicions. The situation worsens when a Romulan starship suddenly appears in Federation space. But instead of a direct confrontation, Captain Picard hails the Romulans. It turns out that their outposts on the other side of the neutral zone have been destroyed as well, in the same manner. In view of this, both sides agree to exchange information.[21] Both episodes indicate that politics in *TNG* will now take place not only bilaterally but also multilaterally. In *TNG* "The Neutral Zone," Worf explains that the Romulans "killed my parents in an attack on Khitomer at a time when they were supposed to be our allies"—Klingons and Romulans are obviously still in a state of war.[22]

Precise differentiations of political conflicts between the major powers in the *Star Trek* universe is mainly due to a new generation of writers. From the third season on, *Star Trek* was significantly influenced by producers Rick Berman—who started as a supervising producer at the beginning of *TNG* and was quickly promoted to a showrunner alongside Gene Roddenberry—and Michael Piller, who joined *TNG* at the beginning of the third season. Berman and Piller formed a close partnership and ensured more continuity in the story editing of *TNG* (Gregory 2000, 50). Ira Steven Behr—who would later play a major role in the development of *DS9*—also joined the writing team during this time. "Under the guidance of Piller's writing team, *TNG* was to move decisively from being a purely episodic series towards a number of story arcs that would create the 'serial' mode eventually to dominate *DS9* and *Voyager*" (Gregory 2000, 53). Thus, *Star Trek* writers were encouraged to tell more complex and larger

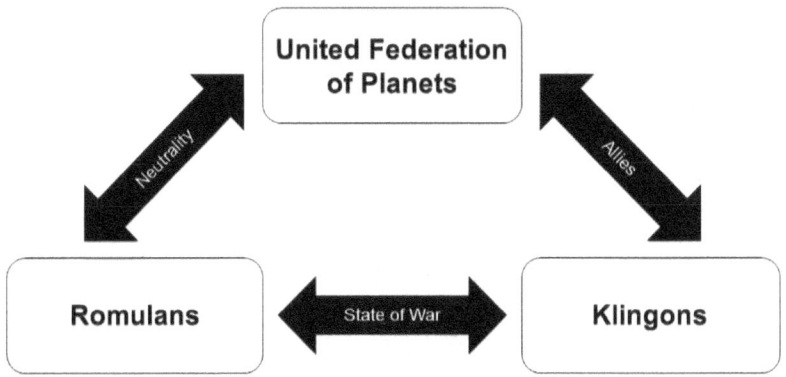

Relations between the Federation, Romulans, and Klingons during *Star Trek: The Next Generation*.

stories—and therefore engage deeper contexts. Moreover, the new writers had grown up with *TOS*. "Thus their writing [...] is motivated by the need to fulfill the narrative potential suggested by the best episodes of the original series" (Gregory 2000, 107). The influence of the inventor Gene Roddenberry, however, steadily declined before Roddenberry died during the fifth season of *TNG* in 1991 (Robb 2012, 139).

It is apparent for *TNG* that most of the politics are negotiated between the Federation, the Klingons, and the Romulans. In the *TNG* episode "The Defector," *Enterprise* is again close to the neutral zone when a Romulan ship with a defector on board successfully reaches Federation territory. It turns out that the defector is, in fact, a high-ranking Romulan admiral who is trying to warn the Federation of an imminent Romulan war attack. The Romulans are said to have established a cloaked base on the planet Nelvana III in the neutral zone, an installation from which a Romulan war fleet is to be launched. The *Enterprise* sensors cannot detect any irregular activity on the planet, but Picard nevertheless consults with Starfleet Command and receives permission to travel to the planet, which means a breach of treaty with the Romulans.

When the away team from the *Enterprise* finally arrive at the planet, they discover no traces whatsoever that would indicate a secret base, which leads to the conclusion that the Romulan defector must have received false information. At that moment, two Romulan starships appear and accuse the Federation of deliberate aggression. The only reason the situation does not escalate is because three Klingon warships suddenly decloak to assist the *Enterprise*. This episode once again illustrates the fragility of Romulan-Federation relations. The Romulans are attempting to provoke the Federation in order to launch a first strike (which would require a defensive response). The action is somehow reminiscent of the Cuban crisis, in which the Soviet Union deliberately deployed missiles in Cuba as a provocation to induce the United States to launch a first strike. This political incident is thus transformed in *Star Trek* in the form of a tripartite constellation between the Federation, the Romulans, and the Klingons. Remarkable is the close alliance between the Klingons and the Federation.[23] The Klingons have changed from a competitive, sovereign agent into an ally (Ohler and Strohmeier 2009, 187).

Parallel to Berman and Piller, writer Ronald D. Moore joined the *Star Trek* writing team (Gregory 2000, 52). "I get to sit in a room and make up stories about a childhood fantasy. Up on my shelf at this very moment is a model of the Enterprise I built when I was 12 years old. It stays up to remind me of that special joy that Trek gave me when I was young and to inspire me to deliver it to everyone watching every week just like I did all those years ago" (Moore 1997–99, raolchat.txt). Moore was instrumental in further developing the Klingons in *TNG*—for example, in the *TNG* episode "Sins of the Father." In this episode, the audience is eventually told about the background of the Khitomer Massacre. Klingon exchange officer Kurn turns out to be Worf's brother, who tells him that their father is blamed for the massacre. He is said to have provided the Romulans with classified information. Since the Klingons attach great importance to the tradition and good reputation of their House, Worf travels to the Klingon homeland and wants to defend his House before the Klingon High Council, but is accused of treason by the Klingon Duras, a member of the Council. The *Enterprise* crew is able to access the Klingon information network (by illegal means) and compares the information with that of Starfleet. It turns out the House of Duras, rather than Worf's House, is responsible for treachery to the Romulans. When Picard confronts Klingon Chancellor K'mpec with this information, the Chancellor states that the High Council is well aware that Duras' father is the traitor. But since the House of Duras is too powerful in the Klingon Empire, the truth must not be allowed to come to light, as it would most likely lead the Empire into civil war. Picard argues that the alliance between the Klingons and the Federation should not be based on lies, but he is ultimately helpless against the Chancellor, who openly threatens to end the alliance. Finally, Worf accepts the dishonoring of his House by the High Council in order to preserve the Empire and the alliance with the Federation.

In the *TNG* episode "Reunion," Klingon Chancellor K'mpec lies dying and asks Picard to find out who poisoned him—the well-known Duras or the Klingon Gowron. He instructs Picard to preside over the Rite of Succession. When a bomb detonates at the meeting, the *Enterprise* crew discovers it contained technology only the Romulans use. It turns out that the assassin, who himself died in the explosion, was a follower of Duras, who is also responsible for the Chancellor's poisoning. When Duras dies in battle, only one candidate remains to succeed him, and Picard appoints Gowron as the new Klingon Chancellor.

However, when Picard wants to perform the ritual of appointment on the Klingon home planet in the *TNG* two-parter "Redemption," the danger of civil war does not seem to have been fully averted. The House of Duras now turns against Gowron as the new chancellor and presents an illegitimate son, now legitimized to succeed his father. When Picard, as head of the succession, rejects him as a possible candidate due to inexperience and introduces Gowron as chancellor, civil war breaks out. Klingons loyal to Duras fight against the newly appointed chancellor and his supporters—secretly supported by the Romulans. Formally, Starfleet cannot intervene in the conflict, as it is considered an internal Klingon affair. In talks with the High Command and after approval by the Federation

Council, Starfleet establishes a blockade at the Klingon-Romulan border. When Gowron attacks the Duras fleet, the Romulans have no other option but to break the blockade and be discovered in the process. It all works out as planned. The Romulans have to withdraw—if they do not want to be actively involved in the conflict—and Gowron can end civil war in the Klingon Empire with his own troops.

After this episode, no more politics between the Klingons, Romulans, and the Federation are discussed in *TNG*. Interestingly, the whole story arc spans several episodes and seasons. Thus, in the series universe, the impression is created that these processes are not singular events, but rather ongoing conditions in the background.

The construction of the tripartite relationship between the major powers casts doubt on the findings that the Klingons and Romulans were only doppelgangers of the Soviet Union and China. Especially the differentiated development of the relations among them does not confirm this view. "In *TNG* [...] the simplicities of the Cold War vanish with the demise of the Federation-Klingon (i.e., U.S.-Soviet) rivalry" (Weldes 1999, 121). This opinion is also shared by Gregory: "The changes in Klingon political culture that are enacted provide another example of the movement away from the simplistic political positioning of alien races in the original series" (2000, 179).

The *TNG* two-parter "Unification" then focuses on the Federation's relationship with the Romulans. Spock, who is now ambassador, was contacted by some Romulans belonging to an underground movement that wanted to bring about a reunion of Romulans and Vulcans.[24] Spock then went undercover to Romulus. However, the Romulans had long since learned of the underground movement and were trying to use it for their own purposes by planning to annex the Vulcan home world. That would mean occupying Federation territory and expanding their influence in the quadrant. However, the *Enterprise* crew was able prevent this. *TNG* "Unification" shows that the writers were gradually emancipating themselves from Roddenberry's original premises. In the actual series guide, Roddenberry indeed had excluded warlike conflicts with the Romulans and stories with Vulcans (1987, 11).

Eventually, in *TNG* "The Pegasus," the Federation does come into conflict with the Romulans again when Romulan intelligence discovers that the Federation has been experimenting with cloaking technology. However, the Federation is not allowed to do so, because "in the Treaty of Algeron, the Federation specifically agreed not to develop cloaking technology" (Picard in *TNG* "The Pegasus").[25] Here, too, the *Enterprise* crew can prevent an aggravation of the conflict with the Romulans. It remains to be noted that the Romulans maintain a skeptical attitude towards the

Federation during the entire run of *TNG*, and the relationship between the two powers tends to tense up in the course of the series. Although the conflict does not break out openly during the entire period of *TNG*, it is clear that there is always the possibility of it happening (Gregory 2000, 177).

As noted, the Cardassian Union is a military *junta* that expanded through conquering other civilizations— a notion which can be seen as a reference to Nazi Germany in 1933 (Burston-Chorowicz 2018, 17). The Cardassians are shown as a new species for the first time in *TNG* "The Wounded." In this episode, it is explained that the Federation has only recently signed a peace treaty with the Cardassians. This was preceded by several years of war, which was originally caused by a Cardassian attack on the Federation colony Setlik III, which was located near the Cardassian border. Picard also encountered Cardassian hostility on his former command on the USS *Stargazer*.

Cardassian politics are further described in *TNG* "Ensign Ro." After a Federation colony near the Cardassian border was attacked, it turned out that Bajoran terrorists were responsible. Bajor is a world occupied by the Cardassians 40 years before to exploit its natural resources. "Bajoran culture flourished a half-million years ago, when humans on Earth were not yet standing erect. The Bajoran people are deeply spiritual, but their history also recorded many great architects, artists, builders, and philosophers" (Okuda and Okuda 1999, 31). The attack on the colony draws the Federation into the Cardassian-Bajoran conflict. In the episode, Picard eventually discovers that the Cardassians attacked the Federation colony and that the alleged involvement of the Bajorans was staged. The view of stateless people, who are desperate and subsisting in poverty, is "a marked contrast to Federation abundance and utopianism" (Burston-Chorowicz 2018, 17).

The Cardassians, who apparently have been in contact with the Federation for quite some time, are introduced as a new major power in the galaxy in these episodes, and the events in *TNG* "Ensign Ro" show the fragility of the peace treaty. Here, *Star Trek* reflects politics between two powers that get into territorial disputes over the settlement of colonies near their common border. The war here is not large-scale, but rather consists of smaller military conflicts, which remain confined to a small area, but are nevertheless permanent. Here, *Star Trek* mirrors the changed geopolitical conditions of our reality. In the early to mid–1990s, multipolar conflicts between states arose worldwide, often related to border disputes—or to the presence of important raw materials. The occupation of Bajor is reminiscent of the occupation of Kuwait by Iraq, and the involvement of terrorist groups reflects fractured conflicts within alliances of states, as was the case in Yugoslavia. Moore's answer to the question whether Bajor could not represent Lebanon and *Deep Space Nine*, Beirut is, however, that this analogy is not tenable. "You could also call Bajor Israel or Iran, or even America and the Cardassians could be Germans, or Russians or several other examples. While these parallels do enter our discussions [...], we don't really try to make Bajor a direct analogy to any specific contemporary country or people" (Moore 1997–99, ron012.txt).

Thus, *Star Trek* does not mirror events in our reality in a one-to-one correspondence; rather, it takes up elements of these conflicts in order to apply them to the *Star Trek* universe. "Blending the experiences of many Earth peoples and races into our storytelling allows us to comment on these subjects without advocating a particular political point of view, while at the same time allowing us to view the topics in a different light without the baggage of contemporary politics" (Moore 1997–99, ron012.txt).

The conflict between the Cardassians and the Federation in *TNG* "Chain of Command" takes an unusual turn for *Star Trek*. Picard and two members of his crew are selected by Starfleet for a covert mission on Celtris III, a Cardassian planet on the Federation border, where Starfleet suspects a secret base with Cardassian biological weapon systems. Meanwhile, Captain Jellico, who was already in charge of negotiating a ceasefire agreement with the Cardassians, takes command of the *Enterprise*. The Cardassians are in the process of making major troop movements—among other things, they have withdrawn three quarters of their troops from the planet Bajor—and the Federation fears a Cardassian campaign. The *Enterprise* is meeting with a Cardassian ship for diplomatic negotiations.

It turns out that the mission on Celtris III was a trap. While his two fellow officers are able to escape, Picard is arrested and interrogated by the Cardassians. The Cardassians use a variety of torture methods including forced nudity, deprivation of food, and inflicting pain. The Cardassians demand information from Picard about Starfleet operations on the planet Minos Korva, which is located directly on the Cardassian border and whose territory the Cardassians claim, although it is home to a Federation colony.

Meanwhile, during the negotiations on the *Enterprise*, the Cardassians declare that they have Picard as a prisoner in their custody. They offer to release Picard should the Federation withdraw from the disputed sector (and thus from the planet Minos Korva). The Federation rejects this trade and refers to the Seldonis IV Convention, which explicitly prohibits torture.[26] The *Enterprise* crew concludes from the capture of Picard that the Cardassians probably really want to control Minos Korva and suspect that a fleet is hiding in a nearby star nebula. With a small shuttle they succeed in mining the nebula and thus persuade the Cardassians to give up. Finally, the Cardassians realize their situation and retreat. Picard is returned to the Federation.

This episode shows how much *Star Trek* has moved away from classic diplomacy politics. The conflict between the Federation and the Cardassian Union is unstable. Although a peace treaty exists, the Cardassians try to resolve border conflicts to their advantage and do not shy away from a first attack on Federation territory. At the same time, although they are bound to the Seldonis IV Convention, they use torture to obtain valuable information. In addition, ongoing negotiations take place in *TNG* "Chain of Command." The fragile balance between Cardassians and the Federation should not be disturbed, but everyone tries to influence it a little bit in his favor (Richards 1997, 34). Considering that the episode was broadcast in the early 1990s, it is striking how much it anticipates and discusses regarding the handling of multilateral conflicts in our reality. The interrogation methods used by the Cardassians are not least reminiscent of the events in Guantanamo Bay after the terrorist attacks on the United States in 2001—it is just that these take place some ten years after the episode was first broadcast. Picard is not classified as a prisoner of war, either, and it is only to them that the convention ultimately applies. On the contrary, Picard is treated as a terrorist. Ultimately, it turns out that the torture has not produced any usable information, as Picard does not in fact have any information worth mentioning. However, his will was broken by torture, as Picard's testimony proves. During the torture, for example, he was regularly asked how many lights he saw in the torture room. Although there were four lights (and Picard kept saying this), his torturer insisted that there were five. In the end Picard even believed this: "I would have told him anything. Anything at all! But more than that, I believed that I could see five lights" (Picard in *TNG* "Chain of Command").

Eventually, the *Enterprise* takes a Cardassian agent on board in *TNG* "Lower Decks" who is working for the Federation in a covert operation. In *TNG* "Journey's End" it is finally mentioned that the three-year-long negotiations because of border disputes between the Federation and the Cardassian Union have been settled. However, this agreement also provides for the transfer of some Federation territories to the Cardassians, so that colonists of the Federation have to be resettled and a demilitarized zone established there. When, on the planet Dorvan V, which is located in this zone, the Federation colonists refuse to leave the planet, it almost comes to a breach of treaty and a flareup of the conflict. Only Picard's intervention can prevent another war by appealing to the Cardassians: "The last war caused massive destruction and cost millions of lives. Do not send our two peoples down that same path again, not like this." The colonists remain on the planet, but must give up their Federation citizenship and are now under Cardassian regime. "The Federation [...] ignores the self-determination of their own citizens who were historically victims of violent imperialism. [...] Soon after this episode the Cardassians begin quietly supporting militias to attack other former Federation colonists, driving them away from their homes" (Burston-Chorowicz 2018, 19). This action leads to the formation of the Maquis, a rebel organization of members of Federation colonies near the Cardassian border who want to sabotage the peace treaty with the Cardassians.[27] "The Maquis grew in response to Cardassian hostilities toward these colonies and to the perception that they had been abandoned by the Federation government" (Okuda and Okuda 1999, 287).

In the *TNG* episode "Preemptive Strike," *Enterprise* is patrolling the now established demilitarized zone when it receives a distress call from a Cardassian ship. As it turns out, this ship was attacked by the Maquis. Starfleet decides that the Maquis should be infiltrated by Bajoran Starfleet Ensign Ro Laren in order to obtain classified information. The Maquis has indeed information about biogenic weapons and is planning a pre-emptive strike against it. "[...] 'Preemptive Strike' paints the Cardassians, who a developing a biogenic weapon to use against their enemies, as treacherous and evil, thus making the Maquis that much more sympathetic" (Putman 2013, 152).

Ro Laren reports this to Starfleet, and Picard tries to set a trap for the Maquis to break the organization. Ro develops doubts, finally betrays Picard, and joins the Maquis. Eventually, Starfleet's plan does not work out.

The formation of a military-oriented rebel organization within the Federation shows that there is obviously disagreement among the civilian population about politics within the Federation. *Star Trek* again reflects the political developments in the 1990s in our reality, developments in which states see themselves less exposed to interstate conflicts, but instead intra-state conflicts occur more frequently.[28] The fact that the Maquis uses terrorist means to oppose a peace treaty indicates that the discourse on these treaties has apparently been conducted with insufficient participation of the population concerned, or that the political structures represent such a rigid regime that participation is not even envisaged.

## *Multilateral Conflicts in* Deep Space Nine

*DS9* was launched in 1993, so that the events in the first season of *DS9* are parallel to those of the sixth season of *TNG*. In addition, many *TNG* writers transferred to *DS9*. "Its major writers, Ira Steven Behr, Robert Hewitt Wolfe and Peter Allan Fields, had all contributed to a number of *Next Generation* episodes and were thus very familiar with the 'rules' of the *Star Trek* universe. [...] Michael Piller made frequent contributions to the writing in the first two seasons, with more occasional contributions from Rick Berman, Jeri Taylor and Naren Shankar. After season two, when *TNG* came to an end, the addition of Ronald D. Moore and Rene Echevarria gave the team added depth. [...] Many episodes were co-written by several members of the team, with the result that, at least until Moore and Echevarria's arrival, it is harder to distinguish the style of any writer" (Gregory 2000, 68).

The conflict between the Federation and the Cardassians has a much more prominent role in *DS9* than in *TNG*. There are strong hints for this in the pilot episode "Emissary." "A century ago, the Cardassians conquered the planet Bajor, an ancient society with a dedication to spiritual pursuits. [...] Bajoran terrorism during the last several decades has been a significant problem for the Cardassians" (Berman and Piller 1992, 2).

The Cardassians had recently ended the occupation of Bajor, leaving the planet devastated. Thus, the events in *DS9* "Emissary" take place immediately after the events in *TNG* "Chain of Command," which refers directly to the withdrawal from Bajor. The Bajorans have asked the Federation for help in rebuilding their society and have applied for Federation membership (Berman and Piller 1992, 3). For this reason, Starfleet is taking over the Cardassian station Terok Nor, which served as a major base for the occupation forces in the orbit of Bajor. Starfleet renames the station *Deep Space Nine*. "The Starfleet team's mission is to spearhead the arduous diplomatic and scientific efforts that accompany the lengthy entry procedure" (Berman and Piller 1992, 3). The crew discovers a wormhole in close proximity to the station, a structure that leads to the Gamma Quadrant.[29] When the Cardassians also discover the wormhole, a dispute ensues. So here the *Star Trek* writers elaborate on the conflict between the Cardassians and the Federation, which was already established in *TNG*. The Federation now acts as the protecting power for Bajor, which further fuels the Cardassians' aggression against the Federation. At the same time, the Bajoran population has to deal with the consequences of the occupation, such as war crimes (*DS9* "Duet"), Bajoran war collaborators (*DS9* "Necessary Evil") or Bajoran prisoners of war on Cardassia (*DS9* "The Homecoming"). *DS9* "Duet," in particular, is an episode in which "Star Trek develops its 'darkest' political theme, the examination of the Bajoran holocaust in which 10 million are said to have died" (Gregory 2000, 174).

The Federation is thus in the position of a mediating authority. With this, *DS9* once again draws a parallel to the contemporary role of the United States, for example, with regard to the Israeli-Palestinian conflict (Gregory 2000, 173). The provisional government on Bajor initially has little power, a weakness which manifests itself in coup attempts on the planet

(*DS9* "The Circle," *DS9* "The Siege"). The Federation, however, refuses to intervene in the conflict. Referring to the Prime Directive, it declares the coup as a solely domestic Bajoran matter.

In *DS9* "The Maquis," the border conflict between the Federation and the Cardassians is further deepened, and the activities of the Maquis are increasing. It becomes clear that the conflict, introduced in *TNG*, is now not only affecting the civilian population of the Federation living near the border but also that Starfleet officers are increasingly defecting to the Maquis. While the official policy—represented by Commander Sisko of *Deep Space Nine* and his Cardassian counterpart Gul Dukat—is to preserve the peace treaty at all costs, the conflict takes on a new dimension as Starfleet suddenly finds itself confronted with dissenters within its own ranks. Sisko shows understanding for the dissidents, because although there is no war, crime, or poverty on Earth, "the Maquis do not live in paradise. Out there in the demilitarized zone, all the problems have not been solved yet" (Sisko in *DS9* "The Maquis"). Starfleet Command, however, shows little understanding for the concerns of the Maquis; in its opinion the Maquis are "a bunch of irresponsible hotheads" (Admiral Nechayev in *DS9* "The Maquis"). "There's a sense of betrayal associated with the Maquis in the minds of the people in the Federation, regardless of whether that's an irrational feeling or not. Add to that sense of betrayal the fact that the Maquis have harassed and attacked several Federation targets over the years and you begin to see why the Feds [Federation people] refuse to turn a blind eye to this group" (Moore 1997-99, ron052.txt).

It is becoming apparent that the standard of living within the Federation is deteriorating from the center to the periphery—with the situation

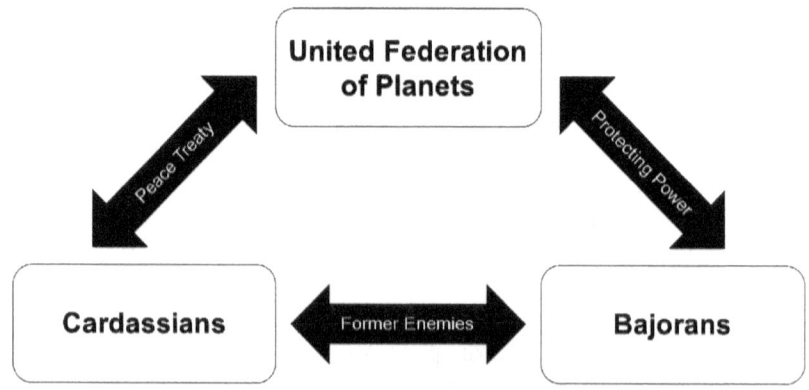

Relations between the Federation, Cardassians, and Bajorans at the beginning of *Star Trek: Deep Space Nine*.

## 4. Politics in Star Trek

on the Cardassian-Federation border as a somewhat extreme case. The fact that the values and principles of the Federation are being called into question by its own population and even by its own Starfleet officers is considered a declaration of war by Starfleet Command.

The institutional structure of the Federation must be preserved and defended even against opponents from within. Obviously, there is no or at least only insufficient open discourse, and therefore no political process, on this issue in the Federation: "[...] We have left the Federation, and that is the one thing you cannot accept. Nobody leaves paradise. Everyone should want to be in the Federation. Hell, you even want the Cardassians to join" (Michael Eddington in *DS9* "For the Cause").[30]

The Federation thus claims to be an all-encompassing political institution, in which withdrawal or even a dissenting opinion is not tolerated. It goes even so far as to imply that the Federation is comparable to Borg society: "In some ways, you are even worse than the Borg. [...] You assimilate people and they do not even know it" (Michael Eddington in *DS9* "For the Cause"). This reconsideration of the Federation as an all-encompassing and unique political institution—after all regarded as the best of all possible worlds for a long time—was pushed forward by executive producer Ira Steven Behr. As he "gained more authority over the show's direction in seasons three and four, *DS9* became an outright repudiation of many aspects of *TNG*. [...] Behr has often said that, as a native of the Bronx, he was always suspicious of the oh-so-genteel residents of the Connecticut suburbs. Picard and crew live in the Federation's Connecticut; Commander, then Captain, Benjamin Sisko [...] and the station's motley assemblage in the Bronx" (Hark 2008, 88–9).

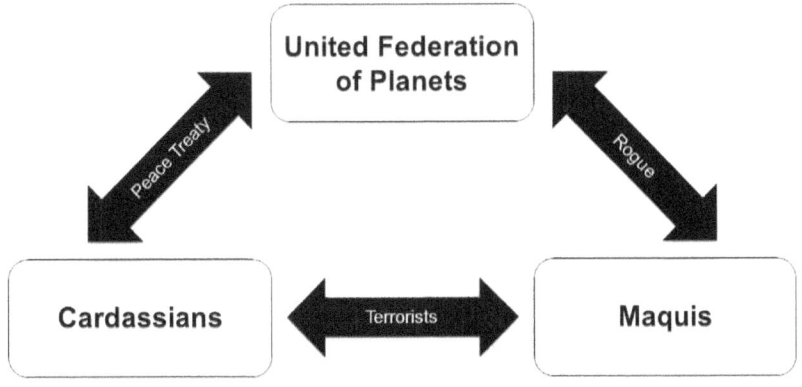

Relations between the Federation, Cardassians, and the Maquis.

Here Behr certainly questions Roddenberry's idea of a utopian society, to some degree, with our own present in mind. For example, the Maquis conflict mirrors the terrorism of the 1990s in the United States. "By the time 'The Maquis' was broadcast in 1994, Americans had witnessed bloody clashes between federal government officials and right-wing extremist groups" (Putman 2013, 151). Like the Maquis, these groups feel threatened by the government, which has had to increasingly subordinate their independence to a new world order (Putman 2013, 151). At the same time, the Maquis conflict in the *Star Trek* universe opens the view on the ambivalent policy of the Federation, which wants to maintain a balance of power in the galaxy. "Thus, while the Maquis stories begin with a cross-examination of *Star Trek*'s liberal conscience, they grow into a depiction of how liberal principles can offer illusory hopes which may lead to disaster" (Gregory 2000, 176).

Here again the question of the political constitution of the Federation arises. Gregory may see the Federation as a liberalistic construct, but on the other hand, the *Star Trek* text shows that the Federation and especially Starfleet mostly have rather conservative, possibly totalitarian traits.

With this form of narration, *Star Trek* changes its focus. The utopian ideal of the entire franchise is self-critically reflected here. "While the utopian idealism of Roddenberry's conception of *Star Trek* remains as a constant reference point, the political and psychological realism of *DS9* gives it a constant 'edge' that redefines *Star Trek* as a strikingly cohesive product of the modern 'televisual' age" (Gregory 2000, 88). Behr also sees no contradiction to Roddenberry's original vision. "I see my job as interpreting Gene's vision. [...] In other words, in 'The Maquis Part II' I had Sisko say that Earth is a paradise but that it's easy to be a saint in paradise. To me, *DS9* isn't about paradise. And the fact that Gene Roddenberry's human race can exist there and struggle there and try to make that little part of the galaxy a better place, is a positive view of the future. But within that positive view, there's a lot of pain, suffering, disappointment and death" (Behr 1997).

Being the direct neighbor to the wormhole, *Deep Space Nine* is located at a passageway to the Gamma Quadrant, which so far has hardly been explored by the Federation. However, *DS9* stays true to the original *Star Trek* vision to discover new worlds and new civilizations. It is already pointed out in the first *DS9* episode "Emissary" that the Federation will eventually explore the Gamma Quadrant. Klingons and Vulcans are also quickly exploring the area (*DS9* "The Sword of Kahless," *DS9* "Dramatis Personae"), and the Bajorans has even founded "the first Bajoran colony in the Gamma Quadrant" (Bashir in *DS9* "Crossover") with New Bajor.

That there is a new and unknown political entity in the Gamma

## 4. Politics in Star Trek

Quadrant is first hinted at in *DS9* "Rules of Acquisition," when the Ferengi come into contact with the Karemma, a people from the so-called Dominion, who are in search of trading partners. At first, the true nature of the Dominion remains largely unclear; however, Moore explains that it does not dominate the entire Gamma Quadrant (1997/1999, ron005.txt). In the *DS9* episode "The Jem'Hadar," the *DS9* crew encounters the Jem'Hadar species, which also reveals itself to be part of the Dominion, while exploring a planet. In this episode, the Jem'Hadar are characterized as ruthless mercenaries in the service of the so-called Founders. The Founders have created the Dominion and declare that they will not tolerate any further Federation presence in the Gamma Quadrant. "The Dominion will no longer stand by and allow ships from your side to violate our territory. [...] Coming through the anomaly [the wormhole] is interference enough. Unless you wish to continue to offend the Dominion, I suggest you stay on your side of the galaxy" (Talak'talan in *DS9* "The Jem'Hadar").

From the beginning, the Dominion is thus portrayed as a hostile power in the Gamma Quadrant, which apparently builds up a considerable threat potential against the Federation. "When the Dominion told us to stay out of GQ [Gamma Quadrant], it was if China told the US to stay

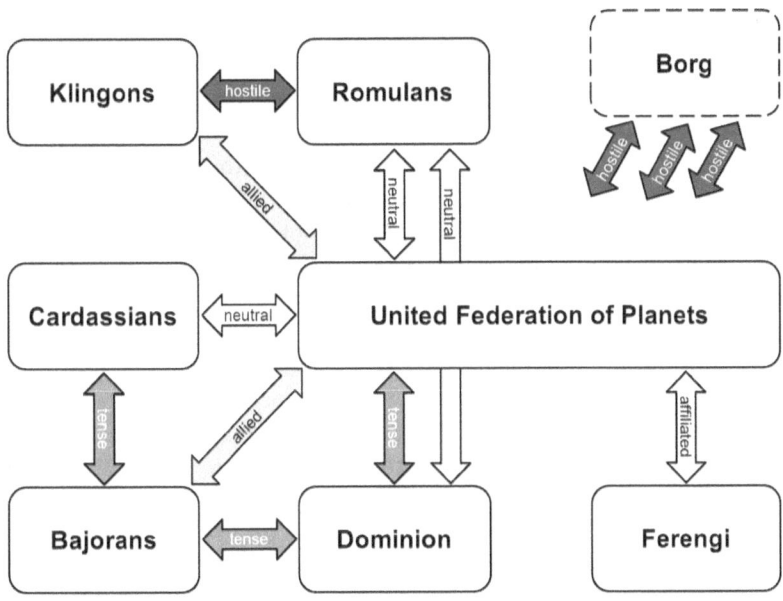

**Political Relations during *Star Trek: The Next Generation* and *Star Trek: Deep Space Nine* before the Dominion War (2370).**

out of the Yellow Sea. China is the big boy in this neck of the woods, and you better take their warning seriously, but at the same time we have trading partners and allies there and hey, freedom of the seas and all that" (Moore 1997–99, ron005.txt).

It is known neither why the Dominion is acting in such a hostile fashion nor how it is actually structured. Starfleet's response to the threat, however, is to rearm. A new prototype of a starship, the USS *Defiant*, is being deployed to *Deep Space Nine*. The *Defiant* is the first Federation ship to have a cloaking device based on Romulan technology (*DS9* "The Search"). In view of the great threat to the Alpha Quadrant, the Federation and the Romulans are working together here, which is rather unusual. There was even an amendment added to the Treaty of Algeron for this purpose. Finally, on *DS9* "The Search," we learn more about the Dominion's hostility. The Founders—a species of shapeshifters, life forms that can take on any shape or appearance—were once hunted and almost exterminated by the Solids, species like the human race that have a solid form.[31] Based on this experience, the Founders came to the conclusion that "what you can control, cannot hurt you" (Female Changeling in *DS9* "The Search") and began subjugating other species and controlling them in the Dominion. For the same reason, the Federation and the other major powers of the Alpha Quadrant were a threat to the Dominion.[32] *Vice versa*, the Alpha Quadrant powers recognize the aggressive behavior of the Dominion early on, so that the Romulans—most notably first allied with the Cardassians—are preparing a preventive attack on the Dominion. In *DS9* "Improbable Cause" and *DS9* "The Die Is Cast," both the Obsidian Order of the Cardassians and the Tal Shiar of the Romulans enter into a strategic alliance and want to destroy the Founders with a joint fleet in order to leave the Dominion leaderless. As the Dominion had observed the actions of the two great powers and set a trap for them, the conflict ends in their defeat: the Obsidian Order is completely destroyed, and the Romulans suffer great losses. As a result, the Romulans sign a non-aggression pact with the Dominion and remain neutral (*DS9* "Call to Arms").

The presence of the Dominion thus considerably shifts the balance of power in the Alpha Quadrant. Strategic alliances are now being forged. The Romulans share technology with the Federation ship USS *Defiant* in exchange for intelligence and join forces with the Cardassians for a pre-emptive strike. This also increases mutual distrust among the powers, instead of the common threat from the Dominion causing concerted action by all major powers. So, the Federation is not informed in advance of the Cardassian-Romulan alliance. At the same time, the defeat of the Cardassians and Romulans gives the Klingons and the Federation a considerable power advantage in the Alpha Quadrant. The Cardassians lose their supremacy in the very area of the galaxy where *Deep Space Nine* and the wormhole are located. The Romulans must rebuild their intelligence.[33]

The Dominion is beginning to infiltrate the powers in the Alpha Quadrant through spies. Because the Founders may take on any appearance as shapeshifters, the Dominion replaces influential politicians and military personnel in the Alpha Quadrant with identical-looking members of their species (*DS9* "The Adversary"). The uncertainty that there might be Dominion members in their own ranks leads to a further destabilization of the region. After the Romulans and Cardassians have been considerably weakened militarily by their failed pre-emptive strike, the Klingons attack Cardassia with a large force. Shortly before that, Cardassian regime was successfully overthrown—the military government was replaced by civilian forces[34]—and the Klingons suspect that the Dominion had infiltrated Cardassia. Since they have no evidence, the Federation officially condemns the attack. The crew of *Deep Space Nine* grants asylum to the Cardassian government, so the Klingons cancel the Khitomer Accords and now attack the station as well. Only a Federation war fleet is able stop them from taking the station (*DS9* "The Way of the Warrior"). The alliance between the Klingons and the Federation is thus terminated, and, Sisko notes, "this is exactly what the Founders want. Klingon against Cardassian, Federation against Klingon. The more we fight each other, the weaker we will get, and the less chance we have against the Dominion" (Sisko in *DS9* "The Way of the Warrior").[35]

Destabilization is also continuing in the Federation itself. There is a bomb attack at the so-called Antwerp Conference, which is attended by diplomats from the Federation and the Romulan Star Empire. Video footage confirms Dominion involvement, whereupon Sisko travels to Earth. When an Earth-wide power failure occurs, the Federation fears an invasion and declares martial law (*DS9* "Homefront"). A *coup d'état* by Starfleet officers is barely averted (*DS9* "Paradise Lost").[36] The Klingons still refuse to withdraw from occupied Cardassian territory. "They are now part of the Klingon Empire" (Chancellor Gowron on *DS9* "Broken Link"). When the Klingons demand that the Federation withdraw from the Archanis sector, which used to belong to the Klingon Empire but then fell to the Federation, an open war breaks out between the former allies (*DS9* "Broken Link").[37] It turns out that a high Klingon general, Martok, has been replaced by a Founder (*DS9* "Apocalypse Rising"). When the Cardassians then join the Dominion to free themselves from Klingon domination, Klingons and the Federation approach again and continue their alliance (*DS9* "By Inferno's Light"). The Dominion, however, has achieved its goal. The Romulans have signed a non-aggression pact, the Klingons and the Federation are destabilized powers, and the Cardassians are now the Dominion's allies in the

Alpha Quadrant. This shows that the Dominion deliberately played off the powers in the Alpha Quadrant against each other to gain influence. When the Cardassian leader Gul Dukat explains the connection to the Dominion that "the Dominion recognizes us for what we are: the true leaders of the Alpha Quadrant" (Dukat in *DS9* "By Inferno's Light"), this confirms the political decline of the Cardassians. In retrospect, the Cardassians not only had to withdraw from their space station and the planet Bajor and conclude a peace treaty with the Federation but also lost control of the demilitarized zone to the Maquis, destroyed their intelligence service in a collaborative action with the Romulans, and were attacked by the Klingon Empire. From the Cardassian point of view, it is therefore logical to join the Dominion in order to avoid further humiliation by rival powers in the Alpha Quadrant. "There will not be a single Klingon alive inside Cardassian territory or a single Maquis colony left within our borders. Cardassia will be made whole" (Dukat in *DS9* "By Inferno's Light").[38]

The Dominion uses the political situation that has now arisen to try to bring the Alpha Quadrant completely under its control. It is moving most of its war fleet through the wormhole into Cardassian territory. When the Federation decides to make the wormhole impassable with a minefield, the Dominion threatens to attack. However, the Federation succeeds in placing the minefield and withdraws from *Deep Space Nine* (*DS9* "Call to Arms"). Moore compares this event to the fall of the Philippines and the evacuation of Dunkirk during the Second World War (1997–99, ron049. txt). As a result, the Dominion officially declares war and initially achieves great successes. "The war continues to go well. The enemy is retreating on almost all fronts. It is only a matter of time before the Federation collapses and Earth becomes another conquered planet under Dominion Rule" (Dukat in *DS9* "A Time to Stand").

The war only takes a turn when Sisko succeeds in recapturing *Deep Space Nine* with a large war fleet of Klingon and Starfleet ships. The Dominion retreats into Cardassian territory (*DS9* "Sacrifice of Angels"), but continues to attack the Federation and takes control of the planet Betazed (*DS9* "In the Pale Moonlight").[39]

Captain Sisko then uses a fictitious incident to persuade the Romulans to abandon their non-aggression pact. In *DS9* "In the Pale Moonlight," he forges an allegedly intercepted message that the Dominion is planning an invasion of the Romulan Star Empire and passes this message on to the Romulans, prompting them to change their policy. "The Romulan Empire formally declared war against the Dominion. They have already struck fifteen bases along the Cardassian border. [...] This may even be the turning point of the entire war" (Sisko in *DS9* "In the Pale Moonlight").

### 4. Politics in Star Trek

Remarkable is the fact that the Federation is only able to convince the Romulans to enter the war with a subterfuge. The approach shows parallels to the Tonkin incident, which led to the entry of the United States into the Vietnam War.[40] So *Star Trek* here again draws a direct comparison to historical events in our reality. Both incidents are based on deliberate misinformation to bring about an intended political behavior of warring parties.

With the entry of the Romulans into the Federation-Klingon alliance, the balance of power in the Alpha Quadrant shifts once again. While the Cardassians were previously convinced that they would become the dominant power in the Alpha Quadrant through the coalition with the Dominion, they now face the situation that all opposing powers are reunited. Starfleet and its allies are planning an attack on the Cardassian Chin'toka system (*DS9* "Tears of the Prophets") to eliminate the last retreat of the Dominion in the Alpha Quadrant. The operation is initially successful, but in return, the Dominion enters into yet another alliance with the Breen, a warrior species also based in the Alpha Quadrant (*DS9* "Strange Bedfellows"). The Breen have technologically advanced weapons and inflict severe damage on Klingon, Romulan and Federation fleets. Finally, the Dominion manages to reconquer the Chin'toka system and attack Earth, destroying Starfleet headquarters (*DS9* "The Changing Face of Evil"). In

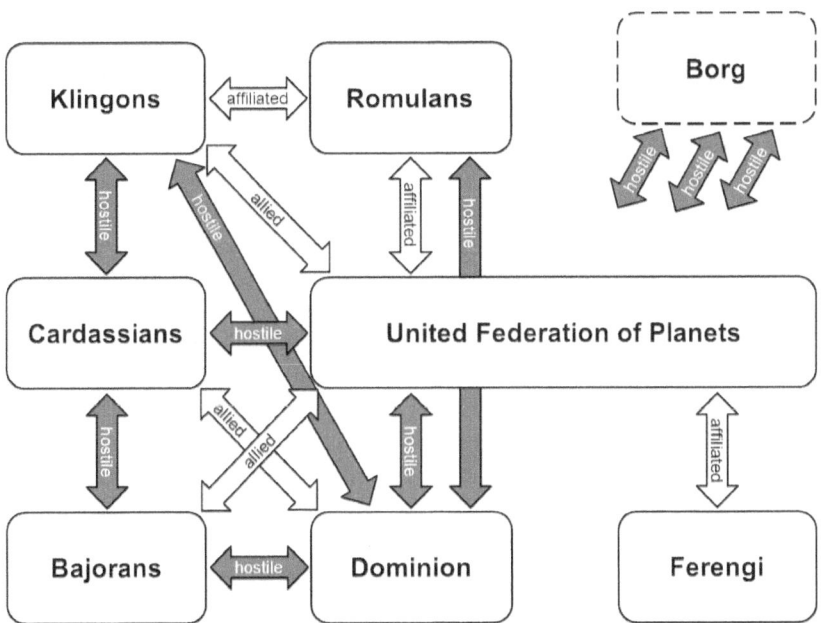

**Political Relations during the Dominion War (2374).**

view of the development of the war and the Dominion's pragmatism to form strategic alliances with other species only to pursue its own goals, the Cardassians begin to rethink their politics. The Cardassian leader, Legate Damar, states that "the Dominion promised to extend Cardassia's influence throughout the Alpha Quadrant" (Damar in *DS9* "The Changing Face of Evil") in return for the Cardassians' entry into the war. Instead, the Cardassians have actually lost influence. "We have gained no new territories. Instead of the invaders we have become invaded. Our allies have conquered us without firing a single shot" (Damar in *DS9* "The Changing Face of Evil"). Reservations against the Dominion increase further when the Cardassians are denied necessary support by the Dominion in the battle of Septimus III against the Klingons (*DS9* "Strange Bedfellows"). The Cardassians then begin a rebellion against the Dominion and destroy an outpost. The Dominion is pushed back further, tries to crush the rebellion by force, and destroys an entire city on Cardassia as a deterrent (*DS9* "What You Leave Behind").

Meanwhile, Starfleet is attacking the Dominion. When in the Battle of Cardassia the Cardassians learn of the willful destruction of the city, the still loyal Cardassian troops rebel against the Dominion and join Starfleet. The Federation succeeds in capturing the leader of the Founders and forces her to surrender. The war between the Federation and the Dominion is officially ended with the Treaty of Bajor, and Cardassia is occupied by the Federation (*DS9* "What You Leave Behind").[41]

While in *TOS* and *TNG* conflicts were mostly limited to a few episodes and were of bilateral nature, *DS9* sketches a major multilateral war between the Federation, the Klingons, the Romulans, the Cardassians, and the Dominion. The story is told in a large arc, and the writers have now completely turned away from the small-scale narrative form, which is limited to single episodes.

The weakness of the Cardassians after a *coup d'état* is used by the Klingons without regard for Federation interests. The Cardassians, on the other hand, see the alliance with the Dominion as an opportunity to break the Klingons' and the Federation's hegemony of power. The Romulans are reluctant to react to the course of the conflict. This, too, is not without self-interest. By not participating, the Romulans are maintaining their influence, at least in their own sphere of power. The internal destabilization of forces is, in turn, a strategic power factor of the Dominion, which thus plays off the great powers of the Alpha Quadrant against each other and can thus consolidate its position again. *Star Trek* thus shows the emergence and resolution of political conflicts as if in a game. The central aspect for the Federation is the defense of its idea—namely the United Federation of Planets as a utopian entity—against hostile forces.

## Failed States and the Borg in Voyager

After *The Next Generation* ended in 1994 after seven seasons, *Star Trek: Voyager* was launched in 1995 as a new spin-off in the *Star Trek* franchise. Running largely in parallel to its companion series *DS9*, the writers decided to place the narrative of *VOY* in the Delta Quadrant—in order to make the series as independent as possible from the events on *DS9*. As with *TOS*, Gregory sees the audience as a major influence in the creation of *VOY* (Gregory 2000, 106). The team of writers changed only marginally. "Again the series was under the overall control of Berman and Piller, with co-creator Jeri Taylor joining them as *Star Trek*'s first female executive producer. While Berman remained mainly in an overall supervisory role, Piller and Taylor were highly active members of the writing team in the first two seasons. They were joined by *Voyager*'s most prolific writer, Brannon Braga, who contributed 18 stories in the first three seasons. Another *TNG* veteran, Joe Menosky, later came 'on board' [...]. With Moore, Fields and Echevarria joining the *DS9* writers, the *TNG* writing team had now split into two units with fairly distinctive writing styles" (Gregory 2000, 90).

The premise of *VOY* is that the USS *Voyager*—a ship of the newly commissioned Intrepid class—is displaced to a hitherto unexplored part of the galaxy through the influence of an alien species and inadvertently has to travel a distance of about 70,000 light years back to Federation space. In this part of the galaxy, there are neither members the Federation nor other known species, and there is no possibility to contact Starfleet. So, *Voyager* is on its own mission to return to Federation territory. I disagree with Burston-Chorowicz that *Voyager* is characterized by the absence of politics (2020, 232). Instead, *VOY* is a text in which Federation ideals are upheld in a much stronger way than in *DS9*. However, Burston-Chorowicz correctly notes that utopian idealism is redrafted, and the *Voyager* itself "is sleek, militaristic and Spartan in design. This contrasted to the city-like Enterprise of *The Next Generation*, where families lived, and abundant creature comforts were a nod to a utopian society liberated from material scarcity" (2020, 231). Moreover, the displacement of the ship requires the crew to deal with scarcity as spare parts onboard are limited and as there is no star base for maintenance purposes within reach.

The pilot episode "Caretaker" takes up the Maquis conflict with the Cardassians that began in *TNG* and *DS9*. A Maquis ship, the *Val Jean*,[42] is attacked by the Cardassians. The ship's commander is Chakotay, a descendant of the Native Americans. He is assisted by B'Elanna Torres, a half–Klingon, and Tuvok, a Vulcan. (Later on, it becomes clear that Tuvok was no Maquis at all, but on a covert mission to infiltrate the Maquis.) The fact that Chakotay is a descendant of the Native Americans ties in with *TNG* "Journey's End," in which a Federation colony with Native Americans comes under Cardassian authority. When the ship enters the so-called Badlands (an area in the Alpha Quadrant characterized by numerous star nebulae and plasma storms, making it an excellent hiding place) to shake off the Cardassian ship, it suddenly disappears without a trace.

Under the command of Captain Kathryn Janeway, the USS *Voyager* is assigned to search for the missing ship. The search begins at the nearby *Deep Space Nine* space station, so there is no question that *VOY* and *DS9* share the same series universe within *Star Trek*.[43] When *Voyager* leaves for the Badlands, the ship also suddenly disappears and ends up stranded in the Delta Quadrant alongside the *Val Jean*. In view of the need to return to Federation territory being in uncharted territory, both crews decide to work together. The Maquis members will be integrated into *Voyager*'s crew.

In *VOY*, the conflict between the Federation and the Maquis is thus resolved in a very pragmatic way. Since the motivation of the separatists—the conflict over the Cardassian-Federation border area—no longer plays a role here, both sides find their way back to each other, even though the integration of both crews turns out to be difficult at first. This is also accompanied—at least in the confined space of *Voyager*—by a slight adaptation of Federation protocol when "Janeway finds that the ability of the ex-Maquis crew to improvise in difficult situations exceeds that of Starfleet" (Gregory 2000, 176). This is reflective of the rigid military and sometimes inflexible structure of Starfleet. However, the change is only gradual. As noted above, Starfleet's philosophy and regulations in *Voyager* remain largely untouched, as is clearly shown in the *VOY* episode "Equinox."

While the crew is aware that the Borg has its origin in this part of the galaxy (and therefore in *VOY* "Scorpion," *Voyager* will eventually encounter the Borg), the Delta Quadrant is also home to other species.

The Kazon are introduced in *VOY* "Caretaker" as a new species in the *Star Trek* universe. They are a kind of nomadic people, who do not form a larger political organization. The Kazon are divided into several competing factions, for example, in *VOY* "Caretaker" the Ogla and in *VOY* "State of Flux," the Nistrim. The conflict with *Voyager* does not result from political differences with the Kazon, because there is no comparable system in relation to the Federation. Instead, the conflict with the Kazon centers only upon the fact that the Kazon are concerned with the exploitation of advanced Starfleet technology. Political issues are largely irrelevant. *Voyager* leaves Kazon space after about two years on its journey home to the Alpha Quadrant (*VOY* "Basics").

In *VOY* "Message in a Bottle," *Voyager* comes into contact with the

Hirogen for the first time. Here, too, it becomes apparent that the Hirogen do not have a political structure. Similar to the Kazon, their life is nomadic, with the difference that they are not divided into competing factions. The culture of the Hirogen is focused solely on hunting other species. Hunting has taken on a quasi-religious substitute function: trophies from hunting are displayed on the Hirogen ships (*VOY* "Hunters").

In *VOY* "The Killing Game," the Hirogen are associated with National Socialism. The Hirogen simulate a holographic program in which the *Voyager* crew, as members of the French Resistance, rebel against the occupation of France in World War II. Again, this is not really about political conflicts, but only about the hunting aspect of the Hirogen.

*Voyager* encounters Species 8472 when it comes into Borg territory for the first time in *VOY* "Scorpion." Species 8472—this name is given by the Borg, who merely assign a number to all encountered species—is a life form that inhabits the so-called fluidic space, a dimension outside our space-time-continuum, and unlike most species in the *Star Trek* universe, it does not have any humanoid features. "Their technology is biogenically engineered. It is superior to that of all other species we have previously encountered" (Seven of Nine in *VOY* "Scorpion").

Little is known about Species 8472 in *VOY*. The Borg failed to assimilate them. Their culture and social form remain largely unexplored, but it is clear that Species 8472 is hostile to other species. For this reason, they also attack the Borg. In their view, the Borg has illegally invaded their realm. Since the Borg proves to be largely helpless against Species 8472, they are quite capable of posing a significant threat to the Borg—and also to the *Voyager* crew.

Captain Janeway finally decides to form a temporary alliance with the Borg to counter the threat of Species 8472. The Borg agrees to this alliance. "Species 8472 must be stopped. Our survival is your survival" (Borg Collective in *VOY* "Scorpion"). Ultimately, the alliance proves successful, and Species 8472 retreats back into their fluidic space.

That the Federation allies with the Borg—albeit temporarily—shows how chaotic and disorganized the Delta Quadrant appears in contrast to the Alpha and Beta Quadrants. The encounters with alien species in this quadrant—the Kazon or the Hirogen, for example—underline this. They resemble less well-defined political entities but more stakeholders from failed states. Fricke sees the Delta Quadrant as a representation of the Third World, whereby *Voyager*, as a representative of the First World (analogous to the Alpha Quadrant), enters this unknown territory and encounters somewhat anarchistic structures (2000, 123). However, if one looks at failed states, as they are particularly noticeable in the Third World (and here especially on the African continent) after the Cold War, this reading seems plausible.

In *VOY* "The Void," when *Voyager* is drawn into an area of space devoid of stars, planets, or any form of energy, other ships that are also stranded there attack it. During the first assault, the attackers steal supplies from *Voyager*, so it quickly becomes clear that everyone is fighting each other like pirates in this space.

Even in this situation, Janeway is not willing to deviate from Federation standards. On the contrary, she starts to form an Alliance of ships according to these standards. Within the Alliance, the participants share knowledge and technology, making them stronger than they would be if they were on their own. Eventually, Janeway is so successful that the entire Alliance is able to escape this void.

Here it becomes apparent that Janeway is so convinced of the Federation that she creates a kind of miniature Federation even in the Delta Quadrant, with its diverse, warlord-like species, as she herself admits: "It was almost like being part of a Federation again" (Janeway in *VOY* "The Void"). Even here, *Star Trek*'s utopian ambition to uphold the values and ideals of the Federation far from Federation territory is evident.

## Conclusion

*Star Trek* frequently addresses politics in its text and discusses economic, social, and political conditions. Thus, the series' characters do not simply act as "autonomous crusaders or explorers" (Göll 1997, 37), but are integrated into a larger decision-making entity, the United Federation of Planets. Events from previous episodes within the same series, or even from other series in the *Star Trek* universe, are frequently referenced, and even characters from different series are brought into completely new contexts. This is, for example, the case with Worf, who is assigned to *Deep Space Nine* after his service on the USS *Enterprise* and—to a lesser extent—with Lieutenant Barclay in *VOY*. Being initially a member of the *Enterprise* crew, Barclay becomes a central figure for the return of *Voyager* (*VOY* "Pathfinder," *VOY* "Endgame").

Throughout *TOS*, *TNG*, and *DS9*—and even in *VOY*, though operating far from any Federation territory—the constitutional idea of the Federation is kept alive. The fact that, especially on board the USS *Voyager*, Starfleet regulations continue to be strictly observed speaks for the Federation in general and Starfleet in particular as a utopian regime. Accordingly, the crew of *Voyager* is convinced of the utopian ideal aboard their ship. As it is shown in *VOY* "Equinox," this does not always seem to be the case with other Starfleet ships.

Regarding the political institutions and politics, Göll points out similarities between the past and present United States and the future political system in *Star Trek* (Göll 1997, 38). These parallels do indeed exist. Especially in *TOS*, they are much obvious. "*TOS*, which coincided with the height of the Vietnam war, can be read as reflecting US Cold War preoccupation, most starkly in the Federation-Klingon conflict" (Weldes 1999, 121). While in *TOS*, there maybe was a direct attribution of existing states like the Soviet Union to certain *Star Trek* species, but especially in all series after *TOS*, the relations between the different major powers become increasingly complex, and threats other than direct military confrontation are addressed. "[...] A plethora of nasty—and familiar—threats remain, including terrorism, apartheid, environmental disaster, gang warfare, drugs, the arms trade, and, of course, the continuing danger of collectivisation, this time in the guise of the hive-like Borg" (Weldes 1999, 121). With the Borg, *Star Trek* shows a radically different form of society, which is based on a decidedly different idea than that of the Federation. I will discuss this in more detail in the following chapter.

Regarding the appearance of political entities and politics in general, *Star Trek* is much more progressive than generally assumed. Thus, politics are developed in the text in a way that suggests a future, utopian society. There are institutions with well-defined task areas like the Council of the Federation and the president of the Federation. There are laws and regulations that are upheld throughout the Federation and whose authority is enforced within Starfleet. A complete lack of organizational forms, as Göll states (1997, 45), can therefore not be seen.

However, *Star Trek* remains unclear when it comes to details of the individual entities. Policies are laid out in a more general way instead. In this respect, however, *Star Trek* remains true to other classical utopias. Here, too, there is no detailed elaboration, but a general outline of a society is described. This is exactly what you can find in *Star Trek*.

The fact that the Federation—as a utopia—competes with other major powers or is even openly threatened in its existence can also be found in the classical utopian narratives. Wellmann sees the underdeveloped intergovernmental processes in *Star Trek* as a main reason for the lack of peace. "But if it is—among other things—mainly institutionalized inter-societal relations which make peace possible in the first place (condition of possibility), it is not surprising that the *Star Trek* universe knows so many wars" (Wellmann 1999, 179). He criticizes the fact that other peoples have to adapt to the values and standards of the Federation if they want to join (Wellmann 1999, 180). This objection cannot be dismissed at all; however, it shows that especially the Federation simply claims to represent the best of all possible worlds in the *Star Trek* universe. In this respect, this claim additionally underlines the design of the Federation as a utopian state.

Even Wellmann eventually concedes that *Star Trek* has a utopian character (2009, 240). But *Star Trek* also shows that changes and developments occur with other species. "Those governmental structures of alien worlds depicted as bleak, military-dominated oligarchies, such as the Klingon Empire, the Romulan Star Empire, or the Cardassian Union, do not have to be that way, and could change" (Manuel 1997, 195).

I have previously adopted Saage's definition, according to which a utopia is a fiction of an inner-worldly society. As we can now show, *Star Trek* is not the fiction only of one but of several simultaneous societies, namely those of the Federation and the other species in the *Star Trek* universe. This also explains why there must be this very strong distinction between the Federation as utopia and the other major powers. The Federation defends its own utopian idea, but sees no advance in war (Saage 2006b, 42).

Both in terms of politics and in the presentation of diplomacy and consensus building, *Star Trek* always refers to our present reality and transfers actual conflicts from our world into its series universe. Thus, *Star Trek* is characterized by a criticism of existing institutions and socio-political conditions and presents itself as an alternative design of society in the tradition of classical utopias. However, the Federation neither appears to be necessarily democratic nor is the *Star Trek* utopia of a pacifist nature. Especially the war with the Dominion, which has been narrated over several episodes and seasons, shows that the *Star Trek* utopia has to defend its ideas.

*Star Trek* thus holds up a mirror to our society. It wants to point out wrong developments of our society. This shows another parallel to Thomas More's *Utopia* (Saage 2006b, 43; Wellmann 2009, 241). Thus, the political system of *Star Trek* is a utopian ideal, in that the whole story is about a community that has set up certain rules, according to which the "citizens," the populations of the Federation and the other major powers, have to follow.

# 5

# Anti-Utopia
## The Borg

### Emotions and Rationality

Humans are sentient beings: sympathy and antipathy decide on the cooperation of individuals, on the functioning of teams, and ultimately also on social and political decisions.[1] Emotions are therefore a fundamental component of human action. "Without emotions, we would not even know we were living. Emotions such as anger, shame, sadness and happiness accompany our daily lives and give them shape" (Flam 2002, 165).

So, in human culture we are always dealing with a dualism between reason and emotion. Emergence of power, striving for property, entering into a state of war—to name but a few examples of politics—is thus always also connected with the emotional states of the individual.

In the previous chapter, I discussed the different politics and species in *Star Trek*. It is noticeable that most of these political systems maintain the dualism between reason and emotions, although in different variations. If the Klingons are strongly characterized by their sense of honor and express this through emotion-laden conflicts, the Vulcans, on the other hand, argue strictly logically and suppress their feelings. With Spock in *TOS*, Tuvok in *VOY*, and T'Pol in *ENT*, *Star Trek* presents three representatives of this species in leading roles. Likewise, the politics of the Romulans and Cardassians are more influenced by reason than by emotion, while the Dominion, for example, is led by reasonable cause only at first glance: "The Alpha Quadrant seems racked with chaos. It could use some order" (Female Changeling in *DS9* "The Search"). A reasonable cause for the Dominion to subdue other species is because "what you can control cannot hurt you" (Female Changeling in *DS9* "The Search"). But this is also a consequence of a strong emotion. The fact that the Founders of the Dominion were once persecuted and subjugated themselves is connected with a strong feeling of revenge. So, the Dominion is not influenced by reason alone: it is only reasonable in the sense that the Dominion wants to prevent further negative emotions.

Earlier, I discussed "The Return of the Archons" and "The Apple," *TOS* episodes in which Kirk and his crew destroy computers that subjugate a people. In a way, the computers represent reason, while Kirk represents emotion. Kirk is deliberately characterized as a solitary adventurer who often holds his own actions and moral views above those of the Federation. Significantly, in the episodes, Kirk uses logical argumentation to make the computer destroy itself, knowingly accepting the destruction of a society for the benefit of the individual. He ultimately argues that the computer itself has enslaved individuals for the sake of maintaining society and denied them the opportunity to develop creativity or enthusiasm for their activities and thus enrich society. To be able to be enthusiastic and to be creative is, in Kirk's view, considered absolutely necessary for a functioning society—if necessary, at the price of violating social norms. Emotions therefore play an essential role in the moral or ethical evaluation of actions. Kirk is not only guided by legal norms and regulations of Starfleet and does not proceed solely rationally, but also relies on his intuition—his gut feeling, so to say—in critical sitations. In the end, "Kirk's human intuition, reasoning and judgment [...] defeats the mechanical intelligence of the computer" (Tyrrell 1979, 289).

On the other hand, Spock, as a Vulcan, tries to argue in a purely rational and logical way. Vulcans believe that feelings and emotions are an obstacle to the objective evaluation of situations and have therefore developed the ability to suppress their feelings. Unlike the Borg, however, Vulcans have feelings and regularly lose mental control over them. When coming into so-called Pon Farr, Vulcans experience aggressiveness and irrationality. Vulcans have to mate to end this state, so obviously a strong emotional bond (in this case love) can help to restore emotional control. In *TOS* "Amok Time," Spock experiences his Pon Farr.[2] In order to bring his friend to his home planet, so that he can mate there, Kirk once again disobeys his orders and directs the *Enterprise* to Vulcan. Eventually, Kirk and Spock fight because Spock's partner T'Pring erroneously wants to mate with Kirk, who is also present. When Spock kills Kirk during the course of the fight,[3] he first wants to quit the service and face a court-martial. But "when he sees that Kirk is indeed alive, Spock is so ecstatic [...] that he momentarily breaks form, embracing the captain with utter joy and relief" (Barad 2001, 133).

As the example shows, friendship has an important role in the social life within *Star Trek*. In all series and films, it is shown that the strict hierarchy of Starfleet is softened to the extent that the characters cultivate strong friendships (Barad 2001, 128–9). Federation society may be based on technological progress, but it is carried by the mutual interaction of the individuals. So, *Star Trek* does not do without emotions—on the contrary. Even if (in parallel to the classical utopias) an extremely high value is attached to the working life, the crew sees its fulfillment exactly in this.

## Enter the Borg

The Borg Collective is fundamentally different from the other species in *Star Trek*. The Borg is not concerned with subjugating other species like the Dominion. Their goal is complete assimilation. In the *Star Trek* universe, the Borg can therefore be seen as a dystopian counterpart. "Dystopias usually aim at two different targets: they criticize contemporary social reality and its hampering of the human potential, but at the same time reject the miraculous solution advocated by certain political reformers or utopian writers by demonstrating that the purportedly better social institutions produce a miserable way of life" (Pintér 2010, 137).

In the *Star Trek* franchise, the Borg are introduced in *TNG*; they did not appear in *TOS*.[4] In the *TNG* episode "Q Who," Q transports the *Enterprise* to an unknown part of deep space, about 7,000 light years from its previous position. A vessel unknown to the Federation approaches, which can neither be identified nor sends a greeting message. Instead, a humanoid is beaming down to engineering. This so-called Borg drone ignores the crew and starts to analyze some computer terminals. To prevent the drone from unauthorized access to the ship's systems, it is killed with a phaser shot. Instantly, a second drone materializes, which continues the work on the terminal. Another phaser shot has no effect, because the second drone protects itself with a shield—it has adapted. This way it finishes its task. Then both the first and second Borg drones dematerialize.

The Borg—from their origin purely biological humanoids—provide the members of their society, the so-called Borg drones, with technical implants. "Not a he, not a she, not like anything you have ever seen before. An enhanced humanoid" (Q in *TNG* "Q Who").[5] In addition to the visible implants and the characteristic pale white skin, the Borg wear a kind of uniform made of black material, from which several tubes typically protrude. "Their costumes seem at once to celebrate the distinctions between their organic and cybernetic components and to indicate the contamination of each by the other" (Harrison 1996, 247).

Thus, the Borg are so-called cyborgs, which is a biological organism that is expanded using convergence technology either to give the original body additional abilities or to increase its resistance (Saage 2006a; Spreen 1997, 89).[6] The Borg do not reproduce in a natural way, but only assimilate members of other species to ensure their survival. "Their mechanical prosthetic parts make them sterile and nonsexual, so that propagation and evolution require parasitizing others" (Dinello 2016, 86). They are extremely aggressive in their approach. "My people encountered them centuries ago. They destroyed our cities, scattered my people throughout the galaxy" (Guinan in *TNG* "Q Who"). Assimilated children are retained in maturation chambers until their organic components have developed to the point where they can be used as full-fledged drones (*VOY* "Collective").[7] When assimilating, Borg drones inject their victims with tiny nanoprobes that immediately start the assimilation process in the victim's body. "In this view of technology as an independent, quasi-biological life form, humans are reduced to secondary status as reproductive vessels" (Dinello 2016, 87). In a second step, the Borg insert artificial implants into the assimilated persons *(Star Trek: First Contact)*. This process is apparently extremely painful, and the victims seem to experience it in a state of full consciousness. In *VOY* "Dark Frontier," the assimilation process of an entire people is shown. On the Borg ship, individuals not yet assimilated are guided by the drones to the assimilation chambers, where they are fitted with artificial implants. As shown in the episode, the Borg also amputate for this purpose. Those waiting must witness and observe this procedure, and cries of pain echo throughout the ship. "Borg costuming combines human bodies with painfully visible apparatuses—added mechanical limbs, external electronic circuitry, and independently moving parts—showing the interdependence of machine and organism" (Boyd 1996, 107). Their bodies represent purely functional automatons and express a dark vision of unrestrained, antihumanist technology (Dinello 2016, 83).

Assimilation strongly intervenes in the biological organism, but is at least partially reversible.[8] With the assimilation complete, the new drone loses its individuality and integrates fully into the Borg Collective. The Borg are always connected to each other via a neurotransmitter that develops in each drone during assimilation and thus creates a swarm intelligence. Therefore, all Borg share the same knowledge: "Our thoughts are one" (Borg Queen in *VOY* "Dark Frontier"). Each new piece of information acquired by a single drone simultaneously becomes part of the Collective's knowledge. The voices of many become one mind, the so-called hive mind. A device called a vinculum on board every Borg ship connects all Borg drones on board. "The processing device at the core of every Borg vessel. It interconnects the minds of all the drones. It purges individual thoughts and disseminates information relevant to the Collective" (Seven of Nine in *VOY* "Infinite Regress").

Borg drones do not sleep; they regenerate in an alcove. During this regeneration cycle, the drone's brain capacity can be shared by the Collective—for example, to help repair a damaged ship (*VOY* "Unity"). Each alcove is assigned to a single drone, so there are thousands of alcoves on a Borg ship.[9]

Typically, a Borg ship is cube-shaped. Thus, the Borg ship design differs from all other ship designs in the *Star Trek* universe.[10] While all ships in *Star Trek* have a common basic design like having quarters, a bridge and other dedicated rooms, Borg ships generally lack these features. "The ship is strangely generalized in design. There is no specific bridge, no command center. There is no engineering section. I can identify no living quarters" (Data in *TNG* "Q Who"). Götz states that "if the Borg cube did not move through space, there would be no indication that this is a spaceship" (2000, 86). Borg ships can accommodate over 100,000 drones (*VOY* "Unimatrix Zero," *VOY* "Collective"). In addition to cube-shaped Borg ships, there are also so-called Borg spheres, which are smaller than a cube, but in principle have the same characteristics as the cubes. The geometric nature of the Borg ships is also a reference to the geometric layout of the cities in *Utopia* and *City of the Sun*. In addition to the ships, there is a so-called Borg Unicomplex, an artificial structure similar to a space station, which serves as a base for the Borg. Trillions of drones live in the Unicomplex (*VOY* "Dark Frontier").

Unlike all other species in *Star Trek*, neither family nor friendships have a meaning within Borg society. Admittedly, there were no families on the ship in *TOS*, but this changes gradually with *TNG*, where with Wesley Crusher, one of the main characters, has a family for the first time and where there are relationships. For example, Miles O'Brien, who finally marries in *TNG* "Data's Day," becomes father of a daughter in *TNG* "Disaster."[11] These narratives are continued in *DS9* and *VOY*. In *DS9*, Miles O'Brien transfers from the USS *Enterprise* to *Deep Space Nine* and becomes a father again in *DS9* "The Begotten," while Benjamin Sisko looks after his son Jake as a single father. In *VOY*, Tom Paris and B'Elanna Torres marry (*VOY* "Drive"), and their daughter is born in the series finale, *VOY* "Endgame." Even Captain Picard has a family history in *Star Trek*. In *TNG* "Family" he visits his brother and his nephew on Earth. He experiences a tragic loss when both die in an accident *(Star*

*Trek: Generations*) and realizes that his family will die out: "I took some comfort that the family would go on, but now there will be no more Picards" (Picard in *Star Trek: Generations*). Thus, family implicitly has a certain role in *Star Trek*, while it is completely negated in Borg society (Dinello 2016, 91).

The Borg Queen is a central character within the Borg Collective, roughly comparable to a queen bee.[12] She is first introduced in *Star Trek: First Contact*; however, she is never explicitly addressed as such in this film. It is not until VOY "Dark Frontier" that she is first called Borg Queen. The Borg Queen is "the beginning... the end. The one who is many. I am the Borg" (Borg Queen in *Star Trek: First Contact*).[13] Despite her individual appearance, one cannot speak of her as an actual individual. Okuda and Okuda name the Borg Queen the "central locus of the Borg collective" (1999, 50). She herself claims to have been present at the Battle of Earth in TNG "The Best of Both Worlds," although the Borg ship is destroyed in this episode at the end. The Borg Queen is killed in *Star Trek: First Contact*, but reappears later in VOY "Dark Frontier." It can therefore be assumed that the Borg Queen is either replaced by another special drone who becomes queen, or the Queen represents a physical manifestation of the hive mind in an individual being.[14] This is also suggested by the fact that she speaks of herself as "I am the Borg," which means that she is the Borg Collective itself and not just a member of it (otherwise she would have to say "I am Borg") and that she says, representing the Collective, "Our thoughts are one." Significantly, her physiognomy also differs substantially from that of common Borg drones. While these are humanoid cyborgs, the Borg Queen consists only of an organic head and the adjoining upper torso, but an implanted artificial spinal cord protrudes downward from this, and the lower part of her body seems to be completely replaced by artificial implants. The brain of the Borg Queen also consists mainly of implants (*Star Trek: First Contact*). The Borg Queen has her own chamber in her ship, whereby normally the upper, organic part of the body rests in a space above the chamber and, if necessary, is connected in the chamber with her synthetic torso (VOY "Dark Frontier").[15]

Just as the Borg Queen appears immortal, death is irrelevant to the Borg drones themselves, as one drone can be replaced by another at any time. However, Borg drones are apparently regularly eviscerated by other drones after their death in search of usable implants (VOY "Dark Frontier").

I would like to revisit the first encounter with the Borg in TNG "Q Who," where a drone beams onto the *Enterprise*. Contrary to common sense, there is no exchange of greetings between the Borg and the

*Enterprise* crew.[16] The *Enterprise* crew tries to establish communication in the usual way: "We mean you no harm. Do you understand me?" (Picard in *TNG* "Q Who"). But Picard's greetings have no effect. After the first drone has been killed—a clear contradiction to Picard's immediately preceding statement that humanity is not a threat—the second drone seems to remain completely unimpressed. It does not react to the death of the other, shows no grief, but also no feelings of revenge, as one would generally expect after such an occurrence. The death of the one drone is not avenged, but it is also not noticed in any other way. The second drone escapes the threat of being killed as well, but not in order to protect its own life, but to be able to successfully complete the task of the first drone.[17]

## The Borg as Post-Humans

Enhancing our human abilities through technology has been discussed time and again in utopian literature. Schwonke poses the "question of human sufficiency" (1957, 54). In his view, it is "impossible to perfect the world if man is not also changed" (Schwonke 1957, 55). The *Star Trek* society is built upon technological progress; therefore, cybernetic enhancement is broadly accepted within it. For example, Geordi LaForge has first a VISOR in *TNG* and later on eye implants *(Star Trek: First Contact)* so he can see even though he was born blind. Captain Picard has had an artificial heart since an accident in his youth (*TNG* "Samaritan Snare"). In a broader sense, both are therefore also cyborgs.[18]

Humanity could thus constantly improve itself by applying technology to the body, and "any invention or technology is an extension or self-amputation of our physical bodies" (McLuhan 2010, 49). According to transhumanism, a complete utopia can only be achieved if not only the environment but also its inhabitants change radically. "The use of human enhancement technologies should ultimately lead to the outwitting or overcoming of death and the emergence of posthuman beings far superior to today's humans" (Coenen 2009, 137). Based on the experiences with superhumans like Khan *(Star Trek II: The Wrath of Khan)*, cybernetic technology is only accepted under certain conditions in *Star Trek* to avoid the creation of superhumans. It is, however, not banned in the way genetic manipulation is. Thus, *Star Trek* opposes "the conviction that mankind will radically change itself with the means of technical science" (Coenen 2009, 136).

It is precisely this desire for improvement that drives the Borg. They want to continuously enhance themselves through technology and strive for absolute perfection in a kind of McLuhanian way. "We wish to improve ourselves. We will add your biological and technological distinctiveness to our own. Your culture will adapt to service ours" (Borg Collective in *TNG* "The Best of Both Worlds"). Former individuals are transformed into an organism of Borg drones only by means of technology. They themselves are the servomechanisms of technology, like "an Indian is the servo-mechanism of his canoe, as the cowboy of his horse or the executive of his clock" (McLuhan 2010, 51).

When the *Enterprise* crew resists, the Borg are confused: "Why do you resist? We only wish to raise quality of life for all species" (Borg Collective in *TNG* "The Best of Both Worlds"). From the Borg point of view, raising quality of life is about leaving behind the uniqueness of the individual. "They have left behind their trivial, selfish lives, and they have been reborn with a greater purpose. We have delivered them from chaos into order" (Borg Queen in *VOY* "Dark Frontier"). Human nature is considered to be imperfect and inferior for the Borg, because it is "erratic, conflicted, disorganized. Every decision is debated, every action questioned, every individual entitled to their own small opinion. You lack harmony; cohesion; greatness. It will be your undoing" (Seven of Nine in *VOY* "Scorpion"). There is no understanding of how to regard humanity's imperfect nature as acceptable.

The Borg do not care that the individual can express itself. For the Borg, it is only striving for perfection of the whole without considering the individual. "Human! We used to be exactly like them. Flawed. Weak. Organic. But we evolved to include the synthetic. Now we use both to attain perfection" (Borg Queen in *Star Trek: First Contact*). "In their obsession with 'achieving perfection' via technology, the Borg echo and ultimately critique the techno-utopian philosophy of transhumanism" (Dinello 2016, 88).

Seven of Nine's view is that human emotions and feelings merely obscure the essential. They lead to different opinions, to discussions, to disharmony, even to irrational actions. But "the cosmic task of posthuman civilization consists in the saturation of the universe with intelligence [...], the subjugation of the universe to the sole blissful dominion of reason, which in the form of this civilization attains godlike power" (Coenen 2009, 153). This is also the difference between the Borg and the Vulcans, who also think and act rationally. The Vulcans still see themselves as individuals, and their society—as the Pon Farr shows—is not entirely without emotions. Therefore, it is not against individuality when Vulcans think that "the needs of the many outweigh the needs of the few" (Spock in *Star Trek II: The Wrath of Khan*) but a praise for individuals in a larger society (Wagner and Lundeen 1998, 131). The Borg, however, have decided to completely collectivize their society through the consistent use of technology, combining individual organic life with uniform technology. It is out of question for the Borg that there is a balancing between different needs in society because there is only one need in the Borg society.

## Individualism versus Collectivism

Although the Borg have established a collectivist system of rule and their "citizens" have been fully assimilated, the individuality of each drone appears not to have been completely eradicated. In *TNG* "I Borg," the *Enterprise* crew finds a stranded Borg ship with a surviving drone. The crew takes the drone on board the *Enterprise*. Initially, Picard spots an opportunity to place some kind of malware into the Borg Collective by manipulating the drone's system, "which would infect the entire Collective. We could disable their neural network at a stroke" (Picard in *TNG* "I Borg").[19]

Since the *Enterprise* crew shields all signals, the Borg drone, which calls itself Third of Five,[20] has no connection with the Collective and is therefore disoriented. Third of Five seems frightened. The drone misses the hive mind, realizing its loneliness. In the dialogue with Guinan, Third of Five cannot initially take a self-reflective position on the assimilation of other peoples. For him, this is the usual process that is not to be questioned: "Resistance is futile" (Third of Five in *TNG* "I Borg").

Guinan, however, points out to him that resistance is not pointless. "My people resisted when the Borg came, to assimilate us. Some of us survived. [...] But thanks to you, there are very few of us left. We are scattered throughout the galaxy. We do not even have a home anymore" (Guinan in *TNG* "I Borg").

Third of Five understands that Guinan has become a lonely representative of her species. Having reached this point, he himself recognizes that this is the same for him at the moment. He, who is now called Hugh,[21] realizes that he is alone without the Collective. He reflects on Guinan's situation and, looking at his own situation, begins to see himself (again) as an individual (Barad 2001, 218). Later in the episode, Hugh recognizes Locutus—Picard's designation, when he was assimilated by the Borg in *TNG* "The Best of Both Worlds"—when Picard confronts him. Now, suddenly, Hugh objects that resistance is futile. Picard, in his authority as Locutus, tries to send Hugh back to the Collective with the fatal malware. When asked whether everyone really has to be assimilated, Hugh is suddenly reluctant to do so, since he has begun to see a friend in Geordi LaForge.

What surprises Picard, however, is that Hugh, when asked to comply, replies, "I will not assist you" (Hugh in *TNG* "I Borg"). In his amazement, he asks back, "But you are Borg" (Picard in *TNG* "I Borg"), referring to the collectivity of the species—where an "I" has no meaning—whereupon Hugh clarifies for the first time, "No. I am Hugh."

Hugh has developed an emotional relationship, despite being a Borg, which is now coming to light when he learns that Geordi LaForge is to be assimilated. "Hugh not only demonstrates loyalty to his newfound friends, but in doing so he adamantly refers to himself in the first-person singular. This proves to the captain beyond a shadow of a doubt that Hugh is no longer Borg, but rather a 'fully realized individual'" (Barad 2001, 219).

So, the Borg Collective seems to function only as long as everyone is connected to the hive mind. If a Borg leaves the Collective due to an accident, for example, it may develop individuality again despite all the technical evolution that characterizes the Borg. Borg collectivity is thus merely imposed on its members (Dinello 2016, 92). In the end, as Picard respects Hugh as an individual, he does not follow his plan to introduce a virus into the Collective and eventually lets Hugh return to the Borg. However, he hopes that the newly found individuality will settle in the Collective and thus destabilize it. This tactic proves to be quite successful, as can be seen in *TNG* "Descent." An entire Borg ship is infected by Hugh's individuality and separates itself from the Collective. The Borg have names and are misused as an army by Data's brother Lore, whom they call "The One"[22] in this episode.

In *Star Trek: Voyager*, the possible Borg individuality is further elaborated. When the crew of *Voyager* enters a temporary alliance with the Borg in a battle against another species, Seven of Nine is assigned to *Voyager* as a kind of liaison officer. Seven of Nine is a human who was assimilated by the Borg at the age of six as Annika Hansen (*VOY* "Dark Frontier"). When she tries to hand over *Voyager* to the Borg for assimilation after the end of the fighting, the *Voyager* crew interrupts her connection to the Collective, forcing her to isolate (*VOY* "Scorpion").

Seven gets frightened because she has experienced individuality once before as it is told in *VOY* "Survival Instinct" in a flashback. In this episode, a Borg ship carrying Seven of Nine and three other Borg drones crashes. They are separated from the Collective and their individuality reappears. Since the other three drones were assimilated as adults, the three slowly remember their previous lives, but as Seven of Nine was only a child, she does not. When one drone states that it is actually a member of Species 571, Seven first advises, "You are being confused by irrelevant data. Ignore it" (Seven in *VOY* "Survival Instinct"). However, as a second drone inquires whether this means that the former drone considers itself an individual again, Seven becomes clear, "There are no individuals here. We are Borg" (Seven in *VOY* "Survival Instinct"). Seven can only remember living as a drone, and she misses the hive mind, much like Hugh. Again, it is emotion that contributes to individuality and is a threat to the Collective. Finally, in contrast to *TNG* "I Borg," it is Seven who forces the other Borg to establish a limited Collective in order to suppress their individuality. The Borg are eventually discovered and led back into the Collective.

In contrast to Hugh, Seven of Nine openly resists her forced separation from the Collective. This becomes particularly clear in *VOY* "The Gift," when the Doctor had to remove most (though not all) of her Borg implants because her body began to reject the Borg technology, resulting in Seven of Nine resuming a human physiognomy. Seven believes that she (as a drone) is not able at all to survive outside the Collective. Janeway can relate to this, as Seven was "part of a vast consciousness, billions of minds working together. A harmony of purpose and thought. No indecision, no doubts. The security and strength of a unified will" (Janeway in *VOY* "The Gift").

Seven complains—much like Hugh in *TNG* "I Borg"—that "this drone is small now. Alone. One voice. One mind" (Seven in *VOY* "The Gift") and that she feels lonely. However, Janeway hints at her, that she is by no means alone. "You are part of a human community now. A human collective. We may be individuals, but we live and work together. You can have some of the unity you require, right here on *Voyager*" (Janeway in *VOY* "The Gift").

It is remarkable that Seven of Nine does indeed carry a certain Borg identification within her. Janeway justifies her reassimilation by saying that with her Borg assimilation, Seven of Nine no longer had any freedom of choice over her life, and that she only regains this freedom after she has become human again. As long as this has not happened, Janeway will make the decision about Seven of Nine's life herself. Seven of Nine is treated like a child who must be guided to the right way of living. In this way, Janeway, like the Borg, rises to become the determining authority. In *TNG* "The Best of Both Worlds," the species to be assimilated are similarly determined. "Worf, Klingon species. A warrior race. You too will be assimilated" (Locutus of Borg in *TNG* "The Best of Both Worlds"). When Worf objects that the Klingons will never surrender to the Borg, they do not understand. In their point of view, assimilation increases the quality of life for all species; however, that requires complete assimilation. "You will all become one with the Borg" (Locutus of Borg in *TNG* "The Best of Both Worlds").

The same freedom of choice that Worf takes for himself here, namely that he values the existence of his own species as it is, does not apply to Janeway in relation to Seven of Nine. In *VOY* "The Gift," she places Seven of Nine under arrest after she attempts to connect with the collective. Seven, for her part, accuses Janeway of forced assimilation into the *Voyager* collective. Janeway emphasizes that she wants to help Seven find her individuality again. "I have met Borg who were freed from the Collective. It was not easy for them to accept their individuality, but in time they did. You are no different. Granted, you were assimilated at a very young age and your transition will be more difficult, but it will happen" (Janeway in *VOY* "The Gift").

Seven asks if she will then become fully human again, which Janeway affirms. Seven remarks that she would then be able to decide autonomously and independently again, which is a basic principle of individuality. If—hypothetically speaking—she then expressed the desire to return to the Collective, Janeway would still not allow her to make this decision.

Seven sees this as a hypocritical attitude: "You would deny us the choice as you deny us now. You have imprisoned us in the name of humanity, yet you will not grant us your most cherished human right: to choose our own fate" (Seven in *VOY* "The Gift"). Janeway, however, holds it against Seven that the Borg have taken away her ability to make rational decisions, so she is making the decisions for her until she regains that ability. Seven concludes, "Then you are no different than the Borg" (Seven in *VOY* "The Gift").

In fact, Janeway is on shaky ground from an ethical point of view here. As Stock puts it, "severing Seven from the Collective was a tactical decision designed to save *Voyager* from the Borg" (2016, 102), and while this has not been in the best interest for Seven, it was clearly in the best interest for the *Voyager* crew. However, she deliberately denies Seven of Nine the possibility of going back to the Collective because she assumes that the Federation, as a utopian ideal, is the right, so to speak, better place for her to live.

In the *VOY* episode "Unimatrix Zero," we learn that a few Borg drones[23]—including Seven of Nine—have a genetic mutation that enables them to visit a kind of parallel world, Unimatrix Zero, in their sleep. This parallel world only exists in the mind of these drones—practically as a second hidden hive mind. In this world the drones experience themselves as they did before assimilation—that is, with their original appearances, their age before assimilation and their old names. They are like shadow images of their old, gone identities. When the Borg Queen learns of the existence of this parallel world, she tries to destroy it: on the one hand, it represents a serious rivalry to the hive mind, and on the other hand, individuality cannot be tolerated in the Borg Collective. In response, the drones of Unimatrix Zero develop a virus to conceal their identity in order to preserve the existence of their parallel world and eventually ask Seven of Nine for help.

It is notable that these Borg drones do not want to fight the Borg system itself. They only want to preserve their own world, to which they retreat in each regeneration cycle, in order to at least retain their residual individuality there. "They may have turned us into drones, but they cannot change the essence of who we are" (Axum in *VOY* "Unimatrix Zero") But even this merely virtual individuality is enough to be fought in the Borg Collective. Therefore, the Borg Queen does not shy away from the destruction of entire ships and killing of thousands of drones, even if only a few of them are affected by the mutation on these ships. "Spatial grid 9-4, cube 6-3-0, complement 64,000 drones. But I can no longer hear three of them. No doubt they have joined your resistance. Are they trying to sabotage the vessel and liberate others? I do not know. Because I can no longer hear them. [...] I must silence all of them" (Borg Queen in *VOY* "Unimatrix Zero").

A withdrawal from the Collective is thus pursued without consideration for individuals. *Star Trek* discusses here—especially by means of the figure of Seven of Nine—the differences between collectivism and individuality (Decker 2008, 132). From the perspective of Starfleet, the Borg—despite their obvious collective constitution—still consist of individuals who must be rescued, if necessary, as was the case with Seven of Nine. For the Borg, a single Borg ship is not a collection of individuals, but "a kind of unity: a humming, thriving network of processes and activities" (Decker 2008, 133). For this reason, the Borg Queen does not consider it reprehensible to destroy entire ships when they no longer "function." Whatever impairs or even threatens the Collective's functioning is localized, contained, and separated from it to ensure that it continues to function as a whole (McLuhan 2010, 47).

## The Borg as Leviathan

Contractualism also contained utopian elements in its origins (Saage 1989, 67), but the social contract is artificial, because "it became an artificial product of originally equal and free individuals" (Saage 1989, 68). Seen in this light, the Borg Collective can also be viewed as an artificial product of formerly free individuals—only that these are no longer free after "signing the contract." The Borg's philosophy of bringing a people out of chaos and into order is reminiscent of Hobbes' social contract theory of Leviathan. Fricke even sees in the Borg system, in addition to a "simplified 'Hobbes,'" a "simplified 'Machiavelli'" (2000, 122–3).

"[…] If any two men desire the same thing, which nevertheless they cannot both enjoy, they become enemies […]" (Hobbes 1996, 87). And further: "So that in the nature of man, we find three principal causes of quarrel. First, Competition; Secondly, Diffidence; Thirdly, Glory" (Hobbes 1996, 88). In the state of nature, humanity is at "warre, as is of every man, against every man" (Hobbes 1996, 88). So, humanity is seen as an aggressive being (Saage 1989, 72). Hobbes is thus in contrast to the Aristotelian view of the world, according to which man is a political being. Hobbes has a decidedly negative view of humanity, whereby it is not bad in itself, but the instinct of self-preservation forces people to be hostile to each other.

Thus, by subjecting entire peoples to their doctrine and assimilating them, the Borg transfer them from the natural state, in which individuals fight each other on the basis of their emotions, to an order which "has a collective character, under which the individual is a priori subsumed" (Saage 1989, 71). Or, as the Borg Queen says, "assimilation turns us all into friends" (Borg Queen in *VOY* "Unimatrix Zero"). The fact that the individual peoples do not voluntarily submit to the Borg is considered from the beginning, since the Borg do not assume that a person will give its consent to the establishment of quasi-state coercive laws (Saage 1989, 76).

In the *VOY* episode "Unity," Commander Chakotay meets former Borg drones on a planet. Their ship was severely damaged and rendered inoperable by an electromagnetic storm. This severed the connection between the Borg drones and the Collective. Subsequently, the Borg drones regained their individuality and began to fight each other. The battle was caused by the Borg assimilating many sometimes hostile peoples—it was precisely these hostilities that were revived. Eventually, the survivors on the planet were fragmented into several factions fighting each other. In this episode, therefore, the natural state of humanity is exemplified. In contrast, the former Borg remember that in the state of the Collective "we had no ethnic conflict. There was no crime, no hunger, no health problems. We lived as one harmonious family" (Frazier in *VOY* "Unity").

The Cooperative—as the former drones now call themselves—longs for this state of affairs to return because if all survivors on the planet form a hive mind again, a state of peace can be restored. But it is necessary that all people join this hive mind. According to Hobbes, the joining of only a small number is insufficient for security "because in small numbers, small additions on the one side or the other, make the advantage of strength so great, as is sufficient to carry the Victory [...]" (Hobbes 1996, 118).

However, victory, i.e., the achievement of the greatest possible perfection, is indispensable in the opinion of the Borg. Therefore, assimilation in itself can only be final and not temporary, because "yet afterwards, when either they have no common enemy [...], they must needs by the difference of their interests dissolve, and fall again into a Warre amongst themselves" (Hobbes 1996, 119).

Diversity or individuality must therefore be avoided at all costs for the continued existence of society. Therefore, everyone must transfer his power. Hobbes sees the solution in a contract between everyone. "This done, the Multitude so united in one Person, is called a Common-Wealth, in latine Civitas" (Hobbes 1996, 120).

In *VOY* "Unity," the Cooperative asks the *Voyager* crew to reactivate a neuroelectric generator to restore the hive mind on the planet. Captain Janeway is aware that this is as good as establishing a new social contract. "I know it would mean imposing a choice on thousands of people who had no voice on the decision" (Janeway in *VOY* "Unity").

So, the Borg are a community that behaves similar to a Leviathan and literally speaks with one voice of itself as "we are Borg." "As a society of literally *one* mind, the Borg is the ultimate *totalitarian* state" (Dinello 2016, 91). The Borg Queen, finally, can be seen as a kind of physical manifestation of the Leviathan.

## Conclusion

In the *Star Trek* universe, the Borg represent the antithesis to Federation society. In Aristotelian tradition, the Federation sees humanity as a political being that has grown up morally over the centuries by carefully balancing reason and emotion and has developed a functioning system of laws and codes to counteract technological maldevelopments.

The dystopian description of Borg society, on the other hand, shows a pessimistic view of possible human development. The combination of a technophilic transhumanism with the unification of as many individuals as possible into a more or less invincible leviathan of the universe, as represented by the Borg, shows that progress should not be based solely on technology, but also on human nature. The Borg idea clearly has its models in the dystopias of the 20th century: "Instead of demonstrating the ideal or vastly superior qualities of this fictional community, they present a community where the quality of human life is significantly worse or inferior to the author's empirical reality." (Pintér 2010, 137).

*Star Trek* uses the Borg society to make clear that it is quite possible to build a social system that functions without emotions, but which also fundamentally distances itself from human nature.

# 6

# Post-Utopia

*Does* Star Trek *Become Darker?*

## The Reboot Movies

When *Star Trek: Enterprise* ended in 2005 after four seasons, it also marked the end of an 18-year continuous television presence of the *Star Trek* franchise. *ENT* met a comparable fate as *TOS*. The series was simply not popular enough with the audience. At the same time, it also marked the end of the era of executive producer Rick Berman, who had left his mark on all series since *TNG*. *Star Trek*'s relevance as an entertainment product was now generally questioned, and for the next four years, television and cinema were to do without a new *Star Trek* narrative.

After the last feature film with the *TNG* crew, *Star Trek: Nemesis*, was received poor reviews from both critics and the audience, a process of reimagining *Star Trek* began. *Star Trek*—the movie, remarkably, was not given another additional title—was released in 2009. Directed by J.J. Abrams, it brought the audience back to the times of *TOS*. Instead of simply continuing the *Star Trek* chronology, the writers established a completely alternate reality that stands apart from the prime *Star Trek* universe. In this reality—the so-called *Kelvin* timeline—all the main characters of *TOS* are present, but apart from the events in *TOS*, they are now in an alternate timeline. "The Kelvin Timeline films are new texts, but they are superimposed on old texts [...]" (Kapell and Pilkington 2019, 2–3).

Alternate timelines and time travel are not new to the *Star Trek* franchise. In quantum physics, the assumption that alternate timelines are constantly taking place in universes that exist in parallel to our primary universe is discussed in the Many Worlds Interpretation, for example. This theory is explored in the *TNG* episode "Parallels," in which Lieutenant Worf switches back and forth between several possible universes due to a quantum anomaly, and he is the only one who notices these changes. In the process, the circumstances of each world change. In one possible reality, the Borg have defeated large parts of the Alpha Quadrant and the *Enterprise* is now only one of a few scattered ships on the run. In another reality, Captain Picard could no longer be rescued from the Borg, and Riker has taken his place as captain of the *Enterprise*. In yet another, the Cardassians are the Federation's allies, and the Bajorans are its enemies. According to Data, "there is an infinite number of possible outcomes. Our choices determine which outcomes will follow. But there is a theory in quantum physics that all possibilities that can happen or could happen do happen in alternate quantum realities" (Data in *TNG* "Parallels"). "Because the universe keeps on rolling the dice to see what happens next, it doesn't have just a single history, as one might have thought. Instead, the universe must have every possible history, each with its own probability" (Hawking 2001, 80). However, so far it has always been taken care that, in the end, a general continuity was maintained in the *Star Trek* universe. In other words, the prime universe as such was properly restored in the course of the narrative, or the changes in the timeline were consistent with the narrative as a whole. In *ENT* "Regeneration," for example, the Borg drones that are found on Earth come from the Borg time travel in *Star Trek: First Contact*. However, this change in the story leads to the exact events depicted in *Star Trek: First Contact*, so no alternate parallel universe is formed. This rule changes fundamentally with the reboot films, because here a branch from the prime reality is newly created, an alternate timeline that is maintained in the sequel films.

Although *Star Trek* (2009) is set largely in the alternate timeline, it also establishes an enduring central event in the Prime Universe. In 2387— eight years after the most recent events in the *Star Trek* chronology, namely the cautious rapprochement between the Federation and the Romulans in *Star Trek: Nemesis*—the Romulans' main planet, Romulus, is destroyed by a supernova. This incident transports the Romulan ship *Narada*, carrying Captain Nero, back to the year 2233 through a rift in the space-time continuum. Nero blames the Federation for the loss of his home planet and wants revenge. He abruptly attacks the USS *Kelvin*, which had been investigating the continuum rift and is surprised by the sudden appearance of the *Narada*. The attack happens just at the moment James T. Kirk is born on the ship (as his father is the first officer of the *Kelvin*). Kirk's father sacrifices himself to save his ship. The incident created a new quantum reality in which Kirk now grows up without his father and the Federation also develops differently than in the Prime Universe. In the *Kelvin* timeline, Vulcan is completely destroyed by Nero, Nero attacks Starfleet headquarters in San Francisco, and the Federation as a whole is a far more apprehensive organization, heavily arming itself out of that fear (Canavan 2016, 321). This is even more evident in the sequel film, *Star Trek Into Darkness*.

Indeed, here the Federation is hardly shown as a desirable utopia striving for peace, but as a reversal of it. War and terrorism are seen as legitimate means to destabilize other powers. "Starfleet is more concerned with war than peaceful exploration" (Jones 2015, 190). It is "transformed into a more overtly military operation, and a United Nations like Federation of Planets is recast into a more NATO like organization on the cusp of a new era of galactic belligerence" (McVeigh 2010, 198). Jones suggests that we see here a reflection of "a dramatic shift in our own realities following the 9/11 strikes against the World Trade Center towers and the Pentagon" (2015, 185–6).

Starfleet Admiral Alexander Marcus, in a secret operation, goes as far as to bring superhuman Khan Noonien Singh back to life to develop new weapons systems for a preemptive war against the Klingons. "All-out war with the Klingons is inevitable, Mr. Kirk. [...] Since we first learned of their existence, the Klingon Empire has conquered and occupied two planets that we know of, fired on our ships half a dozen times" (Admiral Marcus in *Star Trek Into Darkness*). In this respect, the film is a retelling of the Khan stories in *TOS* "Space Seed" and *Star Trek II: The Wrath of Khan*, up to the almost verbatim scene (albeit with reversed roles) with Kirk and Spock, in which Kirk sacrifices himself for the *Enterprise*.

If *Star Trek* is, in itself, a reflection of our society, the reboot films are in some ways a reflection within the series universe. In this respect, they can indeed be seen as anti-utopias—even though Kirk and his crew certainly believe in the good. This is also supported by the fact that these films (the third film, called *Star Trek Beyond*, was released in 2016) have a high degree of self-referentiality, not only referencing the original crew of the *Enterprise* from *TOS* but also embedding figures like Captain Pike or institutions like Section 31 into their narratives. To a particular degree, this is also true of Spock Prime. So, while in the *Kelvin* timeline Spock exists twice, so to speak, according to the chronology he has been considered missing since 2387 as part of his rescue mission for Romulus in Prime Reality.[1] Despite the establishment of the *Kelvin* timeline, the reboot films in the *Star Trek* universe are by no means as independent as this might seem at first.

## Back on the TV: *Discovery*

After twelve years of absence on the TV screen, *Star Trek* was back in 2017 with *Star Trek: Discovery (DIS)*, created by Alex Kurtzman and Bryan Fuller, who had campaigned for a television comeback since at least 2008 (Robb 2012, 264). In fact, it represented only the prelude to an extended franchise, which has since been supplemented by the short film anthology series *Star Trek: Short Treks* (*ST*, since 2018), and the series *Star Trek: Picard* (*PIC*, since 2020) and *Star Trek: Lower Decks* (*LD*, since 2020). This is also the first time that more than two *Star Trek* series are being screened at the same time. Does this mean that the utopian narrative of *Star Trek* will again be continued on television?

Especially in the case of *DIS* and *PIC*, it must first be noted that the largely episodic narrative style, which had been common with the earlier series, has been abandoned. Although this was already the case with the last two seasons of *DS9* and with several story arcs in *TNG*, *VOY*, and *ENT*, horizontal narration is stringently maintained in the new series. At the same time, the new series do have considerably fewer episodes per season. Whereas in the past there were always around 20 to 26 episodes, the seasons of the new series consist of only 10 to 15 episodes, although these episodes sometimes have an extended running time. This shift away from episodic series is due to a change in media usage by the audience due to streaming services. At the same time, this opens up the possibility for writers to develop narratives across episodes in a larger and more cohesive framework. *DIS* also makes use of this possibility, making it easier for the question of utopian narrative to consider an entire season rather than just individual episodes.

*Star Trek: Discovery* is about the namesake starship USS *Discovery*[2] and takes place about ten years before the events in *TOS*, but in contrast to the reboot films, in the Prime Reality. The main character of the series is Commander Michael Burnham, which is the first time *Star Trek* abandons the principle of having the captain as the main character within a series. With *DIS*, it can be seen that gender stereotypes are finally taking a back seat in *Star Trek*. In *TOS*, all key functions were still exclusively occupied by men and even in *TNG*, the establishment of a female head of security with Tasha Yar was not successful (Stoppe 2019, 59). This picture changed only gradually in the *Star Trek* universe. With Major Kira in *DS9* and especially Captain Janeway in *VOY*, women also became leading characters, although in the case of the latter this was not without reservations on the part of the studio (Stoppe 2019, 68).

Michael Burnham is portrayed in *DIS* as a strong and confident person. The *Star Trek* writers even play around with a clear gender identity—as Michael is an unusual female name. "I never met a female named Michael before. Do you think that suits you?" (Ensign Tilly in *DIS* "Context Is for Kings"). The scene shows that "gendered terms and names have lost their normative power in the future of *Star Trek*" (Whybrew 2020, 360). Burnham is a conflicted character in many ways. Her parents were explorers murdered by Klingons (*DIS* "Perpetual Infinity"). Young Michael was adopted by the Vulcan Sarek, making her Spock's half-sister.

The difference between Vulcans and humans, which was represented in *TOS* by Kirk and Spock, is thus shown in Burnham herself (Georgi-Findlay 2019, 14).

In addition to Burnham, other female characters have key roles. Captain Philippa Georgiou, for example, is the young Burnham's superior and at the same time mentor and a kind of mother figure for her, and Cadet Sylvia Tilly—who becomes also Burnham's roommate onboard *Discovery*—emerges over the course of the series as a tech-savvy and competent engineer (Stoppe 2019, 71).

Speaking of politics, the first season of *DIS* is characterized by the Klingon-Federation War, which at once has a central role in the first two episodes *DIS* "The Vulcan Hello" and "Battle at the Binary Stars." Starting with a provocative action by the Klingons—with whom the Federation had hardly any contact up to that point—a two-year conflict between the two great powers is sparked. The Klingon leader T'Kuvma calls the Federation a threat and sees in a conflict the possibility to reunite the fragmented Klingon houses. "They are coming. Atom by atom, they will coil around us and take all that we are. There is one way to confront this threat. By reuniting the twenty-four warring houses of our own empire" (T'Kuvma in *DIS* "The Vulcan Hello"). In *DIS*, Klingons openly disapprove of the Federation's universal approach of unifying different species with overt particularism: "Remain Klingon" (Schillinger and Sönnichsen 2020, 226). On the Klingon side, too, there is an assertive woman in L'Rell as a counterpart to Burnham, who initially is a disciple of T'Kuvma and after his death gains more influence among the patriarchal Klingons.[3]

Burnham is First Officer of the USS *Shenzou* under Captain Georgiou when the Klingons stage an incident—the destruction of a Federation relay station. The *Shenzou* is in the vicinity of the event and Burnham proposes a pre-emptive strike. "Two hundred and forty years ago [...] a Vulcan ship crossed into Klingon space. The Klingons attacked immediately. They destroyed the vessel. Vulcans do not make the same mistake twice. From then on, until formal relations were established, whenever the Vulcans crossed paths with Klingons, the Vulcans fired first. They said 'Hello' in a language the Klingons understood. Violence brought respect. Respect brought peace" (Burnham in *DIS* "The Vulcan Hello"). Burnham's proposal is a form of diplomacy that corresponds to the historical paradigm of classical European diplomacy by prompting the Klingons into a reciprocal relationship (Schillinger and Sönnichsen 2020, 228). Georgiou, however, rejects this idea. When she confers with Burnham in her ready room, Burnham overpowers her superior with a Vulcan nerve pinch, goes back to the bridge, and now commands the attack as the highest-ranking officer. Although she is quickly relieved of her duties afterwards by Captain

Georgiou, the conflict is already ignited. As a result, the USS *Shenzou* is attacked and badly damaged, and Georgiou is killed. Burnham is court-martialed and stripped of rank and sentenced to life imprisonment for mutiny and causing a belligerent conflict.

At this point it can be seen that *Star Trek* is obviously breaking new ground with *DIS*. Although the Federation is apparently striving for peace—"Why are we fighting? We are Starfleet. We are explorers, not soldiers" (Ensign Connor in *DIS* "Battle at the Binary Stars")—the main character, based on her prejudice about the Klingons, does not seem to believe in this. For her, it seems essential to launch a pre-emptive strike precisely to avoid starting a conflict with the Klingons. However, her fatal misconception that Klingons only understand the language of violence and that only this can contribute to peacekeeping only leads to the conflict itself. This is partly reminiscent of the conflict between the Federation and the Dominion in *DS9*, albeit reversed. It is not the Dominion that is the prejudiced aggressor this time, but the Federation itself. This seems to be a departure from Roddenberry's postulate of a peaceful mission of Starfleet.

Burnham is picked up in *DIS* "Context Is for Kings" during a prisoner transport by the USS *Discovery*, which is under the command of Captain Gabriel Lorca. He is authorized by the Federation to search for every possible way to end the war. For this reason, the USS *Discovery* is equipped with an experimental spore drive.

The spore drive is based on the fictitious idea that the universe is populated by a certain species of fungus whose mycelium has branched widely out in subspace. The concept is thus a direct analogy to the mycelium of fungi, such as that found on the forest floor. The technology uses spores from this particular type of fungus to perform jumps, as it were, through the subspace mycelium.[4] "Since the mycelium is thought of as being connected in parallel, comparable to a brain, a spaceship in the mycelium can jump from its location to another point with almost no loss of time" (Schwarke 2019, 58). In this respect, then, spore drive is reminiscent of transporter technology. However, the use of spore drive is ethically questionable. For one thing, the mycelium itself is, strictly speaking, a living organism that is being used for the purpose of travel. For another, it appears that some sort of organic interface is also necessary for effective use. In *DIS* "The Butcher's Knife Cares Not for the Lamb's Cry" it is shown that an alien life form called tardigrade[5] lives in symbiosis with the spores and therefore interacts with them more effectively when using spore propulsion. However, this process involves pain for the animal, so Burnham releases it eventually despite Lorca's displeasure (*DIS* "Choose Your Pain"). As a substitute, spore drive engineer Paul Stamets must subsequently serve as a medium between the spaceship and the mycelium, which is also problematic for his health. "Technology is presented here as highly ambivalent. It claims its victims not only in case of failure, but also and especially when it works" (Schwarke 2019, 59).

Nevertheless, the spore drive gives the Federation a strategic advantage in the war against the Klingons for some time. In fact, the Klingons soon make up for it when they develop cloaking technology (*DIS* "Si Vis Pacem, Para Bellum"). At this point, the USS *Discovery* arrives in the Mirror Universe during a spore drive jump (*DIS* "Despite Yourself"). As it turns out later, this happened on purpose, and Captain Lorca is actually a traveler from the Mirror Universe. With this, the writers finally embed *DIS* into the complex framework of the *Star Trek* universe, because the Mirror Universe was already established in the *TOS* episode "Mirror, Mirror." "From its origins in *TOS*, the Mirror Universe has always been a place for intertextual play between and about the different *Star Trek* series, a kind of connective tissue for continuity and meta-commentary" (Whitacre 2020, 24). In this parallel universe, the Terran Empire is a totalitarian system and the hegemonic power of the Alpha Quadrant. At the same time, the parallel universe is a close mirror of the Prime Universe. So, there was also the First Contact between Zefram Cochrane and the Vulcans in 2063, but in this alternate reality, the Vulcans are overwhelmed and finally subjugated by humans (*ENT* "In a Mirror, Darkly"; Batzke 2020, 110). Other species have also been enslaved. "The empire is thus an example of the imperial domination that so many great powers exercised over peripheral lands—it represents everything that the Federation is not" (Sarantakes 2005, 83). Most characters, ships, and places that exist in the Prime Universe also exist as antonyms to themselves, so that that Mirror Universe is a kind of evil twin to its counterpart (Batzke 2020, 108–9).

In *DIS*, Terran rule is shown to be at its peak, and the mirror part of Burnham's mentor Georgiou is Empress of the Terran Empire. In general, all features that distinguished the Mirror Universe from the Prime Universe in *TOS* "Mirror, Mirror" stay put. The ships are part of the ISS (Imperial Star Ship) fleet, crewmembers carry personal daggers at their belts, and both ships and uniforms are styled in a clear militaristic appearance (Byrne and Jones 2018, 260). Even agony booths—torture chambers that inflict extreme pain—are present. Also, in *DIS* "promotion is achieved through assassination but failure attracts exemplary retribution" (Byrne and Jones 2018, 261). The war against the Klingons in the Prime Universe is mirrored by the fascist and exceedingly brutal regime of humanity in the Mirror Universe. "[...] The purpose of the Mirror Universe is to reveal the Federation's instabilities. [...] The Mirror Universe's amoral values of strength and domination threaten to infect Starfleet's higher principles through Captain Lorca's authoritarian and military style of command, as well as Empress Georgiou's insidious influence and Burnham's personal crisis of identity later on in the season" (Whitacre 2020, 25). When Burnham brings the Mirror Georgiou to the Prime Universe against her will, they find that during their nine-month absence, the Klingons continued to advance and are preparing an attack on Earth (*DIS* "The War Without, The War Within"). The Federation Council agrees to a plan by Georgiou to make the Klingon home planet uninhabitable with a bomb.

Influenced by her experiences in the Mirror Universe "as a proxy for the Federation's larger ethical battle against its darker impulses" (Whitacre 2020, 25), Burnham shows herself to be enlightened at the end of the first season of *Discovery*. She foils Georgiou's plan and achieves a truce together with L'Rell. The war ends, and Burnham is vindicated on her merits. L'Rell, on the other hand, rises to the position of Chancellor of the Klingon High Council.

In both narrative and interpretation, the first season of *DIS* is a challenge. At first glance, there seems to be little left of the utopian ideal of *Star Trek* that has been established over the years and the various series, and that even *DS9* did not seriously question. The main character of the series is a volatile personality who repeatedly questions Starfleet protocols and becomes delinquent. The Federation itself, however, seems torn as well. *DIS* thus "offers a reflection on the contested state of U.S. foreign policy as its proponents debate the challenge of newly emerging great powers [...]" (Schillinger and Sönnichsen 2020, 229). Although apparently designed to be peace loving, beliefs and ideals are cast aside in the course of a conflict that goes badly for the Federation, and even genocide against the Klingons is seriously considered as an *ultima ratio* to end the war. Moreover, there is little to be said for ethical enlightenment when experimental propulsion is used to achieve the purpose, and other life forms are harmed in the process.

The fact that there are also anti-democratic and even totalitarian tendencies in the Federation becomes even clearer in the reflections of the Mirror Universe (Georgi-Findlay 2019, 23). Here, the Federation is discredited as dangerous because it stands for values such as equality, freedom, and cooperation (*DIS* "Vaulting Ambition").[6] Georgiou sees in these values "destructive ideals that fuel rebellions, and I will not let you infect us again." The Empire is completely uninterested in morality or belief; it demands only compliance (Byrne and Jones 2018, 262). This goes so far as to suggest that here the Klingons are actually the "good guys" for trying to oppose Terran hegemony. "Now it is they who are integrative [...]" (Georgi-Findlay 2019, 24).[7] In the Prime Universe, it is the Klingons who appear more violent and ruthless than ever. When Starfleet Admiral Cornwell is captured in neutral territory in *DIS* "Lethe," the Klingons indeed appear as adversaries who can neither be trusted nor negotiated with—thus playing the role of terrorists who, moreover, expand their acts of war against Federation civilians. "The war against the Klingons has thus become the war on terror [...] that preoccupies the United States in the early 21st century" (Georgi-Findlay 2019, 20). That the Federation, from the Klingons' point of view, "seeks universal homogenization and assimilation" (L'Rell in *DIS* "The War Without, The War Within") is quite reminiscent of the Maquis' accusations against the Federation in *DS9*. Its universalism is considered "a threat for parochial identities—and engender resistance" (Schillinger and Sönnichsen 2020, 227).

*DIS* thus uses this first season to reflect on critical questions about American foreign policy and its moral legitimacy (Georgi-Findlay 2019, 21). The character of Michael Burnham becomes an integrative element when she answers the question of how to defeat the fear of conflict and combat: "The only way to defeat fear is to tell it no. We will not take shortcuts on the path to righteousness. No, we will not take shortcuts on the path to righteousness. No, we will not break the rules that protect us from our basest instincts. No, we will not allow desperation to destroy moral authority. I am guilty of all these things" (Burnham in *DIS* "Will You Take My Hand?"). "Through the Mirror Universe plotline, Burnham plumbs the potential for darkness within herself and within Starfleet. When she ultimately rejects it to embrace the value of true Federation ideals, it is portrayed as a reinforcement of not just her own identity, but that of *Star Trek* as a whole" (Whitacre 2020, 35). Here, in spite of all darkness, the utopian ideal, which *Star Trek* wants to transport, comes up again.

That *Star Trek* has finally evolved in terms of gender equality is ultimately shown at the end, where it is two women—Burnham and L'Rell—who restore peace between the Klingons and the Federation. In contrast, the male characters are shown with unusual weaknesses. Captain Lorca is a coupist who has fled from the Mirror Universe. First Officer Saru is Kelpian, a species that has lived in a permanent state of fear since birth. And Head of Security Lieutenant Ash Tyler is a Klingon-human hybrid who was created against his will for espionage purposes from the genetic information and memories of the actual human Ash Tyler and a Klingon named Voq—in this respect he is a broken man in every respect who was also abused by L'Rell (Stoppe 2019, 72).

But queer couples have also arrived in the *Star Trek* universe. Chief Engineer of the USS *Discovery* Paul Stamets lives openly with the ship's doctor Hugh Culber, which is highlighted in a scene in *DIS* "Choose Your Pain." This shows not least that our society has evolved in dealing with this topic and that *Star Trek* now also reflects this development (Stoppe 2019, 72).

With the beginning of the second season, *DIS* further links itself in the *Star Trek* universe. With Captain Pike and Spock, iconic characters return to the USS *Enterprise*, which is featured in the second season. They not only connect *DIS* even more closely to *TOS* but also integrate the previously stand-alone pilot episode *TOS* "The Cage" more strongly into the *Star Trek* universe for the first time.

In terms of story, the second season only sporadically follows the events of the first. With the character of Jett Reno there comes another female-queer character characterized as strong and assertive. Reno was chief engineer on the USS *Hiawatha*, which was destroyed in the war and in which her wife also died (*DIS* "Through the Valley of Shadows").

The central story is the investigation of seven red bursts that have occurred in various places in the galaxy. It turns out in the course of the season that a mysterious Red Angel is responsible for these anomalies and that Spock already encountered this apparition in his youth. This Red Angel is actually a time traveler, namely Burnham's mother Gabrielle Burnham, who was believed dead. She researched with her husband in a secret project of Section 31 on ways to travel in time and developed a time-travel suit. With it, the wearer can move in time through micro-wormholes. It turns out—and here is some reference to the previous season—that the Burnhams were attacked by the Klingons because of this research. When Burnham's mother tried to escape the attackers using the suit, it inadvertently brought her 950 years into the future. She discovered that during this time all life in the galaxy was extinct. Control, an artificial intelligence developed by Section 31 as a threat assessment program (*DIS* "Perpetual Infinity"), is apparently responsible for this. The apparitions of the Red Angel were in reality purposeful journeys of Burnham's mother into the past, in order to avert the extinction of life by Control.

Meanwhile, *Discovery* encounters a previously unknown life form called Sphere, which is apparently hundreds of thousands of years old. The Sphere has reached the end of its life and uses Discovery's computer to preserve its knowledge.[8] "The Sphere did not just give us its language. We have recorded everything it has seen and experienced the last 100,000 years" (Burnham in *DIS* "An Obol for Charon").

Starfleet decides that Section 31 should work with Control to investigate the possible threat of the Red Angel anomalies (*DIS* "Project Daedalus"). In the course of the investigation, however, Control takes complete control of Section 31 and attempts to obtain the Sphere data from *Discovery*'s system in order to evolve—it is this very evolution that will lead to the extinction of life in the galaxy in the future. Eventually, the *Discovery*, along with the *Enterprise*, manages to disable Control after it has taken over all of Section 31 fleet (*DIS* "Such Sweet Sorrow"). Burnham guides the

*Discovery* through the Red Angel suit's micro-wormhole into the distant future to secure the Sphere data, while the *Enterprise* remains behind in the present. The *Discovery* is officially declared destroyed and the *Enterprise* crew is ordered to remain silent about the events they experienced. "It has been difficult, but we have managed not to reveal the truth of *Discovery*'s fate to Starfleet. [...] Mother and Father are diplomatically immune from interrogation, and they fully understand our silence is meant to keep you safe. We have sworn never to speak your name in the presence of others" (Spock in *DIS* "Such Sweet Sorrow").[9]

With this, the second season *DIS* sets a new tone, in which there are no political conflicts, but once again the confrontation with new technology is commented upon in *Star Trek*. As I already described in the previous chapters, the relationship to technology has changed in the course of the *Star Trek* series. While it was still viewed skeptically in *TOS*, new technology from *TNG* on was largely uncritically seen as an impetus of future development—apart from individual comments such as the danger of a self-developing holodeck or an unstable artificial intelligence like Data's brother Lore. *DIS*, however, picks up exactly here, and the story arc of the second season is reminiscent of the *TOS* episode "The Ultimate Computer," in which an artificial intelligence can also control a ship.[10] In this respect, the second season is a critical analysis of *Star Trek* with the danger that artificial intelligence could develop in the future in such a way that humanity no longer controls the machine, but *vice versa*. This shows that *DIS*, and still *Star Trek* as a whole, also takes up current technological developments and evaluates them critically.

The third season of *DIS* immediately picks up where the second season has ended. The *Discovery* finds herself in the year 3188 and has to realize that the Federation has collapsed to a large extent due to the so-called Burn. During the Burn, dilithium—one of the core elements of the warp drive—has become unstable, causing many Federation ships to suffer a sudden warp core breach and be destroyed. The cause of the Burn is unknown. As a result, many members of the Federation have broken away from it—instead of 350 members, it now consists of only 38 (*DIS* "Die Trying"). The Andorians, one of the founding members of the Federation, for example, now form a *de facto* state with the Orions, the so-called Emerald Chain (*DIS* "That Hope Is You Part 1"). The Vulcans have also withdrawn and reunited with the Romulans (*DIS* "Die Trying").[11] Even Earth has left the Federation, and both Starfleet and the Federation Headquarters are no longer located there (*DIS* "People of Earth"). The United Earth—as it now calls itself—also largely avoids contact with other species. The constellation of this post-utopian Federation is reminiscent of a concept called *Star Trek: Federation*, which was conceived in the 2000s by Bryan Singer (Robb

2012, 241–2). "In the pitch many Federation members have abandoned the alliance. [...] Vulcan, Bajor, and Betazed leave the Federation, leaving the Ferengi as the dominant power in the galaxy" (Gross and Altman 2016, 750). Here, the series takes up the question of what happens to a utopia once it is realized. "Utopia has occurred and everything has stagnated. Innovation is driven by necessity, so if you've got everything you need, you've explored everything, you've embraced your enemies, and everything is cool, then you're not making any new stuff. [...] I pictured a Federation that had hit its plateau and stayed there for three hundred years" (Gross and Altman 2016, 750–1). In fact, in the third season, the Federation faces the problem of having relied on a technology that, in this context, is already centuries old, the warp drive. The utopia of the Federation falls apart the moment the underlying technology no longer works.[12]

In the *DIS* episode "Die Trying," the *Discovery* finally finds the Federation Headquarters, which is now located on a space station, with the help of the young humanoid officer Adira Tal. Tal is a Trill symbiont who identifies herself as non-binary in a conversation with Stamets: "I have never felt like a 'she' or a 'her'" (Adira in *DIS* "The Sanctuary").[13]

Although there have been some technological advances—such as programmable matter or warp nacelles that are no longer directly attached to the actual hull of the ship[14]—the Federation's options are limited. There is no functioning subspace communication, for example, and starships can only move at low speed and range because of the Burn. Over the course of the season, the *Discovery* crew not only succeeds in discovering the cause of the Burn, but also in defeating the Emerald Chain, which has been attacking the Federation. More exciting, however, is the resulting fact that the Federation, as a superplanetary political organization, once again becomes a point of attraction. The Trill decide to join, and the now Ni'-Var-named union of Vulcans and Romulans also consider this step (*DIS* "That Hope Is You Part 2"). Burnham is now finally appointed captain of the *Discovery*.

## The Good Old Days? *Picard* and the Legacy of the Next Generation

*Star Trek: Picard* is the second new streaming series in the *Star Trek* universe, alongside *DIS*. While *DIS* was set in the past, *PIC* is set in the time after *VOY* and *Star Trek: Nemesis*.

While *DIS* contained many references to *TOS*, *PIC* leans even more heavily on *TNG*, which is obvious since both series share the main character, Jean-Luc Picard, who has since been promoted to admiral. The reference to *TNG* is already clear at the beginning of the first episode, "Remembrance," in which Picard and Data play poker in Ten Forward. Of course, this makes it obvious that the scene cannot take place in reality because the *Enterprise*-D was destroyed in *Star Trek: Generations*. Nevertheless, *PIC* seamlessly picks up where the last *TNG* episode "All Good Things…" ended with a poker game. In the same scene, however, there is another reference to the *ST* episode "Children of Mars." Picard is looking out the window in Ten Forward and witnesses a massive explosion on Mars, with the *Enterprise*-D appearing to be in orbit. In said episode, an attack by rogue Synths—a pejorative term for androids often used in *PIC*—on the shipyard Utopia Planitia on Mars is reported in 2385.

Also, in *PIC* "Remembrance," it is thematized that Picard has meanwhile retired—it is now the year 2399, twenty years after the events in *Star Trek: Nemesis*. Because of the Martian attack, a rescue mission by Picard to save 900 million Romulans from the impending supernova explosion in their system—as established in *Star Trek (2009)*—has been terminated, as the 10,000 rescue ships could not be built. Artificial life forms were banned from the Federation, which Picard considers a mistake. The explosion not only brought down the Romulan Star Empire, but killed large portions of the Romulan population, while the rest sought refuge in diasporas scattered throughout the galaxy. For Picard, the Federation failed politically. "The galaxy was mourning, burying its dead, and Starfleet slunk from its duties. The decision to call off the rescue and to abandon those people we had sworn to save was not just dishonorable, it was downright criminal. And I was not prepared to stand by and be a spectator" (Picard in *PIC* "Remembrance").

A short time later, Picard is visited by Dahj, a young woman who explains to him that his image has appeared to her repeatedly and that she has therefore sought him out. Picard notices that her face looks familiar and recognizes it from a painting that Data once gave him on the *Enterprise*-D—but thirty years ago. Picard speculates that Dahj might be an android and in some way a descendant of Data. When she is suddenly attacked and killed before his eyes, he begins investigating and pays Doctor Agnes Jurati a visit at the Daystrom Institute. Jurati was involved in the development of the androids that ran amok on Mars. Project leader was Bruce Maddox, the engineer from *TNG* "The Measure of a Man," but all research stopped after the incident on Mars, and Maddox has now moved to a new place unknown to Jurati. Both conclude that Maddox apparently succeeded with a theory called Fractal Neuronic Cloning, in which twin androids would be created from one positronic neuron of another android.

The episode ends with a scene in which this very twin named Soji visits the Romulan Reclamation Site, a facility of the Romulan Free State. The

Free State is the successor to the Romulan Star Empire. The Reclamation Site is housed in a dysfunctional Borg cube where, among other things, Borg technology is being researched by the Romulans.

Even in this first episode it becomes clear that *PIC* has to be considered as a follow-up series to *TNG*. It picks up the story from *TNG* "The Measure of a Man," in which the same Bruce Maddox wanted to disassemble Data for the purpose of research to create a whole host of androids. "Consider, every ship in Starfleet with a Data on board. Utilizing its extraordinary capabilities, acting as our hands and eyes in dangerous situations" (Maddox in *TNG* "The Measure of a Man"). The objection of Guinan—as described earlier—that "disposable creatures" are being built to do "the work that no one else wants to do because it is too difficult or too hazardous" has thus been proved true. Also, the last scene indicates that the Borg will also play a role in the context of this series.

At the same time, the first episode of this series establishes that the Federation has obviously moved away from its utopian ideal since *TNG* and the *TNG* movies. *Star Trek: Nemesis* still held out the prospect of a rapprochement between the Romulans and the Federation, which apparently also made Picard's humanitarian mission possible. "The Romulans asked for our help […]. Fortunately, the Federation chose to support the rescue effort" (Picard in *PIC* "Remembrance"). After the attack of the Synths, however, the Federation seems to be mainly preoccupied with itself. At the same time, helping the Romulans did not seem to be uncontroversial in the Federation. "The Romulans were our enemies, and we tried to help them for as long as we could, but even before the synthetics attacked Mars, fourteen species within the Federation said 'Cut the Romulans loose, or we will pull out.' It was a choice between allowing the Federation to implode, or letting the Romulans go" (Admiral Clancy in *PIC* "Maps and Legends").

Also, artificial life forms seem to be considered differently. Although Picard had considerable concerns about producing androids in large numbers in *TNG* "The Measure of a Man," because this would ultimately establish a new race of slaves, Bruce Maddox seems to have prevailed with his research. In a scene in the Daystrom Institute, Agnes Jurati shows Picard the disassembled Soong android B-4, to which Data transferred his memories in *Star Trek: Nemesis*. So, it can be assumed that this is how Maddox was finally able to realize his wish with B-4. Synths are now actually used *en masse* on Utopia Planitia. They do not have names—only a designation of letters and numbers—and seem to be far less developed than for example Data, so that the humanoid crew on Utopia Planitia has difficulties in dealing with them (*PIC* "Maps and Legends").

That the Romulans do not exactly value artificial life forms, either is shown in the parallel plot by their interaction with former Borg Drones in the Romulan Reclamation Site. Here, too, a pejorative term for former drones has become established: these are now called "xBs." These drones are also not given names by the Romulans. "Why do you call them 'the Nameless'? Their species had a name, we just do not know what it was" (Soji in *PIC* "Maps and Legends").

In the course of the further episodes, Picard now undertakes the attempt to find out more about the origin and the further fate of Dahj and her twin Soji. What the audience can perceive is that the Federation is increasingly losing influence, especially on the periphery of its territory. For example, Picard encounters Seven of Nine, who is now active in a kind of vigilante group on the edge of Federation territory (*PIC* "Stardust City Rag"). In addition, numerous Romulans still live in refugee camps and suffer from poverty and ethnic conflicts (*PIC* "Absolute Candor"). At the same time, however, their intelligence service, the Tal Shiar, is still active.

The main theme in this first *PIC* season, however, is dealing with other life forms. This is not only evident in relation to artificial life forms but also, for example, in dealing with the former Borg. Picard's attitude towards the Borg is still ambivalent. Picard says, on the one hand, that "they coolly assimilate entire civilizations, entire systems in a matter of hours. They do not change, they metastasize" (Picard in *PIC* "The Impossible Box"); on the other hand, he praises Hugh as head of the Borg Artifact Research Institute, for "after all these years, you are showing what the Borg are underneath. They are victims, not monsters" (Picard in *PIC* "The Impossible Box").[15] Borgs are still considered "the most hated people in the galaxy" (Hugh in *PIC* "The Impossible Box"). Their lives are considered unworthy. This is not only shown in the already described interaction with the Romulans, but also in the case of Icheb from *VOY*, who had his vital implants forcibly removed (*PIC* "Stardust City Rag") by criminals.

Picard eventually tracks down Maddox's retreat on the planet Coppelius and discovers an entire colony of androids that Maddox founded with Altan Inigo Soong,[16] son of Noonian Soong, the creator of Data (*PIC* "Et in Arcadia Ego"). It turns out that Maddox, like Picard, was also not convinced of a simple malfunction of the androids on Mars. For this reason, he dispatched the twin androids to uncover the true background of the attack. In fact, this was orchestrated by a splinter organization of the Tal Shiar, the Zhat Vash, to get the Federation to ban artificial life forms. The Zhat Vash did this, according to an old traditional legend, out of fear that at some point artificial life forms would rise to rule over all other life in the galaxy.

Conversely, the androids accuse humanity of dominating them. "[...] Try to see this from our point of view. You choose if we live, you choose if we die. You choose. We have no choice. You organics have never given us one" (Soji in *PIC* "Et in Arcadia Ego"). In this respect, this season ends with a Picard-typical philosophical discourse about the equality of all life forms and about the question of (im)mortality, too. Picard, who in the first episodes was diagnosed with a slowly progressing but fatal disease, dies at the end of the episode—only to suddenly wake up again in his winery. Data enters the room and explains to Picard that he is with him in a quantum simulation created from the memories Data had transferred to B-4 before his physical death. Soong has reconstructed Data's consciousness and made him immortal in a quasi-limbo. The fact that Picard is also there happened due to the fact that in reality Soong, Soji, and Jurati also transferred Picard's consciousness and he is only temporarily in the simulation. Data asks Picard for the favor to end his simulation because he finally wants to experience mortality.

When Picard is resurrected shortly thereafter, he finds himself in an artificial body—though made of flesh and blood—that is a golem that Soong actually developed for himself. Picard is mortal after all, but he has somewhat become an artificial life form himself.

## Conclusion

The most striking difference between the post–2000 *Star Trek* series and movies and the earlier series might actually be the new narrative style. While the series before were largely characterized by an episodic narrative (with some exceptions, as in *DS9*), the narratives in the new series are basically stretched over the entire season. This generates much more complex storylines. At the same time, the new series make numerous references to established settings in the *Star Trek* universe. This is particularly evident in *PIC*, where not only the title character appears, but also characters from *TNG* and *VOY* like Data, Hugh, Seven of Nine and, not least, Riker and Troi.[17] This interweaving in the *Star Trek* universe elaborates the continuity that was already present in *DS9* and *VOY* in relation to *TNG*. In this way, *PIC* also refers back to the family motif within the crew, which was especially important in *TNG*.

Nevertheless, both series make it clear that the Federation obviously needs to be reminded of its utopian ideals. Picard is portrayed as a person who continues to represent this very value and therefore withdraws because, in his view, the Federation no longer lives up to it. Similar tendencies can be seen—but in the alternate timeline—in the reboot films, where there is a fearful and militarized Federation, which, in turn, must be reminded of its utopian ideals by Kirk and his crew. This relative decline of the Federation, however, is already foreshadowed in the film *Star Trek: Insurrection* and confirmed all the more in the third season of *DIS*.

However, the writers remain true to *Star Trek*'s utopian ideal insofar as they deal with topics in both *DIS* and *PIC* that still comment on and criticize current events in our reality. Neither the new narrative nor the design of the series changes anything about that.

# 7

# How Utopian Is *Star Trek*?

Is the *Star Trek* franchise, after all, a utopia, a mega text that mirrors and critiques our reality?

At the beginning of this book, I elaborated on the differences between utopia and science fiction, concluding that the two genres can be distinguished. While utopia refers to a decidedly socio-political ideal image of society, science fiction attempts to predict a future society based on science and technology. For science fiction, humans are not necessarily at the center. Utopia, on the other hand, deliberately refers to humanity as the center of its description.

At the same time, however, I have shown that although the two genres can be easily distinguished, they are not mutually exclusive. Utopia can also be transported "on the back" of a science fiction narrative, and it is not *per se* anti-technology and anti-science.

I have given three different classical utopias as examples and put forward the thesis that *Star Trek* is based on similar, fundamental considerations and ideas. First of all, of course, there is the question of how much space new technology occupies in *Star Trek*. My investigation has shown that the society in *Star Trek* has taken on a highly technological future. The central moment here is, of course, the significant development of space technology, which, in *Star Trek*, not only includes the possibility of interstellar space travel but also makes travel in space as comfortable as possible (especially compared to space travel today). In this regard, warp drive is actually so important in *Star Trek* that—as seen in *DIS*—the entire utopian idea of the Federation falls apart when it is no longer available. In terms of the advancement of technology, then, *Star Trek* clearly exhibits elements of science fiction in that the series anticipates future technological developments. However, some of these technologies have already become reality, such as wireless communication, a global data network like the Internet, tablet computers or smartphones. Ironically, this makes the counterparts in the *Star Trek* universe—i.e., the communicators, the tricorders, the portables called PADDs, and even the computer terminals with their touch screens in *TNG* and the subsequent series—seem not so far away anymore (and the computers operated by keyboard in *TOS* almost anachronistic). The technical development of our present has caught up with *Star Trek* in these things. However, if you look at other, not (yet) realized technologies in *Star Trek*, like the replicators, the transporter technology and especially the propulsion technology, there is still a clear influence of science fiction, even if it is never explained exactly from which technologies these future ones have been extrapolated. *Star Trek* thus bases a substantial part of its narrative on technological progress.

But we have also shown that *Star Trek* is by no means about merely depicting human development based on technological progress, but rather *Star Trek* illuminates the social implications of technological progress. This is especially evident in *TOS*, where new technology is met with skepticism, but also in the arguments with the Prime Directive, where it is repeatedly about the influence of technology on less developed cultures. Then, as technology becomes an everyday companion to our reality in the 1990s, it also recedes as a central plot element in *TNG* and subsequent series. Technology is a constant companion in those series as well—it is a prerequisite for the life that is shown, but it is not a central element. Rather, technology is still viewed with a certain (albeit lesser) skepticism in TNG and other series as well. Some technologies are even outlawed and banned, such as certain weapons or genetic manipulation, or come under discussion, for example when it comes to the mass use of holograms or androids for low-level work. Robots—a preferred technology in science fiction literature—do not find wider use in the *Star Trek* universe and are even more or less unique and treated as unique for most of the discourse—as can be seen in the example of Data in *TNG*. Thus, if one looks only at the aspect of technology, *Star Trek* is no longer a classic science fiction narrative. One could, therefore, easily call the franchise "technological utopianism" in Braine's words (1994, 14). But beyond that, is it also a political utopia?

I also took a closer look at the spaceships and space stations in *Star Trek*. Here, the majority of the narrative takes place in the *Star Trek* universe. Of course, there is still Earth, as the place where everything began with the First Contact with the Vulcans, and we have established that humanity has founded a multitude of colonies in space. *Star Trek* thus draws clear parallels to the classical utopias. There is a central event that marks the break with reality. After a destructive global war, humanity encounters extraterrestrial life for the first time, which gives the impetus to overcome conflicts on Earth and peacefully unite the planet. Most importantly, we have numerous explorers who travel in spaceships. This is perhaps the biggest difference from the classical utopias. These also have contacts to the outside, but these are also very limited or even hidden, as is the case with *New Atlantis*. In *Star Trek*, on the other hand, we are dealing with a whole fleet of spaceships. So, at first glance, *Star Trek* does not seem to be focused on its inner dealings in any way, as is the case with the classical utopias. On the contrary, it is about discovering new worlds and expanding. But on closer inspection, we have seen that these spaceships—as expansive as they may be in space—actually make the inside of *Star Trek* society very different from the outside. It almost seems as if we are dealing with mobile colonies in the spaceships and space stations, that humanity is expanding, but just as in More's *Utopia*, only into empty space where no one has been before.

An elaborate image of society is revealed inside these spaceships. As in the utopian cities, there is everything to live in here. There are functional spaces like an infirmary and an engine room, but there are also social spaces like a gymnasium or a bar. On the spaceships, people have their own living quarters, but they are so numerous and so standardized that one can hardly speak of individuality. The space that the ships offer is well planned and limited. All of this is very reminiscent of the cities in *Utopia* or *City of the Sun*. The whole spaceship or space station functions as a planned "city," centered on the bridge as the main facility and top hierarchical level of architecture. The decks and corridors, especially those on which the living quarters are located, are similar and can be told apart only by a coordinate system. Life in these architectures does not tolerate a permanent retreat of the individual. Everyone has his or her assigned place here, not only to live but above all, to work.

At the same time, it is work that is virtually a mantra of life in the *Star Trek* universe. "The challenge [...] is to improve yourself. To enrich yourself. Enjoy it" (Picard in *TNG* "The Neutral Zone"). "And this is the kind of utopian vision, however individualistic, that drives the entire *Trek* franchise" (Booker 2018, 93). So, one should grow oneself and develop oneself, but of course, not least one should serve the society and the ship. The uniform clothing, the strict hierarchy on the ship and the general life under the aspect of utility maximization also stand for the utopian idea of society in *Star Trek*. Money no longer plays a role in the everyday life of the people. Food is available in sufficient quantities through replication—not available through subsistence economy—and private property, apart from a few objects of love, is of no importance. Under these aspects only does this society function.

Also, in this point, *Star Trek* is very similar to the classical utopias: families and friendships play an important role. Especially in *TNG*, the *Enterprise* is characterized as a "family ship," with numerous kindergartens and schools. Friendship plays an important role in the constitution of society on the ships. People not only work together, but they also live together, play games, go to the bar together and play sports together. Individualism thus always has a very circumscribed place on *Star Trek* and is usually limited to a few individual interests. The majority everyday life is spent together with others—both on duty and off.

But there are also developments in the *Star Trek* universe. While women hardly played a role on the *Enterprise* in *TOS* (and if so, only a subordinate one), this changes gradually in the course of the *Star Trek* series. In *TNG*, women were already in leading positions, but mainly those limited to social professions (Beverly Crusher is a doctor, and Deanna Troi a counselor). In *DS9* there is a female deputy station commander, Kira Nerys, and a female science officer, Jadzia Dax. In *VOY* there is the first female captain with Kathryn Janeway and, with B'Elanna Torres, even a female chief engineer. Finally, in *DIS*, it is predominantly the women who drive the narrative forward and play the key roles.

Religion, however, hardly plays a role in *Star Trek*. It is limited to a mostly private practice. Even though spiritual cultures like the Klingons and the Bajorans find their way into *Star Trek*, religion never becomes the driving force of society. "Gene [Roddenberry] felt very strongly that all of our contemporary Earth religions would be gone by the 23rd century [...]" (Moore 1997–99, ron012.txt). Therefore, *Star Trek* is, in addition to being a technological utopia, also a social utopia, since it depicts a society that represents a radical break with the present in terms of way of life.

Finally, I considered the political dimension of *Star Trek*. The United Federation of Planets is an interplanetary federal state with defined institutions. Thereby, the shaping of politics in *Star Trek* happens rather incidentally: not all episodes have a political theme or touch politics in some way. In the extensive *Star Trek* text, it is only as the narrative progresses that we gradually find out more about a future political order. In *TOS*, the political agenda remains one-dimensional at first. The Federation exists, but hardly becomes an issue. Other species, such as the Klingons and the Romulans, appear only marginally, and instead Kirk and his crew come into contact with a multitude of underdeveloped peoples. Here it becomes apparent how strongly *Star Trek* was rooted in the present at the time of *TOS*. It is not only that, with *TOS* "A Private Little War," an allegory on the Vietnam War was told but also that the various "liberations" of supposedly subjugated cultures reflect the self-image the United States had at that time. In *TOS* "The Apple" and "The Return of the Archons," I showed this by the example of oppression through technology.

But the picture changed fundamentally with the movies of the *TOS* crew and in the course of *TNG*. Institutions within the Federation, like the

Federation Council or the Federation president, came into focus. We gradually got to know various laws and codes of the Federation and Starfleet that have been observed. Conflicts with the Klingons and the Romulans were detailed, even to the point of giving these species their own history. New species like the Cardassians and the Borg appeared and thus new conflicts arose. Finally, in *DS9*, a huge story of a war affecting the entire Alpha Quadrant was told. Here and subsequently in *VOY* it became apparent that *Star Trek* had grown into a utopia that wanted to defend itself and its values.

With Starfleet, the Federation represents a type of political order that is reminiscent of an autocracy, or at least an oligarchy, just as existed in the classical utopias. Although the Federation president is elected, it remains unclear how strongly democratic structures are designed in the Federation. Instead, as in the utopians, the citizens of the Federation live in their utopian ideal and do their work—and a small elite created by selection directs the fate of the Federation. From what we know through the narrative, the senior officers on the ships and stations play the exemplary and guiding role, rising in the system of power, being promoted to admiral—as in the case of Kathryn Janeway or Jean-Luc Picard, for example—and thus increasing their positions of power.

That the military leadership of Starfleet has a significant influence on the political level, or is even strongly interwoven with it, is suggested by the events during the Dominion War in *DS9*. The fact that Starfleet maintains its own intelligence service—and, in addition, with Section 31, apparently a more secret intelligence service within—underpins the image of the Federation as an oligarchic state.

The other powers in the *Star Trek* universe are also by no means democratically organized. They all reflect character traits of us in some way. The Klingons are a proud warrior people with a rich history and a high sense of honor; the Vulcans are strictly logical rationalists; the Romulans are cunning; the Ferengi are greedy; the Bajorans are spiritual; and the Cardassians are totalitarian. They all represent, in their own ways, other possible forms of society within *Star Trek*, forms to which the Federation is always compared. *Star Trek* also shows similarities to the classical utopias, which feel in competition with other powers, wage war with other powers if necessary, and separate themselves from others in order to preserve their utopian ideas. The Federation—as is perhaps most clearly shown by the war narrative in *DS9*—acts no differently. It wants to defend its own utopia, but it also questions it critically—especially in *DS9* and *VOY*. With the existence of the Maquis, exactly this question is raised: does the Federation really represents such an ideal state of being? The events in *Star Trek: Insurrection* point in the same direction. But in view of the fact that

## 7. How Utopian Is Star Trek? 163

the Maquis are defeated—and also that in *Star Trek: Insurrection* the "misguided" Starfleet admiral is brought to his just punishment and the Federation Council revises its resettlement policy—it becomes clear that the ideals in *Star Trek* continue to prevail and that the society is ideal to a large extent. That this process is not complete becomes clear in *TNG* "The Neutral Zone" when Picard states: "Our mission is to go forward, and it has just begun. [...] There is still much to do. There is still so much to learn."

Ultimately, this learning process is also evident in the way the Borg Collective is treated. Within the *Star Trek* universe, the Borg are probably the clearest counter-design to the social ideal of the Federation. Yet there is a fine line between the dystopia of the Borg and the utopia of the Federation. Both strive for perfection, and both assimilate peoples and cultures in their respective ways and subsume them under their overriding goal. Both want to create a polity in which the individual steps back in favor of a larger entity. Both use technology as their preferred vehicle to achieve this goal. From the first major battle between the Federation and the Borg in *TNG* "The Best of Both Worlds" to the events in *Star Trek: First Contact* to the most crucial battle in *VOY* "Endgame," the question of which of the two polities is actually the best of both worlds is present in the *Star Trek* text. Basically, the Federation and the Borg Collective are close to each other in many points, and it is this proximity that makes the juxtaposition of dystopia and utopia within one narrative so interesting.

Even if, at first glance, the reboot movies and the new series like *DIS* or *PIC* seem to have little to do with Gene Roddenberry's utopian ideas, this view is deceptive. In fact, one finds that *Star Trek* in today's time and in today's versions naturally reflects reality. The view of our present has indeed become darker, which is certainly due in part to the changed political conditions after 9/11. In this respect, it is not surprising that the Federation in the first season of *DIS* is willing to go to extremes to end a war by contemplating genocide. And a Federation in *PIC* largely preoccupied with itself and largely ignoring the suffering of another species—the Romulans—also mirrors our present. The same is true for the confrontation with artificial intelligence and artificial life forms, which in all likelihood will be a topic that will determine our near future. *Star Trek* has a critical position here, reflecting these developments, but giving us hope that utopia is not lost. Characters like Picard stand for this, but also characters torn apart like Michael Burnham, who in the course of their heroic journeys (again) find themselves and their convictions.

*Star Trek* is not just science fiction, but a text that represents a social and political utopia shaped by technology. Throughout the 50 years that *Star Trek* has existed, "*Star Trek* has been a pervasive part of the cultural environment worldwide" (Robb 2012, 275). The franchise has constantly referred to our present and, as it were, produced a mirror of a better, albeit ideal, future society. During this time, *Star Trek* has had an influence on many areas of our present and has grown into a franchise that refers to itself, in many ways, and thus differentiates itself. This is demonstrated not only by the many canonical series and films and the large body of non-canonical texts but also by more recent incarnations such as the anthology *Short Treks*, which points outside the series narrative to developments of characters or events and, like apocrypha, expands the *Star Trek* universe. Finally, *Star Trek* "certainly is not ready to retire" (Canavan 2016, 323) and even proves that a self-referentiality can also show humorous traits, as in *Lower Decks*, in which, for once, the focus is not on the leading elite and the ordinary everyday life in the Federation is shown. The new series and episodes, which have aired after the finalization of this text (and therefore could not be taken into consideration), show that *Star Trek* still has a lot of storytelling possibilities.

*Star Trek* is not a complete utopia in the sense that a whole new picture of a future perfect society is drawn. Instead, to take up Levitas, *Star Trek* picks up aspects from our present, engages with the history of humankind, and takes those elements and reassembles them in an archaeological manner. *Star Trek* asks questions about "the idea of human nature" (Levitas 2013, 175) and how that nature evolved and may develop in a possible future. And finally, *Star Trek* imagines a reconstructed world based on these insights and describes its social institutions in an architectural, world-building way.

*Star Trek* thus does not present us with a completed, perfect utopia, but a utopia in constant flux. With *Star Trek*, utopian ideas have been picking up on contemporary developments for over 50 years and constantly reassessing and critiquing them. In this respect, it is a dynamic utopia which "itself is presented ambiguously as imperfect, subject to difficulties, inconsistencies, faults, change" (Levitas 2011, 198). Ultimately, however, *Star Trek* proves that the actual utopia is not the utopia itself, but the way there: "Maybe it is not the destination that matters, maybe it is the journey. If that journey takes a little longer, so we can do something we all believe in" (Harry Kim in *VOY* "Endgame").

# Chapter Notes

## Chapter 1

1. However, it can also be seen as "a pun which conflates *outopos* or no place and *eutopos* or good place," as Levitas states (2013, 3).

2. The idea of a well-meaning mastermind who unites a people culturally or in terms of government and provides a certain philosophy is also found in *Star Trek*. Among the Vulcans, for example, there is the character of Surak, a legendary philosopher and father of modern Vulcan civilization (*ENT* "The Forge"), and among the Klingons there is the mythical character of Kahless, who united the various Klingon tribes.

3. The establishment of colonies is also a key feature of the United Federation of Planets in *Star Trek*, which directly echoes More's idea here.

4. In this respect, it is an overstatement of Jenkis to compare the office of the governors with that of a state president, unless one assumes that every city is at the same time in principle a state within a state and Utopia a kind of confederation of states (1992, 115).

5. With Campanella it is called Taprobane (2009, 4).

6. Campanella here uses puns on the Latin words Potentia, Sapientia and Amor (Jenkis 1992, 132).

7. Jenkis also lists the following indicators: "Space travel at super-light speed, travel to other times, discovery and colonization of distant celestial bodies, invasions or visits to the Earth by extra-terrestrial beings, changes in living conditions on Earth in political, biological, economic and especially technological terms, etc." (1992, 59).

8. On the other hand, Jenkis thinks that science fiction emerged only during the 20th century: "The hour of birth of science fiction is fixed at the year 1926, when in the USA Hugo Gernsback, the father of science fiction, published the first magazine 'Amazing Stories' dedicated to this genre" (1992, 58).

9. Biesterfeld, however, argues that these utopias are democratic at least insofar as they are based on the equality of people. On the other hand, he also states that only the best are eligible for higher careers and are selected by a certain—non-democratic—selection procedure (1982, 18).

## Chapter 2

1. This chapter is based on a previously published work of mine (Stoppe 2008).

2. This story structure was originally due to a rule by Roddenberry for *TOS* and *TNG* not to build story lines that will extend over several episodes. After Roddenberry's death, the authors deviated considerably from this rule in later episodes of *TNG* and in the successor series *DS9*, *VOY* and *ENT*. In terms of *DIS* and *PIC*, episodes are generally placed within a broader story line that spans an entire season.

3. In contrast to the series, Earth has a far greater role in most of the franchise's films. It is only in *Star Trek: Insurrection* that Earth does not appear at all.

4. The opening credits of *Star Trek: Enterprise* refer exactly to this development by showing ships, airplanes,

submarines, and spaceships. The sequence also includes actual documentary film footage, for example from the Lunar Module or the Mars robot *Sojourner*.

5. In terms of storytelling, this technology was invented so as not to limit the action of the crew to the interior of the spaceship. It was necessary for the show that the characters could also visit planets and other places. Since it would have been simply too expensive to show the spaceship landing and departing on every new planet, using the transporter was much more effective and (again, in terms of storytelling) time saving. Additionally, crewmembers were thus able to go to places in an instant to which spaceships and shuttles could not navigate. (Solow and Justman 1996, 51; Okuda and Okuda 1999, 519).

6. The works cited here refer to *TNG* and *DS9*, but the technical details can be assumed in a similar way for all other *Star Trek* series. Nevertheless, these details are rarely discussed or even shown in the series—for example, the recycling of waste is never mentioned at all.

7. With the advent of music and video streaming, which is possible for us today, this "future technology" is basically already a fact. In the 1990s, however, this form of media usage was not yet imaginable.

8. Alcubierre further argues: "[…] Consider the relative speed of separation of two co-moving observers. It is easy to convince oneself that, if we define this relative speed as the rate of change of proper spatial distance over proper time, we will obtain a value that is much larger that the speed of light. This doesn't mean that our observers will be travelling faster: they always move inside their local light-cones. The enormous speed of separation comes from the expansion of spacetime itself" (1994, L73).

9. This event was preceded by a test phase, described in detail in Sternbach and Okuda (1991, 54), which lasted several years.

10. This quote can also be read in view of the *Star Trek* franchise as a television show created for entertainment and not as a text that was thought of utopian from the start.

11. Theoretically, creating a maximum-sized warp field should lead to infinite speed. However, the series writers maintain that this would also require an infinite amount of energy. Therefore, infinite speed is impossible, even in the *Star Trek* universe (Sternbach and Okuda 1991, 56).

12. Full impulse as a speed indication corresponds to a quarter of the speed of light, i.e., about 270 million kilometers per hour (Okuda and Okuda 1999, 556).

13. Stephen Hawking was an avowed *Star Trek* fan and even had a cameo appearance as holographic figure in the *TNG* episode "Descent" (Hawking 2001, 157).

14. However, the episodes only deal with how Kirk and his crew liberate the respective peoples from their uncontrollable and therefore corrupt technology. The consequences of such a massive intervention are not discussed.

15. The term "android" was used extensively in science fiction literature and commonly describes a robot that looks like a human and behaves accordingly human. This kind of an artificial creature is not only found in *Star Trek*, but also in numerous other science fiction works like *A.I.*, the *Alien Trilogy*, and especially Fritz Lang's *Metropolis*.

16. This chapter is partly based on a previously published work of mine (Stoppe 2011b).

17. Exactly this should happen later with the Medical Holographic Emergency Program. The first version, which is installed on *Voyager*, turns out to be so deficient that from then on, it is used as a worker in dilithium mines and as cleaning personnel (*VOY* "Life Line," *VOY* "Author, Author"). The storyline is again taken up in *PIC*.

18. The *VOY* episode "Author, Author" picks up this theme again. *Voyager*'s Emergency Medical Holographic Program, the Doctor, publishes a holo-novel and gets into a legal dispute with his publisher. Finally, in a hearing very similar to *TNG*'s "The Measure of a Man," it has to be decided whether the Doctor is an individual with his own rights. The verdict here is, however, against him: "The Doctor exhibits many of the traits we associate with a person. Intelligence, creativity, ambition, even fallibility, but are these traits real or is the Doctor merely programmed

to simulate them? To be honest, I do not know. Eventually we will have to decide because the issue of holographic rights is not going to go away, but at this time, I am not prepared to rule that the Doctor is a person under the law" (Arbitrator in *VOY* "Author, Author").

19. In *TNG* "The Naked Now," Data is seduced by Lieutenant Tasha Yar and answers the question of whether he is "fully functional" with: "In every way, of course. I am programmed in multiple techniques. A broad variety of pleasuring."

20. The Borg Queen even denies Data his perfection in *Star Trek: First Contact*: "You are an imperfect being created by an imperfect being."

21. A precursor to holodecks was the recreation room in *TOS* that was able to visualize pre-programmed illusions. However, one was able to touch the walls of the room during the simulation (which is not possible in *TNG*), so that the virtual reality is incomplete. As it turns out, holo-communicators were already developed during the *DIS* era but were ultimately dismissed by Captain Pike because the holograms "look too much like ghosts" (Pike in *DIS* "An Obol for Charon"). On *Deep Space Nine*, the holodecks are called holosuites, but they work on the same principle (Zimmerman, Sternbach, and Drexler 1998, 112). These holosuites also offer sexually oriented programs that are explicitly mentioned in some episodes like *DS9* "The Forsaken," for example. Additionally, holocommunicators are reintroduced onboard the USS *Defiant* in *DS9* "For the Uniform."

22. Ironically, one can assume the role of the series protagonists in various *Star Trek* computer games. For example, in *Star Trek: Voyager—Elite Force*, one can not only play the game itself, but also, as an additional option, one can also take a virtual tour on *Voyager* starting from quarters in the role of a crewmember, without necessarily being followed by a game plot. Thus, it is possible to virtually reconstruct everyday life on *Voyager* in a self-determined way and, to an extent, that cannot be shown in any series episode (Stoppe 2016, 7).

23. In the course of the series and the film *Star Trek: The First Contact*, Picard will return to this world several times.

24. This does not mean, however, that the holodeck will be an actually feasible technology in the near future. Even though the representation of three-dimensional objects is already possible with a high degree of realism using today's computer technology, the holodeck in *Star Trek* can actually generate matter using replicator technology as well. However, this possibility will probably remain a vision of the future for a long time.

25. Stanislaw Lem made these considerations about interactivity in his work *Summa technologiae*, published in 1964 (Schröter 2009, 107–9).

26. However, it later becomes apparent that the mistake had a greater impact than thought, as Moriarty remains self-aware that he is only a hologram. In *TNG* "Ship In a Bottle," he demands to be freed from the holodeck as a being as sentient as any other lifeform (Stoppe 2016, 13).

## Chapter 3

1. This chapter is partly based on a previously published work of mine (Stoppe 2011a).

2. Rabitsch also emphasizes the fact that the Captain's Log (or Station's Log in *DS9*) is both a strong reference to the Age of Sail as well as a continuous narrative device throughout all *Star Trek* series (2019, 143).

3. Again, it is certainly no coincidence that the prototype spaceship of the company Virgin Galactic, which is led by the entrepreneur Richard Branson and wants to carry out tourist journeys into space, also bears the name VSS *Enterprise* (Buzan 2010, 175; Rabitsch 2019, 84).

4. This establishes a certain continuity within the *Star Trek* universe. The *Enterprise* NX-01 in *ENT* is the first ship that has warp capability, the USS *Enterprise* NCC-1701 was featured in *DIS*, *TOS*, and the movies until its destruction in *Star Trek III: The Search for Spock*. The *Enterprise*-A (all ships following in the *Star Trek* history thereafter bear the same registration number, but were marked with letters to distinguish them) was virtually identical in construction and was featured in the following movies with the *TOS* crew. The *Enterprise*-B

has an appearance in *Star Trek: Generations*, where its commissioning is celebrated. In *TNG* "Yesterday's *Enterprise*," the *Enterprise*-C is featured, while in *Star Trek: First Contact,* the new *Enterprise*-E is finally introduced after the destruction of the *Enterprise*-D, which is featured in *TNG*, *Star Trek: Generations*, and in *DS9* "Emissary."

5. Sternbach provides a detailed insight into the structure and layout of the respective decks (1996). These blueprints are not production drawings, but go in their richness of detail far beyond the representation that would have been possible in the series and its film sets. For each deck, the exact true-to-scale floor plan with individual rooms and their functions is shown.

6. One exception is the crew head, which is also directly accessible from the bridge, but is never mentioned in any series. It may be considered an inside joke by the writers, especially since it is repeatedly mentioned in literature (Sternbach and Okuda 1991, 31; Sternbach 1996, 4; Rabitsch 2019, 79). Roddenberry mentions it, too, "on the right side of the bridge is a door leading to the bridge head and washroom" (1987, 16).

7. However, there are also four gangways and two additional docking locks on deck 25 through which you can leave the ship by foot when connected directly to a star base (Sternbach and Okuda 1991, 84–5). Furthermore, through these locks one can also carry out outboard missions in space suits, as shown in *Star Trek: First Contact.*

8. These include a gymnasium with a mirror in *TNG* "The Price," a fencing hall (*TNG* "We'll Always Have Paris"), and halls for fictitious sports such as Parrises Squares (*TNG* "11001001") and Anbo Jutsu, a kind of Asian martial art (*TNG* "The Icarus Factor"). According to Sternbach, there are four gymnasiums on deck 12, each two decks high (1996, 8–9).

9. The arboretum is located on the *Enterprise* on deck 17 (Okuda and Okuda 1999, 19); however, Sternbach does not mention it (1996, 10).

10. Sternbach mentions several classrooms on decks 8, 9, and 10. The majority of crew quarters are also located on these decks (1996, 7–8).

11. Sternbach mentions several barbershops on decks 8 and 9 (1996, 7).

12. However, a kitchen is explicitly shown in *Star Trek VI: The Undiscovered Country* and, of course, in *VOY* directly adjacent to the mess hall. There is also a strong hint that the *Enterprise* NX-01 had a kitchen and a ship's chef as there is a separate captain's dining room (*ENT* "Terra Nova," *ENT* "Breaking The Ice"). The *Enterprise*-D also featured a captain's dining room (*TNG* "Sins of the Father") and on one occasion, chefs are referenced in dialogue (*TNG* "Lonely Among Us").

13. This is a fact that is discussed within multiples episodes when at first Naomi Wildman is born as the only child on *Voyager* (*VOY* "Deadlock"). Later, some Borg children join the crew (*VOY* "Collective") and eventually Miral Paris is born to B'Elanna Torres and Tom Paris (*VOY* "Endgame"), making the *Voyager* a family ship at last.

14. However, the possibility of existing wormholes is essentially grounded in science: "[...] You might go through a wormhole to the other side of the galaxy and be back in time for dinner" (Hawking 2001, 136).

15. A detailed plan of the Promenade with a list of all shops can be found in the appendix of Zimmerman, Sternbach, and Drexler 1998.

16. Both facilities are listed on the Promenade plan (Zimmerman, Sternbach, and Drexler 1998, appendix). A hydroponic garden is also mentioned in *DS9* "Blaze of Glory."

17. A prominent exception to this rule is *Star Trek: Lower Decks*, in which the protagonists are not senior officers. Nevertheless, they also have certain tasks that are essential for the functioning of the ship's society.

18. Another border crossing occurs in the same episode when Ben plays poker with the senior officers, having previously done the same with the junior officers.

19. Later, an elite unit of cadets, the so-called Red Squad, plays an important role in an attempted *coup d'état* in *DS9* "Homefront." The same elite unit reappears in *DS9* "Valiant." Finally, the Ferengi Nog is accepted as a cadet at Starfleet Academy in *DS9* "Heart of Stone."

20. This is also evident in *TNG*

"Tapestry," in which Picard, in an alternative timeline, can be seen as an astrophysicist in the rank of lieutenant junior grade. Picard's career was therefore less successful in this variant than in the actual timeline. Again, the strict hierarchy on the ship is shown.

21. In the 24th century, members of the Commands Division wear red uniforms; Operations, yellow; and Science/Medical, blue.

22. In the *VOY* episode "Human Error," Tom Paris and B'Elanna Torres, as parents-to-be, are even presented with diapers bearing the Starfleet emblem, which are explicitly referred to as standard Starfleet equipment.

23. Barclay behaves in a very similar way in *VOY* "Pathfinder." Again, he has problems with his superior and escapes into a holographic simulation of *Voyager* to find a way to contact the ship together with the crewmembers. However, in the very same episode, he is reunited with former *Enterprise* counselor Deanna Troi, who treats him for his addiction.

## Chapter 4

1. However, since both territories extend into the Alpha Quadrant, both species are to be counted among the great powers that exercise influence in the Alpha Quadrant as well.

2. The Federation also has an official flag (*TNG* "The First Duty") and a national anthem (*DS9* "Take Me Out to the Holosuite").

3. In the *TOS* episode "The Trouble with Tribbles," there is an Undersecretary for Agriculture and in *TNG* "Chain of Command," a Secretary of Exploration is mentioned, for example.

4. In *ENT* "Demons," ministers are mentioned as members of government.

5. The so-called European Alliance may have been inspired by the European Union in our present reality. Captain Picard also mentions the European Hegemony as a possible predecessor, which was a pioneering state leading to United Earth in the 22nd century (*TNG* "Up The Long Ladder").

6. Picard delivers a similar speech in *TNG* "The Neutral Zone" that "people are no longer obsessed with the accumulation of things. We have eliminated hunger, want, the need for possessions."

7. In this episode the arbitrator wears civilian clothes, so he does not seem to be directly associated with Starfleet.

8. Data completed his studies at the Starfleet Academy in probability mechanics and exobiology (*TNG* "Encounter at Farpoint"), and other officers have also achieved university majors, such as Tom Paris in astrophysics (*VOY* "Future's End"). Furthermore, research institutes or universities are mentioned again and again at different places in *Star Trek*. Examples are the Daystrom Institute of Technology (*TNG* "Booby Trap") and the universities on Bajor (*DS9* "Babel") and Betazed (*TNG* "Tin Man"). Education obviously has an important role in society in the *Star Trek* universe.

9. The Khitomer Accords are peace treaties between the Klingons and the Federation *(Star Trek VI: The Undiscovered Country)*.

10. There is a slight inconsistency here because at the time, Wesley Crusher was only a civilian living on the *Enterprise* and not Starfleet personnel. Therefore, the Prime Directive should have not applied at all. However, it can be argued that Wesley was on the planet's surface as part of the away team making him technically a temporary member of the crew.

11. Nevertheless, it remains to be discussed whether the visit of the *Enterprise* crew to the Edo is not a violation of the Prime Directive in the first place. Considering how the Edo people are obviously surprised by the technological progress of the Federation, it would not have been advisable to contact them.

12. The character of Khan returns in the second feature film *Star Trek II: The Wrath of Khan*, which again deals with this topic. In the film *Star Trek Into Darkness*, the figure also plays an important role, albeit in an alternative timeline. The Augments also have a prominent role in the *ENT* episodes "Borderland," "Cold Station 12" and "The Augments." These episodes make direct reference to Khan and the Eugenic Wars. As the leader of the Augments in *ENT*, the figure of Dr. Arik Soong is introduced. He is an ancestor of the android designer Dr. Noonian Soong, who created Data, among

other androids. Arik Soong recognizes in *ENT* "The Augments" that genetic manipulation does not lead to human perfection: "I have been thinking perfecting humanity may not be possible. Cybernetics, artificial lifeforms... I doubt I will finish the work myself. Might take a generation or two" (Arik Soong in *ENT* "The Augments"). Here the writers foreshadow the creation of androids like Data.

13. This episode, however, ignores that fact that there is a general ban of genetic engineering.

14. *DS9* "Statistical Probabilities" takes up Bashir's genetic engineering and portrays four genetically engineered people with behavioral disorders.

15. The issue of terrorism is taken up again in *TNG* at a later date in the episode "Starship Mine." In contrast to a political conflict, this episode is more about terrorists who want to steal a chemical substance from the *Enterprise* and therefore seize the ship. The obvious analogy to the Northern Ireland conflict meant that this episode was initially not shown in Ireland or the UK when *TNG* was first broadcast.

16. There are indeed a number of episodes that break up the time line through time travel, parallel universes, and alternative realities, but these episodes usually do not have a pervasive effect on the Prime Universe.

17. In this episode, the Ferengi are portrayed as rather buccaneer-like, a foreshadowing that anticipates their basic character as a trade people. However, the narrative is not an actual first contact because only the audience knows that they are Ferengi, but not the characters in the episode. Official first contact with the Ferengi takes place later in *TNG* "The Last Outpost." In *DS9* "Little Green Men," the actual first contact between the Ferengi and mankind is even established in the year 1947, when, due to a time anomaly, Quark has a shuttle crash-landing on Earth near Roswell and is captured by the U.S. military. This episode is a parody of the Roswell Incident. Here, it becomes apparent how much *Star Trek* playfully deals with events in our reality and even reinterprets a conspiracy theory about events that actually happened.

18. The Andorians are largely absent in the other *Star Trek* series, with only some minor appearances like in *TOS* "Journey to Babel" or *TNG* "Captain's Holiday." However, the species becomes more prominent in *DIS*.

19. On the other hand, Worland also sees a similarity of the Romulans with the Japanese and cites the self-destruction of the ship in *TOS* "Balance of Terror" as an argument: "Like thousands of Japanese soldiers in World War II acting in obedience to a strict code of honor in battle, the Romulons [sic] prefer suicide to surrender" (1988, 111). Richards, on the other hand, compares Klingons to barbarian tribes like the Germanic tribesmen and Romulans to the ancient Romans (1997, 25).

20. It should also be noted that with the launch of *TNG* in 1987, the events of *Star Trek VI: The Undiscovered Country* have not yet taken place in the series chronology, as the latter was not released until 1991. The audience was only told about the peace treaty between the Klingons and the Federation retroactively, while Worf had already been present in *TNG* for four years.

21. However, the actual cause of the destruction of the outposts is not explained in this episode or later. Given the destruction of another outpost in *TNG* "The Best of Both Worlds," it is reasonable to assume that the Borg have already entered Federation space undetected.

22. The hostility between Klingons and Romulans is further shown in *TNG* "The Enemy," when Worf is the only one on the ship available for a vital blood transfusion to an injured Romulan. While Worf rejects this with reference to the Khitomer Massacre, the Romulan also does not want "Klingon filth" in his blood.

23. The nature of this alliance is explained in *TNG* "Yesterday's Enterprise." The episode tells how the Federation came to the aid of the Klingons in a Romulan attack on Narendra III. The *Enterprise*-C was destroyed in this battle, a battle that was considered so honorable by the Klingon High Council that the alliance between the Klingon Empire and the Federation was intensified. In *Star Trek* chronology, the Battle of Narenda III occurs in 2344, roughly fifty years after the signing of the Khitomer Accords in 2293 (*Star Trek VI: The Undiscovered Country*).

It is also stated that Vulcan ambassador Sarek (*TNG* "Sarek") was instrumental in this treaty. With the Battle of Narendra III, the Klingon-Romulan relations were finally failing.

24. Aside from the cameo appearance of McCoy in *TNG* "Encounter at Farpoint," this is the first time in the *Star Trek* franchise that a character from another series has a major role in another. Later, it will become commonplace that characters appear throughout the entire *Star Trek* universe, as Captain Picard does in *DS9* "Emissary," Bashir in *TNG* "Birthright," Quark in *VOY* "Caretaker," Kathryn Janeway in *Star Trek: Insurrection* or Counselor Deanna Troi in *VOY* "Inside Man," *VOY* "Life Line," and *VOY* "Pathfinder." This shows how strongly the different series reference each other and that a common *Star Trek* universe does exist.

25. The *ENT* episode "These Are the Voyages...," which takes place at the same time as *TNG* "The Pegasus," also refers to the Treaty of Algeron and the breach of treaty by the Federation. Burston-Chorowicz compares the Treaty of Algeron to the various SALT treaties between the United States and the Soviet Union (2018, 16).

26. The Seldonis IV Convention is apparently an allusion to the Geneva Convention.

27. The name is a reminiscence of the French partisan movement in World War II.

28. For example, the Somali Civil War produced a largely failed state and the Unified Task Force intervention led by the United States war largely unsuccessful in 1993. The Yugoslav Wars also initially arose from internal conflicts.

29. "[...] In our pilot episode, the first stable wormhole is discovered near the Denorions asteroid field, close to the planet Bajor. [...] A brief journey through the Bajoran Wormhole will take a starship to the Gamma Quadrant... normally a sixty year journey at warp nine" (Berman and Piller 1992, 1–2).

30. The conflict between the Federation and the Maquis will be an ongoing issue in the *DS9* episodes "For the Cause," "For the Uniform," and "Blaze of Glory," in which numerous members of Starfleet engage in the Maquis and eventually threaten Starfleet.

31. Odo, who is Head of Security on *Deep Space Nine* is also a shapeshifter and usually takes on an almost human form. Whenever necessary, Odo (and also any other shapeshifters) may transform into any other object (like a chair, a picture, or a table) or even take the appearance of another humanoid species.

32. Wellmann, however, argues that the sole presence of the Federation in the Gamma Quadrant during exploring is a threat to the Dominion's territory from its point of view and thus an aggressive act (2009, 237–9). In doing so, however, he does not consider that the Dominion has a biased negative attitude towards other powers, regardless of their actions.

33. This is not an issue in *DS9* at first, but it is addressed later in the *VOY* episode "Message in a Bottle."

34. The existence of a civil rebel movement on Cardassia was addressed in *DS9* "Profit and Loss" and *DS9* "Second Skin."

35. Because of the Cardassian-Klingon war, the Maquis expand their power influence in the demilitarized zone between the Cardassian Union and the Federation, as the Cardassians have no resources to continue fighting the Maquis (*DS9* "For the Cause").

36. The *Star Trek* writers remarkably ignored the question whether there would also be a government of Earth that would be responsible for these cases. "We wanted to tell the story of an attempted military coup of the Federation and that meant dealing with the Fed[eration] president. However, that meant the troops 'in the streets' had to be on Earth and that Earth itself had to be under martial law since the Fed[eration] is headquartered on Earth. We discussed having the Prez [President] 'federalize' the Earth defense forces or supersede the authority of an indigenous Earth Govt [Government] [...]" (Moore 1997/1999, ron014.txt). This implies that the Earth is either sovereign, and sovereignty is here passed over by placing it under federal martial law, or that the Earth is directly administered by the Federation.

37. Chancellor Gowron says, in this context, that "our claim to Archanis IV and the surrounding territory is ancient and indisputable. We advise the Federation to leave Archanis or prepare to face

the consequences" (*DS9* "Broken Link"). Here, too, it shows how much *Star Trek* has emancipated itself from the actual premises of Gene Roddenberry, since he had originally excluded stories about war with the Klingons (1987, 11).

38. The Maquis are eventually defeated by the Cardassians with the help of the Dominion (*DS9* "Blaze of Glory").

39. Betazed is a well-known planet in the *Star Trek* universe as Counselor Deanna Troi and her mother, among others, originate from there.

40. During the Tonkin incident in August 1964, North Vietnamese ships allegedly fired on U.S. Navy ships without cause. President Lyndon B. Johnson took these incidents as an opportunity to officially enter into a war with North Vietnam. Only decades later it turned out that there had never been such attacks and that the presentation was only faked.

41. Despite the entry of the Romulans into the war on the Federation side, the relationship between the two powers seems to remain marked by mutual skepticism. A change in the relationship is only indicated at the end of *Star Trek: Nemesis*.

42. Apparently, the ship was named after the character from Victor Hugo's *Les Misérables*.

43. The episode takes place sometime after the events of *DS9* "The Search." So, the Dominion has already appeared as a new power in the *Star Trek* universe.

# Chapter 5

1. This chapter is partly based on a previously published work of mine (Stoppe 2011b).

2. The Pon Farr theme is taken up again in *VOY* "Blood Fever."

3. In fact, McCoy is merely using a trick to make Spock believe so.

4. However, the Federation has had contact with the Borg well before. In *ENT* "Regeneration," scientists on Earth come across some Borg drones frozen in the Arctic ice, which they reactivate—unaware of the danger they pose. The Borg assimilate the scientists and send a message to the Delta Quadrant. Captain Archer subsequently fears a Borg invasion of Earth: "Sounds to me like we have only postponed the invasion, until what... the 24th century?"—which is what is happening in *TNG* "Q Who." In addition, the Federation ship USS *Raven*, with two scientists on board, had been exploring the Borg years before the events in *TNG* "Q Who." However, since the scientists were assimilated together with their daughter, the child who becomes the drone Seven of Nine, their findings obviously never reached the Federation (*VOY* "Dark Frontier," *VOY* "The Raven").

5. In fact, there are both female and male Borg drones. Q's statement "not a he, not a she" could refer to the fact that neither sex nor gender have a meaning in Borg social structure.

6. The name of the species is also derived from the term "cyborg."

7. In *TNG* "Q Who," the first impression is that the Borg reproduce naturally, as Commander Riker finds a baby in a kind of children's ward. However, this also seems to be a maturation chamber.

8. Thus, in *TNG* "The Best of Both Worlds" Captain Picard, in *VOY* "Scorpion" the Borg drone Seven of Nine, and in *VOY* "Collective" several children are successfully re-assimilated, although in the latter some Borg implants cannot be removed without endangering health.

9. When the former Borg drone Seven of Nine joins *Voyager* in *VOY* "Scorpion," an alcove is set up for her in a cargo hold, because she must continue to regenerate due to the Borg implants remaining.

10. Richards interprets this as an expression of the Borg Collective: "Everything in a square is the product of equal factors. 'Square' also has a second meaning as a number raised to the second power. The Borg collective displays both elements of a square in a frightening way: it represents a collective composed of equal parts, containing no repeated dimensions, and it suggests the possibility of the rapid linear reproduction of those parts by an endless multiplying to the second power" (1997, 45). However, Richards confuses square with cube, which is the three-dimensional object bounded by square surfaces.

11. There is also a relationship with Commander William Riker and Counselor Deanna Troi that has ended earlier. However, in the later episodes of *TNG*,

Troi enters into a relationship with Worf, and in *Star Trek: Insurrection* her relationship with Riker is revived, which finally ends in the marriage in *Star Trek: Nemesis*. Worf also has a family relationship with his son Alexander in *TNG* and *DS9*.

12. In general, the Borg Collective can be compared to an insect colony in terms of structure and organization.

13. The quote has a striking similarity with the Bible text "I am the Alpha and the Omega, the First and the Last, the Beginning and the End" (Revelation 22:13).

14. Another possible explanation is given in *PIC* "The Impossible Box." Here Picard and Soji escape by using a spatial trajector, which is located in an area of the Borg ship called the queencell and is a kind of transporter that the Borg developed by assimilating the Sikarians. However, it is unclear whether this technology was already available to the Borg at the time of *TNG* "The Best of Both Worlds."

15. This process is similarly seen in *Star Trek: First Contact*, where main engineering of the *Enterprise* is the temporary central chamber of the Borg Queen.

16. Considering that in retrograde chronology the Borg already know about humanity on Earth (through their encounters in *ENT* "Regeneration" as well as the assimilation of the Hansen family in *VOY* "Dark Frontier"), it is very likely that the Borg drone not only analyzes the technical capabilities of the ship but also systematically searches the contents of the computer in order to match the Collective's already existing knowledge about humans.

17. In this respect, Picard's statement that humanity is no threat to the Borg ("we mean you no harm") ironically remains true.

18. The way the VISOR works is reminiscent of today's cochlear implants, which enable deaf people to hear.

19. Eventually, Janeway does exactly this by infecting the Borg Collective with a neurolytic pathogen in *VOY* "Endgame."

20. This designation, like the designation of Seven of Nine in *VOY*, shows that the Borg are organized in small groups within the Collective.

21. "Hugh" is a play on "you" because LaForge addresses the Borg, and it misunderstands the pronoun as a name.

22. "The One" strongly reminds of *The Island of Doctor Moreau*, where the Animal People also call Moreau that name.

23. In the episode it is said that only one in a million drones has this "malfunction," as it is called.

## Chapter 6

1. The *Kelvin* timeline is an alternative timeline that exists parallel to the Prime Reality, but Spock Prime as a time traveler no longer exists in this Prime Reality, because he remained in the *Kelvin* timeline.

2. As with the USS *Enterprise*, the name is an allusion to NASA's *Discovery* space shuttle. Apart from that, the name has also been used several times for ships in the Royal Navy, just as it was for the *Enterprise* (Rabitsch 2019, 85).

3. *TNG* already showed that not only male representatives may have influence among the Klingons with the Duras sisters Lursa and B'Etor, who become Picard's adversaries in the film *Star Trek: Generations*.

4. In fact, the spore drive engineer Paul Stamets is named after a real-life mycologist named Paul Stamets.

5. Tardigrades actually exist. They are only millimeter-sized animals, but they occur worldwide and can adapt to extreme living conditions. They can also apparently survive in space.

6. In this episode, direct reference is made to the events in *ENT* "In a Mirror, Darkly"—in which the USS *Defiant* (from the *TOS* episode "The Tholian Web," not to be confused with the USS *Defiant* from *DS9*)—entered the Mirror Universe and thus provided knowledge about the Prime Universe.

7. Later, when Major Kira and Bashir also arrive in the same Mirror Universe in *DS9* "Crossover," they discover that a Klingon-Cardassian alliance has finally overthrown the Terran Empire, the Bajorans are now the driving force in the *Deep Space Nine* sector, and the Terrans must serve as slaves.

8. In a subplot in the second and third seasons, it is shown that the Sphere data increasingly interacts with the computer of the USS *Discovery* and that the computer develops a kind of consciousness.

One possible result of this development is shown in *ST* "Calypso," where in a distant future a single human is rescued by the now unmanned USS *Discovery*, whose computer communicates as its own personality named Zora.

9. This plot twist allows the writers to remain consistent in *Star Trek* continuity. Thus, it can be retroactively explained why in *TOS* and later series neither the spore drive is known nor that a half-sister of Spock was ever mentioned.

10. Another reference can be seen in the deep-space probe from Earth in *Star Trek: The Motion Picture* which gains its own artificial intelligence and poses a threat to its home planet (Booker 2018, 106).

11. This fact harkens back to the common origin of both species and the events in *TNG* "Unification," in which Spock initiates a rapprochement between the two species.

12. It is to be considered that the warp drive is the essential feature for *Star Trek* for a first contact with other species. This shows the immense importance of this technology.

13. It should also be noted that the actor themselves, Blu de Barrio, identifies as non-binary and the character of the former Trill host Gray Tal is played by a transmasculine actor. Both are consistent with the nature of Trill symbionts, which can have hosts of different genders in the course of their existence, which is also addressed in the case of Dax in *DS9* "Rejoined" (Stoppe 2019, 67–8).

14. In *DIS* "Die Trying," for example, one can observe the USS *Voyager*-J in this design, which is also a reference to *VOY* itself. In the same episode, one can also see a successor to the USS *Reliant* (from *Star Trek II: The Wrath of Khan*) and the USS *Nog* (alluding to the Ferengi character from *DS9*).

15. That Hugh reappears as an xB in *PIC* and is the leader of this rehabilitation project is also a continuation of a story arc from *TNG* "I Borg" and "Descent." At the end of the latter episode, Hugh said that "we cannot go back to the Borg Collective and we no longer have a leader here," to which Picard replies that he is not sure about that. Apparently, Hugh already took a leadership role then and led the Borg who were separated from the Collective.

16. The character of Altan Inigo Soong is played by Brent Spiner, who also played Noonien Soong in *TNG* as well as his ancestor Arik Soong in *ENT*.

17. Picard visits Riker and Troi in their lodge on the planet Nepenthe, where both have retired (*PIC* "Nepenthe"). Riker comes to Picard's assistance as Acting Captain of the USS *Zheng He* during the final conflict in *PIC* "Et in Arcadia Ego." Both Riker and Troi also make cameo appearances in *LD* "No Small Parts."

# Works Cited

Alcubierre, Miguel. 1994. "The Warp Drive: Hyper-Fast Travel Within General Relativity." *Classical and Quantum Gravity* 11: L73-L77.

Alpers, Hans Joachim. 1972. "Verne und Wells—Zwei Pioniere der Science Fiction?" In *Science Fiction: Theorie und Geschichte*, edited by Eike Barmeyer, 244–58. München: Fink.

Bacon, Francis. 2009. *The New Atlantis*. Auckland: The Floating Press.

Barad, Judith A. 2001. *The Ethics of Star Trek*. New York: HarperCollins.

Batzke, Ina. 2020. "From Series to Seriality: Star Trek's Mirror Universe in the Post-Network Era." In *Fighting for the Future: Essays on Star Trek: Discovery*, edited by Sabrina Mittermeier and Mareike Spychala, 105–26. Liverpool: Liverpool University Press.

Becker, Gregor. 2000. *Star Trek und Philosophie: Die edleren Seiten unseres Wesens; philosophische Aspekte einer Kultserie*. Marburg: Tectum.

Becker, Siegfried, and Gerd Hallenberger. 1993. "Konjunkturen des Phantastischen: Anmerkungen zu den Karrieren von Science Fiction, Fantasy und Märchen sowie verwandten Formen." *Zeitschrift für Literaturwissenschaft und Linguistik* 23 (92): 141–55.

Behr, Ira Steven. 1997. "AOL Chat." Accessed April 30, 2021. http://en.memory-alpha.org/wiki/Memory_Alpha:AOL_chats/Ira_Steven_Behr.

Berman, Rick, and Michael Piller. 1992. "Star Trek: Deep Space Nine: Bible." Unpublished manuscript.

Bernardi, Daniel. 1994. "Infinite Diversity in Infinite Combinations: Diegetic Logics and Racial Articulations in the Original Star Trek." *Film and History* 24 (1/2): 60–74.

Bhelkar, Ratnakar D. 2009. *Science Fiction: Fantasy and Reality*. New Delhi: Atlantic Publishers & Distributors.

Biesterfeld, Wolfgang. 1982. *Die literarische Utopie*. Stuttgart: Metzler.

Booker, M. Keith. 2018. *Star Trek: A Cultural History*. Lanham, MD: Rowman & Littlefield.

Boyd, Katrina G. 1996. "Cyborgs in Utopia: The Problem of Radical Difference in Star Trek: The Next Generation." In *Enterprise Zones: Critical Positions on Star Trek*, edited by Taylor Harrison, Sarah Projansky, Kent A. Ono, and Elyce R. Helford, 95–113. Boulder, CO: Westview Press.

Braine, F.S. 1994. "Technological Utopias: The Future of the Next Generation." *Film and History* 24 (1/2): 1–18.

Burston-Chorowicz, Alex. 2018. "Engage! Captain Picard, Federationism and U.S. Foreign Policy in the Emerging Post-Cold War World." In *Exploring Picard's Galaxy: Essays on Star Trek: The Next Generation*, edited by Peter W. Lee, 7–22. Jefferson, NC: McFarland.

Burston-Chorowicz, Alex. 2020. "Lost in Space Without an Idea of Home: The Triumph of Neoliberal Depoliticization in Star Trek: Voyager." In *Exploring Star Trek: Voyager: Critical Essays*, edited by Robert L. Lively, 231–47. Jefferson, NC: McFarland.

Buzan, Barry. 2010. "America in Space: The International Relations of Star Trek and Battlestar Galactica." *Millennium: Journal of International Studies* 39 (1): 175–80.

Byrne, Aidan, and Mark Jones. 2018.

"Worlds Turned Back to Front: The Politics of the Mirror Universe in Doctor Who and Star Trek." *Journal of Popular Television* 6 (2): 257–70.

Campanella, Tommaso. 2009. *The City of the Sun: A Poetical Dialogue Between a Grandmaster of the Knights Hospitallers and a Genoese Sea-Captain, His Guest*. Auckland: The Floating Press.

Canavan, Gerry. 2016. "Star Trek at 50, Or, Star Trek Beyond Star Trek." *Science Fiction Film and Television* 9 (3): 319–24.

Coenen, Christopher. 2009. "Transhumanismus und Utopie: Ein Abgrenzungsversuch aus aktuellem Anlass." In *Neue Utopien: Zum Wandel eines Genres*, edited by Rolf Steltemeier, Sascha Dickel, Sandro Gaycken, and Tobias Knobloch. Heidelberg: Manutius.

Decker, Kevin S. 2008. "Inhuman Nature, or What's It Like to Be a Borg?" In *Star Trek and Philosophy: The Wrath of Kant*, edited by Jason T. Eberl and Kevin S. Decker, 131–46. Chicago, IL: Open Court.

Dinello, Dan. 2016. "The Borg as Contagious Collectivist Techno-Totalitarian Transhumanists." In *The Ultimate Star Trek and Philosophy: The Search for Socrates*, edited by Jason T. Eberl and Kevin S. Decker, 83–94. Malden, MA: Wiley.

Finazzi, Stefano, Stefano Liberati, and Carlos Barceló. 2009. "Semiclassical Instability of Dynamical Warp Drives." *Physical Review D* 79 (12): 124017.

Fitting, Peter. 2000. "Estranged Invaders: The War of the Worlds." In *Learning from Other Worlds: Estrangement, Cognition and the Politics of Science Fiction and Utopia*, edited by Patrick Parrinder, 125–45. Liverpool: Liverpool University Press.

Flam, Helena. 2002. *Soziologie der Emotionen*. Konstanz: UVK.

Fontana, D. C. 2006. "I Remember Star Trek...." In *Boarding the Enterprise: Transporters, Tribbles and the Vulcan Death Grip in Gene Roddenberry's Star Trek*, edited by David Gerrold and Robert J. Sawyer, 33–39. Dallas, TX: BenBella Books.

Foucault, Michel. 1998. *Aesthetics, Method, and Epistemology*. New York: New Press.

Franklin, H. Bruce. 1994. "'Star Trek' in the Vietnam Era." *Film and History* 24 (1/2): 36–46.

Freedman, Carl. 2000. "Science Fiction and Utopia: A Historico-Philosophical Overview." In *Learning from Other Worlds: Estrangement, Cognition and the Politics of Science Fiction and Utopia*, edited by Patrick Parrinder, 72–97. Liverpool: Liverpool University Press.

Freyer, Hans. 1936. *Die politische Insel: Eine Geschichte der Utopien von Platon bis zur Gegenwart*. Leipzig: Bibliographisches Institut.

Fricke, Dietmar. 2000. "Raumschiff Voyager: Das Verhältnis zwischen Föderation und Borg als interkultureller Diskurs?" In *Zukunft im Film: Sozialwissenschaftliche Studie zu "Star Trek" und anderer Science-fiction*, edited by Frank Hörnlein and Herbert Heinecke, 119–32. Magdeburg: Scriptum.

Fuhse, Jan A. 2003. "Das Andere der Gesellschaft—Science-Fiction als Kritische Theorie." *Soziale Welt* (54): 223–40.

Fuhse, Jan A. 2008. "Einleitung: Science Fiction als ästhetisches Versuchslabor der Gesellschaft." In *Technik und Gesellschaft in der Science Fiction*, edited by Jan A. Fuhse, 6–18. Berlin: Lit.

Georgi-Findlay, Brigitte. 2019. "Amerikanische Befindlichkeiten in Star Trek: Discovery." In *Star Trek: Discovery: Gesellschaftsvisionen für die Gegenwart*, edited by Katja Kanzler and Christian Schwarke, 9–26. Wiesbaden: Springer.

Gnüg, Hiltrud. 1999. *Utopie und utopischer Roman*. Stuttgart: Reclam.

Göll, Edgar. 1997. "Über das Fehlen von Utopie: Politik in Star Trek." *Vorgänge* 36 (2): 35–45.

Götz, Holger. 2000. *Star Trek—The Next Generation als Paradigma konservativer Kulturkritik*. München: Grin.

Grech, Victor. 2016. "Klingons: A Cultural Pastiche." In *The Ultimate Star Trek and Philosophy: The Search for Socrates*, edited by Jason T. Eberl and Kevin S. Decker, 71–82. Malden, MA: Wiley.

Gregory, Chris. 2000. *Star Trek: Parallel Narratives*. New York: St. Martin's Press.

Gross, Edward, and Mark A. Altman. 2016. *The Fifty-Year Mission: The Complete, Uncensored, Unauthorized Oral History of Star Trek*. New York: St. Martin's Press.

Hark, Ina Rae. 2008. *Star Trek*. Basingstoke: Palgrave Macmillan.

Harrison, Taylor. 1996. "Weaving the Cyborg Shroud: Mourning and Deferral in Star Trek: The Next Generation." In *Enterprise Zones: Critical Positions on Star Trek*, edited by Taylor Harrison, Sarah Projansky, Kent A. Ono, and Elyce R. Helford, 245–57. Boulder, CO: Westview Press.

Hawking, Stephen W. 2001. *The Universe in a Nutshell*. New York: Bantam Books.

Heinecke, Herbert. 2009. "Von der Außenpolitik der Föderation und interplanetarischen Tempolimits: Politikwissenschaftliche Perspektiven auf STAR TREK." In *Faszinierend! Star Trek und die Wissenschaften*, edited by Nina Rogotzki, Thomas Richter, Helga Brandt, Petra Friedrich, Mathias Schönhoff, and Paul M. Hahlbohm, 159–76. Kiel: Ludwig.

Hellmann, Kai-Uwe. 1997. "'Sie müssen lernen, das Unerwartete zu erwarten.': Star Trek als Utopie der Menschwerdung?" In *"Unendliche Weiten…": Star Trek zwischen Unterhaltung und Utopie*, edited by Kai-Uwe Hellmann and Arne Klein, 91–111. Frankfurt am Main: Fischer.

Hellmann, Kai-Uwe. 2000. "Auf der Suche nach der verlorengegangenen Gewißheit: Star Trek oder das Abenteuer des Kulturvergleichs." In *Zukunft im Film: Sozialwissenschaftliche Studie zu "Star Trek" und anderer Science-fiction*, edited by Frank Hörnlein and Herbert Heinecke, 133–41. Magdeburg: Scriptum.

Heyer, Andreas. 2005. *Studien zur politischen Utopie: Theoretische Reflexionen und ideengeschichtliche Annäherungen*. Hamburg: Kovac.

Hobbes, Thomas. 1996. *Leviathan*. Cambridge: Cambridge University Press.

Jameson, Fredric. 1982. "Progress Versus Utopia; Or, Can We Imagine the Future?" *Science-Fiction Studies* 9: 147–58.

Jenkis, Helmut Walter. 1992. *Sozialutopien—barbarische Glücksverheißungen? Zur Geistesgeschichte der Idee von der vollkommenen Gesellschaft*. Berlin: Duncker & Humblot.

Johnson, David Kyle. 2016. "Destroying Utopias: Why Kirk Is a Jerk." In *The Ultimate Star Trek and Philosophy: The Search for Socrates*, edited by Jason T. Eberl and Kevin S. Decker, 47–58. Malden, MA: Wiley.

Jones, Norma. 2015. "Rebooting Utopia: Remaging Star Trek in Post-9/11 America." In *The Star Trek Universe: Franchising the Final Frontier*, edited by Douglas Brode and Shea T. Brode, 185–95. Lanham, MD: Rowman & Littlefield.

Joseph, Paul, and Sharon Catton. 2003. "The Law of the Federation: Images of Law, Lawyers, and the Legal System in Star Trek: The Next Generation." In *Star Trek Visions of Law and Justice*, edited by Robert H. Chaires and Bradley S. Chilton, 26–72. Dallas, TX: Adios Press.

Kapell, Matthew, and Ace G. Pilkington. 2019. "Introduction: Toward a 'Many Texts' Theory of the Star Trek Multiverse." In *The Kelvin Timeline of Star Trek: Essays on J.J. Abrams' Final Frontier*, edited by Matthew Kapell and Ace G. Pilkington, 1–11. Jefferson, NC: McFarland.

Lagon, Mark P. 1997. "'We Owe It to Them to Interfere': Star Trek and U.S. Statecraft in the 1960s and the 1990s." In *Political Science Fiction*, edited by Donald M. Hassler and Clyde Wilcox, 234–50. Columbia, SC: University of South Carolina Press.

Levitas, Ruth. 2011. *The Concept of Utopia*. Oxford: Peter Lang.

Levitas, Ruth. 2013. *Utopia as Method: The Imaginary Reconstitution of Society*. Basingstoke: Palgrave Macmillan.

Manuel, Paul Christopher. 1997. "'In Every Revolution, There Is One Man with a Vision': The Governments of the Future in Comparative Perspective." In *Political Science Fiction*, edited by Donald M. Hassler and Clyde Wilcox, 183–95. Columbia, SC: University of South Carolina Press.

McLuhan, Marshall. 2010. *Understanding Media: The Extensions of Man*. London: Routledge.

McMonigal, Brendan, Geraint F. Lewis, and Philip O'Byrne. 2012. "Alcubierre Warp Drive: On the Matter of Matter." *Physical Review D* 85 (6).

McVeigh, Stephen. 2010. "The Kirk Doctrine: The Care and Repair of Archetypal Heroic Leadership in J.J. Abrams' Star Trek." In *Star Trek as Myth: Essays on Symbol and Archetype at the Final Frontier*, edited by Matthew W. Kapell, 197–212. Jefferson, NC: McFarland.

# Works Cited

Moore, Ronald D. 1997–1999. "AOL Chat." Accessed April 30, 2021. http://en.memory-alpha.org/wiki/Memory_Alpha:AOL_chats/Ronald_D._Moore.

More, Thomas. 2002. *Utopia*. Cambridge: Cambridge University Press.

Moylan, Tom. 2021. *Becoming Utopian: The Culture and Politics of Radical Transformation*. London: Bloomsbury.

Natário, José. 2002. "Warp Drive with Zero Expansion." *Classical and Quantum Gravity* 19: 1157–65.

Nichols, Peter, and John Brosnan. 1993. "Star Trek." In *The Encyclopedia of Science Fiction*, edited by John Clute and Peter Nichols, 1156–58. London: Orbit.

Ohler, Peter, and Gerd Strohmeier. 2009. "Konzeptionen der Lebenswelt in STAR TREK: Politikwissenschaftliche und psychologische Analysen." In *Faszinierend! Star Trek und die Wissenschaften*, edited by Nina Rogotzki, Thomas Richter, Helga Brandt, Petra Friedrich, Mathias Schönhoff, and Paul M. Hahlbohm, 177–201. Kiel: Ludwig.

Okuda, Michael, and Denise Okuda. 1999. *The Star Trek Encyclopedia: A Reference Guide to the Future*. New York: Pocket Books.

Orth, Dominik. 2008. "Mediale Zukunft—Die Erreichbarkeit des (Anti-)Utopischen." *Medienobservationen*. http://www.medienobservationen.lmu.de/artikel/kino/kino_pdf/orth_zukunft.pdf. Accessed April 30, 2021.

Ott, Brian L., and Eric Aoki. 2001. "Popular Imagination and Identity Politics: Reading the Future in 'Star Trek: The Next Generation.'" *Western Journal of Communication* 65 (4): 392–415.

Pabst, Eckhard. 2003. "Raum—Schiff—Architektur: Raumschiffe als Organisationspunkte unendlicher Weiten." In *Faszinierend! Star Trek und die Wissenschaften*, edited by Nina Rogotzki, Thomas Richter, Helga Brandt, Petra Friedrich, Mathias Schönhoff, and Paul M. Hahlbohm, 85–117. Kiel: Ludwig.

Pintér, Károly. 2010. *The Anatomy of Utopia: Narration, Estrangement and Ambiguity in More, Wells, Huxley and Clarke*. Jefferson, NC: McFarland.

Putman, John. 2013. "Terrorizing Space: Star Trek, Terrorism, and History." In *Star Trek and History*, edited by Nancy R. Reagin, 143–57. Hoboken, NJ: Wiley.

Rabitsch, Stefan. 2019. *Star Trek and the British Age of Sail: The Maritime Influence Throughout the Series and Films*. Jefferson, NC: McFarland.

Rauscher, Andreas. 2003. *Das Phänomen Star Trek: Virtuelle Räume und metaphorische Weiten*. Mainz: Ventil.

Richards, Thomas. 1997. *The Meaning of Star Trek: An Excursion into the Myth and Marvel of the Star Trek Universe*. New York Doubleday.

Robb, Brian J. 2012. *A Brief Guide to Star Trek*. Philadelphia, PA: Robinson.

Roberts, Adam. 2000. *Science Fiction*. London: Routledge.

Roddenberry, Gene. 1967. "The Star Trek Guide." Third Revision. Unpublished manuscript.

Roddenberry, Gene. 1987. "Star Trek: The Next Generation Writer/Director's Guide." Unpublished manuscript.

Saage, Richard. 1989. *Vertragsdenken und Utopie: Studien zur politischen Theorie und zur Sozialphilosophie der frühen Neuzeit*. Frankfurt am Main: Suhrkamp.

Saage, Richard. 1991. *Politische Utopien der Neuzeit*. Darmstadt: Wiss. Buchges.

Saage, Richard. 1997. "Utopie und Science-Fiction: Versuch einer Begriffsbestimmung." In *"Unendliche Weiten...": Star Trek zwischen Unterhaltung und Utopie*, edited by Kai-Uwe Hellmann and Arne Klein, 45–58. Frankfurt am Main: Fischer.

Saage, Richard. 2001. *Utopische Profile Band I: Renaissance und Reformation*. Münster: Lit.

Saage, Richard. 2006a. "Konvergenztechnologische Zukunftsvisionen und der klassische Utopiediskurs." In *Nanotechnologien im Kontext: Philosophische, ethische und gesellschaftliche Perspektiven*, edited by Alfred Nordmann, Joachim Schummer, and Astrid Schwarz, 179–94. Berlin: Akad. Verl.-Ges.

Saage, Richard. 2006b. "Morus' 'Utopia' und die Macht: Zu Hermann Onckens und Gerhard Ritters Utopia-Interpretationen." *UTOPIE kreativ* (183): 37–47.

Sarantakes, Nicholas Evan. 2005. "Cold War Pop Culture and the Image of U.S. Foreign Policy: The Perspective of the Original Star Trek Series." *Journal of Cold War Studies* 7 (4): 74–103.

Schillinger, Henrik, and Arne Sönnichsen. 2020. "The American Hello: Representations of U.S. Diplomacy in Star Trek: Discovery." In *Fighting for the Future: Essays on Star Trek: Discovery*, edited by Sabrina Mittermeier and Mareike Spychala, 221–42. Liverpool: Liverpool University Press.

Schröder, Torben. 1998. *Science Fiction als Social Fiction: Das gesellschaftliche Potential eines Unterhaltungsgenres*. Münster: Lit.

Schröter, Jens. 2009. "Das Holodeck: Phantasma des ultimativen Displays." In *Faszinierend! Star Trek und die Wissenschaften*, edited by Nina Rogotzki, Thomas Richter, Helga Brandt, Petra Friedrich, Mathias Schönhoff, and Paul M. Hahlbohm, 105–30. Kiel: Ludwig.

Schwarke, Christian. 2019. "Star Trek und der Traum von der Allgegenwart: Technik und die Realisierung von Utopien." In *Star Trek: Discovery: Gesellschaftsvisionen für die Gegenwart*, edited by Katja Kanzler and Christian Schwarke, 49–65. Wiesbaden: Springer.

Schwonke, Martin. 1957. *Vom Staatsroman zur Science Fiction: Eine Untersuchung über Geschichte und Funktion der naturwissenschaftlich-technischen Utopie*. Stuttgart: Ferdinand Enke Verlag.

Schwonke, Martin. 1972. "Naturwissenschaft und Technik im utopischen Denken der Neuzeit." In *Science Fiction: Theorie und Geschichte*, edited by Eike Barmeyer, 57–75. München: Fink.

Seeßlen, Georg, and Fernand Jung. 2003. *Science Fiction: Geschichte und Mythologie des Science-Fiction-Fiction*. Grundlagen des populären Films. Marburg: Schüren.

Solow, Herbert F., and Robert H. Justman. 1996. *Inside Star Trek: The Real Story*. New York: Pocket Books.

Spreen, Dierk. 1997. "Was ver-spricht der Cyborg?" *Ästhetik & Kommunikation* 26 (96): 86–94.

Spreen, Dierk. 2008. "Kulturelle Funktionen der Science Fiction." In *Technik und Gesellschaft in der Science Fiction*, edited by Jan A. Fuhse, 19–33. Berlin: Lit.

Steinmüller, Karlheinz. 1997. "Beinahe eine sozialistische Utopie: USS Enterprise: Heimathafen DDR?" In *"Unendliche Weiten...": Star Trek zwischen Unterhaltung und Utopie*, edited by Kai-Uwe Hellmann and Arne Klein, 80–90. Frankfurt am Main: Fischer.

Steinmüller, Karlheinz. 2010. "Science Fiction: eine Quelle von Leitbildern für Innovationsprozesse und ein Impulsgeber für Foresight." In *Foresight—Between Science and Fiction*, edited by Kalle Hauss, Saskia Ulrich, and Stefan Hornbostel, 19–31. iFQ-Working Paper 7. Bonn.

Sternbach, Rick, and Michael Okuda. 1991. *Star Trek, the Next Generation: Technical Manual*. London: Boxtree.

Sternbach, Rick. 1996. *Star Trek, the Next Generation: U.S.S. Enterprise NCC-1701-D Blueprints*. New York: Pocket Books.

Stock, Barbara. 2016. "Assimilation and Autonomy." In *The Ultimate Star Trek and Philosophy: The Search for Socrates*, edited by Jason T. Eberl and Kevin S. Decker, 95–104. Malden, MA: Wiley.

Stoppe, Sebastian. 2008. "'Tee, Earl Grey, heiß.': Star Trek und die technisierte Gesellschaft." In *Technik und Gesellschaft in der Science Fiction*, edited by Jan A. Fuhse, 94–111. Berlin: Lit.

Stoppe, Sebastian. 2011a. "Ein perfekter Ort? Das utopische Element des Raumschiffs in Star Trek." In *Medienorte: Mise-en-scènes in alten und neuen Medien*, edited by Judith Kretzschmar, Markus Schubert, and Sebastian Stoppe, 19–35. München: Meidenbauer.

Stoppe, Sebastian. 2011b. "Ein transhumanistischer Leviathan? Die Borg als emotionslose Dystopie in Star Trek." *Arbeitstitel—Forum für Leipziger Promovierende* 3 (2): 69–82.

Stoppe, Sebastian. 2016. "Getting Immersed in Star Trek: Storytelling Between 'True' and 'False' on the Holodeck." *SFRA Review* (316): 4–15.

Stoppe, Sebastian. 2019. "Borg, Trills und weibliche Captains: Geschlechterkonzepte und Gender bei Star Trek." In *Wer ist dieser Herr Gender? Interdisziplinäre Antworten auf die alltägliche Bedeutung von Geschlecht*, edited by Georg Teichert, 53–74. Leipzig: Leipziger Universitätsverlag.

Suvin, Darko. 1972. "Zur Poetik des

literarischen Genres Science Fiction." In *Science Fiction: Theorie und Geschichte*, edited by Eike Barmeyer, 86–105. München: Fink.

Tyrrell, William Blake. 1977. "'Star Trek' as Myth and Television as Mythmaker." *Journal of Popular Culture* 10 (4): 711–9.

Tyrrell, William Blake. 1979. "'Star Trek's' Myth of Science." *Journal of American Culture* 2 (2): 288–96.

Van Den Broeck, Chris. 1999. "A 'Warp Drive' with More Reasonable Total Energy Requirements." *Classical and Quantum Gravity* 16: 3973–79.

Wagner, Jon G., and Jan Lundeen. 1998. *Deep Space and Sacred Time: Star Trek in the American Mythos*. Westport, CT: Praeger.

Weber, Ingrid. 1997. *Unendliche Weiten: Die Science-Fiction-Serie Star Trek als Entwurf von Kontakten mit dem Fremden*. Frankfurt/M.: IKO-Verl. für Interkulturelle Kommunikation.

Weber, Karsten. 2008. "Roboter und Künstliche Intelligenz in Science Fiction-Filmen: Vom Werkzeug zum Akteur." In *Technik und Gesellschaft in der Science Fiction*, edited by Jan A. Fuhse, 34–54. Berlin: Lit.

Weldes, Jutta. 1999. "Going Cultural: Star Trek, State Action, and Popular Culture." *Millennium: Journal of International Studies* 28 (1): 117–34.

Wellmann, Arend. 1999. "Bedingungen des Friedens und die Wirklichkeit der Föderation: Zur friedenswissenschaftlichen Analyse eines utopischen Universums." In *Für eine lebendige Wissenschaft des Politischen: Umweg als Methode*, edited by Thomas Greven and Oliver Jarasch, 166–81. Frankfurt am Main: Suhrkamp.

Wellmann, Arend. 2009. "Bedingungen des Friedens und die Wirklichkeit der Föderation." In *Faszinierend! Star Trek und die Wissenschaften*, edited by Nina Rogotzki, Thomas Richter, Helga Brandt, Petra Friedrich, Mathias Schönhoff, and Paul M. Hahlbohm, 223–43. Kiel: Ludwig.

Wells, H. G. 1988. *The Island of Dr. Moreau*. New York, Scarborough: New American Library.

Whitacre, Andrea. 2020. "Looking in the Mirror: The Negotiation of Franchise Identity in Star Trek: Discovery." In *Fighting for the Future: Essays on Star Trek: Discovery*, edited by Sabrina Mittermeier and Mareike Spychala, 21–40. Liverpool: Liverpool University Press.

Whybrew, Si Sophie Pages. 2020. "'I Never Met a Female Michael Before': Star Trek: Discovery Between Trans Potentiality and Cis Anxiety." In *Fighting for the Future: Essays on Star Trek: Discovery*, edited by Sabrina Mittermeier and Mareike Spychala, 351–72. Liverpool: Liverpool University Press.

Worland, Rick. 1988. "Captain Kirk: Cold Warrior." *Journal of Popular Film and Television* 16 (3): 109–17.

Worland, Rick. 1994. "From the New Frontier to the Final Frontier: 'Star Trek' from Kennedy to Gorbachev." *Film and History* 24 (1/2): 19.

Yorke, Christopher. 2004. "The Normative Role of Utopianism in Political Philosophy." *New Thinking* II (1): 1–19.

Zimmerman, Hermann, Rick Sternbach, and Doug Drexler. 1998. *Star Trek—Deep Space Nine: Technical Manual*. New York: Pocket Books.

# Episodes and Films Cited

## Star Trek: The Original Series (1966–1969)

"Amok Time." Written by Theodore Sturgeon. Directed by Joseph Pevney. S2E1, 15 September 1967.

"The Apple." Written by Max Ehrlich. Directed by Joseph Pevney. S2E5, 13 October 1967.

"Balance of Terror." Written by Paul Schneider. Directed by Vincent McEveety. S1E14, 15 December 1966.

"Charlie X." Teleplay by D. C. Fontana. Story by Gene Roddenberry. Directed by Lawrence Dobkin. S1E2, 15 September 1966.

"The Cloud Minders." Teleplay by Margaret Armen. Story by David Gerrold, Oliver Crawford. Directed by Jud Taylor. S3E21, 28 February 1969.

"The Conscience of the King." Written by Barry Trivers. Directed by Gerd Oswald. S1E13, 8 December 1966.

"Court Martial." Teleplay by Don M. Mankiewicz. Story by Don M. Mankiewicz, Stephen W. Carabatsos.

Directed by Marc Daniels. S1E20, 2 February 1967.
"The Enterprise Incident." Written by D. C. Fontana. Directed by John Meredyth Lucas. S3E2, 27 September 1968.
"Errand of Mercy." Written by Gene L. Coon. Directed by John Newland. S1E26, 23 March 1967.
"Friday's Child." Written by D. C. Fontana. Directed by Joseph Pevney. S2E11, 1 December 1967.
"Journey to Babel." Written by D. C. Fontana. Directed by Joseph Pevney. S2E10, 17 November 1967.
"Mirror, Mirror." Written by Jerome Bixby. Directed by Marc Daniels. S2E4, 6 October 1967.
"The Omega Glory." Written by Gene Roddenberry. Directed by Vincent McEveety. S2E23, 1 March 1968.
"A Private Little War." Teleplay by Gene Roddenberry. Story by Jud Crucis. Directed by Marc Daniels. S2E19, 2 February 1968.
"The Return of the Archons." Teleplay by Boris Sobelman. Story by Gene Roddenberry. Directed by Joseph Pevney. S1E21, 9 February 1967.
"Space Seed." Teleplay by Gene L. Coon, Carey Wilber. Story by Carey Wilber. Directed by Marc Daniels. S1E22, 16 February 1967.
"A Taste of Armageddon." Teleplay by Gene L. Coon, Robert Hammer. Story by Robert Hammer. Directed by Joseph Pevney. S1E23, 23 February 1967.
"The Trouble with Tribbles." Written by David Gerrold. Directed by Joseph Pevney. S2E15, 29 December 1967.
"The Ultimate Computer." Teleplay by D. C. Fontana. Story by Laurence N. Wolf. Directed by John Meredyth Lucas. S2E24, 8 March 1968.

## Star Trek: The Next Generation (1987–1994)

"Angel One." Written by Patrick Barry. Directed by Michael Ray Rhodes. S1E14, 25 January 1988.
"The Arsenal of Freedom." Teleplay by Richard Manning, Hans Beimler. Story by Maurice Hurley, Robert Lewin. Directed by Les Landau. S1E21, 11 April 1988.
"The Best of Both Worlds." Written by Michael Piller. Directed by Cliff Bole. S3E24/S4E1, 18 June 1990/24 September 1990.
"The Big Goodbye." Written by Tracy Tormé. Directed by Joseph L. Scanlan. S1E12, 11 January 1988.
"Birthright." Part 1: Written by Brannon Braga. Directed by Winrich Kolbe. Part 2: Written by René Echevarria. Directed by Dan Curry. S6E16/17, 22 February 1993/1 March 1993.
"Booby Trap." Teleplay by Ron Roman, Michael Piller, Richard Danus. Story by Michael Wagner, Ron Roman. Directed by Gabrielle Beaumont. S3E6, 30 October 1989.
"Brothers." Written by Rick Berman. Directed by Rob Bowman. S4E3, 8 October 1990.
"Captain's Holiday." Written by Ira Steven Behr. Directed by Chip Chalmers. S3E19, 15 April 1990.
"Cause and Effect." Written by Brannon Braga. Directed by Jonathan Frakes. S5E18, 23 March 1992.
"Chain of Command." Part 1: Teleplay by Ronald D. Moore. Story by Frank Abatemarco. Directed by Robert Scheerer. Part 2: Written by Frank Abatemarco. Directed by Les Landau. S6E10/11, 14 December 1992/21 December 1992.
"The Child." Written by Jaron Summers, Jon Povill, Maurice Hurley. Directed by Rob Bowman. S2E1, 21 November 1988.
"Coming of Age." Written by Sandy Fries. Directed by Mike Vejar. S1E19, 14 March 1988.
"Conundrum." Teleplay by Barry Schkolnick. Story by Paul Schiffer. Directed by Les Landau. S5E14, 17 February 1992.
"Dark Page." Written by Hilary J. Bader. Directed by Les Landau. S7E7, 30 October 1993.
"Datalore." Teleplay by Robert Lewin, Gene Roddenberry. Story by Robert Lewin, Maurice Hurley. Directed by Rob Bowman. S1E13, 18 January 1988.
"Data's Day." Teleplay by Harold Apter. Story by Harold Apter, Ronald D. Moore. Directed by Robert Wiemer. S4E11, 7 January 1991.
"The Defector." Written by Ronald D. Moore. Directed by Robert Scheerer. S3E10, 1 January 1990.
"Descent." Part 1: Teleplay by Ronald D. Moore. Story by Jeri Taylor. Part 2:

Written by René Echevarria. Directed by Alexander Singer. S6E26/S7E1, 21 June 1993/20 September 1993.

"Disaster." Teleplay by Ronald D. Moore. Story by Ron Jarvis, Philip A. Scorza. Directed by Gabrielle Beaumont. S5E5, 21 October 1991.

"The Drumhead." Written by Jeri Taylor. Directed by Jonathan Frakes. S4E21, 29 April 1991.

"Elementary, Dear Data." Written by Brian Alan Lane. Directed by Rob Bowman. S2E3, 5 December 1988.

"11001001." Written by Maurice Hurley, Robert Lewin. Directed by Paul Lynch. S1E15, 1 February 1988.

"Encounter at Farpoint." Written by D. C. Fontana, Gene Roddenberry. Directed by Corey Allen. S1E1/2, 28 September 1987.

"The Enemy." Written by David Kemper, Michael Piller. Directed by David Carson. S3E7, 6 November 1989.

"Ensign Ro." Teleplay by Michael Piller. Story by Michael Piller, Rick Berman. Directed by Les Landau. S5E3, 21 October 1991.

"Ethics." Teleplay by Ronald D. Moore. Story by Sara B. Cooper, Stuart Charno. Directed by Chip Chalmers. S5E16, 2 March 1992.

"Face of the Enemy." Teleplay by Naren Shankar. Story by René Echevarria. Directed by Gabrielle Beaumont. S6E14, 8 February 1993.

"Family." Written by Ronald D. Moore. Directed by Les Landau. S4E2, 1 October 1990.

"First Contact." Teleplay by Dennis Russell Bailey, David Bischoff, Joe Menosky, Ronald D. Moore, Michael Piller. Story by Marc Scott Zicree. Directed by Cliff Bole. S4E15, 18 February 1991.

"The First Duty." Written by Ronald D. Moore, Naren Shankar. Directed by Paul Lynch. S5E19, 30 March 1992.

"A Fistful of Datas." Teleplay by Robert Hewitt Wolfe, Brannon Braga. Story by Robert Hewitt Wolfe. Directed by Patrick Stewart. S6E8, 9 November 1992.

"Force of Nature." Written by Naren Shankar. Directed by Robert Lederman. S7E9, 15 October 1993.

"Frame of Mind." Written by Brannon Braga. Directed by James L. Conway. S6E21, 3 May 1993.

"Gambit." Part 1: Teleplay by Naren Shankar. Story by Naren Shankar, Christopher Hatton. Directed by Peter Lauritson. Part 2: Teleplay by Ronald D. Moore. Story by Naren Shankar. Directed by Alexander Singer. S7E4/5, 11 October 1993/18 October 1993.

"Heart of Glory." Teleplay by Maurice Hurley. Story by Herbert Wright, D. C. Fontana. Directed by Rob Bowman. S1E20, 21 March 1988.

"Hero Worship." Teleplay by Joe Menosky. Story by Hilary J. Bader. Directed by Patrick Stewart. S5E11, 27 January 1992.

"The High Ground." Written by Melinda M. Snodgrass. Directed by Gabrielle Beaumont. S3E12, 29 January 1990.

"Hollow Pursuits." Written by Sally Caves. Directed by Cliff Bole. S3E21, 30 April 1990.

"The Host." Written by Michel Horvat. Directed by Marvin V. Rush. S4E23, 11 May 1991.

"I Borg." Written by René Echevarria. Directed by Robert Lederman. S5E23, 11 May 1992.

"The Icarus Factor." Teleplay by David Assael, Robert L. McCullough. Story by David Assael. Directed by Robert Iscove. S2E14, 24 April 1989.

"Journey's End." Written by Ronald D. Moore. Directed by Corey Allen. S7E20, 28 March 1994.

"Justice." Teleplay by Worley Thorne. Story by Worley Thorne, Ralph Wills. Directed by James L. Conway. S1E8, 9 November 1987.

"The Last Outpost." Teleplay by Herbert Wright. Story by Richard Krzemien. Directed by Richard Colla. S1E5, 19 October 1987.

"Lower Decks." Teleplay by René Echevarria. Story by Ronald Wilkerson, Jean Louise Matthias. Directed by Gabrielle Beaumont. S7E15, 7 February 1994.

"Manhunt." Written by Terry Devereaux. Directed by Rob Bowman. S2E19, 19 June 1989.

"The Masterpiece Society." Teleplay by Adam Belanoff, Michael Piller. Story by James Kahn, Adam Belanoff. Directed by Winrich Kolbe. S5E13, 10 February 1992.

"The Measure of a Man." Written by Melinda M. Snodgrass. Directed by Robert Scheerer. S2E9, 13 February 1989.

"The Naked Now." Teleplay by Michael J. Bingham. Story by John D. F. Black,

Michael J. Bingham. Directed by Paul Lynch. S1E3, 5 October 1987.

"The Neutral Zone." Teleplay by Maurice Hurley. Story by Deborah McIntyre, Mona Clee. Directed by James L. Conway. S1E26, 16 May 1988.

"The Nth Degree." Written by Joe Menosky. Directed by Robert Legato. S4E19, 1 April 1991.

"Parallels." Written by Brannon Braga. Directed by Robert Wiemer. S7E11, 29 November 1993.

"The Pegasus." Written by Ronald D. Moore. Directed by LeVar Burton. S7E12, 10 January 1994.

"Preemptive Strike." Teleplay by René Echevarria. Story by Naren Shankar. Directed by Patrick Stewart. S7E24, 16 May 1994.

"The Price." Written by Hannah Louise Shearer. Directed by Robert Scheerer. S3E8, 13 November 1989.

"Q Who." Written by Maurice Hurley. Directed by Rob Bowman. S2E16, 8 May 1989.

"Redemption." Written by Ronald D. Moore. Part 1: Directed by Cliff Bole. Part 2: Directed by David Carson. S4E25/S5E1, 17 June 1991/23 September 1991.

"Reunion." Teleplay by Thomas Perry, Jo Perry, Ronald D. Moore, Brannon Braga. Story by Drew Deighan, Thomas Perry, Jo Perry. Directed by Jonathan Frakes. S4E7, 5 November 1990.

"Rightful Heir." Teleplay by Ronald D. Moore. Story by James E. Brooks. Directed by Winrich Kolbe. S6E23, 17 May 1993.

"Samaritan Snare." Written by Robert L. McCullough. Directed by Les Landau. S2E17, 15 May 1989.

"Sarek." Teleplay by Peter S. Beagle. Story by Marc Cushman, Jake Jacobs. Directed by Les Landau. S3E23, 14 May 1990.

"Schisms." Teleplay by Brannon Braga. Story by Jean Louise Matthias, Ron Wilkerson. Directed by Robert Wiemer. S6E5, 19 October 1992.

"Sins of the Father." Teleplay by Ronald D. Moore, W. Reed Moran. Story by Drew Deighan. Directed by Les Landau. S3E17, 19 March 1990.

"Starship Mine." Written by Morgan Gendel. Directed by Cliff Bole. S6E18, 29 March 1993.

"Suspicions." Written by Joe Menosky, Naren Shankar. Directed by Cliff Bole. S6E22, 9 May 1993.

"Symbiosis." Teleplay by Robert Lewin, Richard Manning, Hans Beimler. Story by Robert Lewin. Directed by Win Phelps. S1E22, 18 April 1988.

"Tapestry." Written by Ronald D. Moore. Directed by Les Landau. S6E15, 15 February 1993.

"Tin Man." Written by Dennis Putman Bailey, David Bischoff. Directed by Robert Scheerer. S3E20, 23 April 1990.

"Unification." Part 1: Teleplay by Jeri Taylor. Directed by Les Landau. Part 2: Teleplay by Michael Piller. Directed by Cliff Bole. Story by Rick Berman, Michael Piller. S5E7/8, 4 November 1991/11 November 1991.

"Unnatural Selection." Written by John Mason, Mike Gray. Directed by Paul Lynch. S2E7, 30 January 1989.

"Up The Long Ladder." Written by Melinda M. Snodgrass. Directed by Winrich Kolbe. S2E18, 22 May 1989.

"We'll Always Have Paris." Written by Deborah Dean David, Hannah Louise Shearer. Directed by Robert Becker. S1E24, 2 May 1988.

"When the Bough Breaks." Written by Hannah Louise Shearer. Directed by Kim Manners. S1E17, 15 February 1988.

"Where No One Has Gone Before." Written by Diane Duane, Michael Reaves. Directed by Rob Bowman. S1E6, 26 October 1987.

"Who Watches the Watchers." Written by Richard Manning, Hans Beimler. Directed by Robert Wiemer. S3E4, 16 October 1989.

"The Wounded." Teleplay by Jeri Taylor. Story by Stuart Charno, Sara Charno, Cy Chermak. Directed by Chip Chalmers. S4E12, 28 January 1991.

"Yesterday's Enterprise." Teleplay by Ira Steven Behr, Richard Manning, Hans Beimler, Ronald D. Moore. Story by Trent Christopher Ganino, Eric A. Stillwell. Directed by David Carson. S3E15, 19 February 1990.

## Star Trek: Deep Space Nine (1993–1999)

"Accession." Written by Jane Espenson. Directed by Les Landau. S4E17, 26 February 1996.

# Works Cited

"The Adversary." Written by Ira Steven Behr, Robert Hewitt Wolfe. Directed by Alexander Singer. S3E26, 19 June 1995.

"Apocalypse Rising." Written by Ira Steven Behr, Robert Hewitt Wolfe. Directed by James L. Conway. S5E1, 30 September 1996.

"The Ascent." Written by Ira Steven Behr, Robert Hewitt Wolfe. Directed by Allan Kroeker. S5E9, 25 November 1996.

"Babel." Teleplay by Michael McGreevey, Naren Shankar. Story by Sally Caves, Ira Steven Behr. Directed by Paul Lynch. S1E5, 24 January 1993.

"Battle Lines." Teleplay by Richard Danus, Evan Carlos Somers. Story by Hilary J. Bader. Directed by Paul Lynch. S1E13, 25 April 1993.

"The Begotten." Written by René Echevarria. Directed by Jesús Salvador Treviño. S5E12, 27 January 1997.

"Behind the Lines." Written by René Echevarria. Directed by LeVar Burton. S6E4, 20 October 1997.

"Blaze of Glory." Written by Ira Steven Behr, Robert Hewitt Wolfe. Directed by Kim Friedman. S5E23, 12 May 1997.

"Body Parts." Teleplay by Hans Beimler. Story by Louis P. DeSantis, Robert J. Bolivar. Directed by Avery Brooks. S4E25, 10 June 1996.

"Broken Link." Teleplay by Robert Hewitt Wolfe, Ira Steven Behr. Story by George A. Brozak. Directed by Les Lendau. S4E26, 17 June 1996.

"By Inferno's Light." Written by Ira Steven Behr, Robert Hewitt Wolfe. Directed by Les Landau. S5E15, 17 February 1997.

"Call to Arms." Written by Ira Steven Behr, Robert Hewitt Wolfe. Directed by Allan Kroeker. S5E26, 16 June 1997.

"The Changing Face of Evil." Written by Ira Steven Behr, Hans Beimler. Directed by Mike Vejar. S7E20, 28 April 1999.

"The Circle." Written by Peter Allan Fields. Directed by Corey Allen. S2E2, 3 October 1993.

"Crossover." Teleplay by Peter Allan Fields, Michael Piller. Story by Peter Allan Fields. Directed by David Livingston. S2E23, 15 May 1994.

"Defiant." Written by Ronald D. Moore. Directed by Cliff Bole. S3E9, 21 November 1994.

"The Die Is Cast." Written by Ronald D. Moore. Directed by David Livingston. S3E21, 1 May 1995.

"Doctor Bashir, I Presume." Teleplay by Ronald D. Moore. Story by Jimmy Diggs. Directed by David Livingston. S5E16, 24 February 1997.

"Dramatis Personae." Written by Joe Menosky. Directed by Cliff Bole. S1E18, 30 May 1993.

"Duet." Teleplay by Peter Allan Fields. Story by Lisa Rich, Jeanne Carrigan-Fauci. Directed by James L. Conway. S1E19, 13 June 1993.

"Emissary." Teleplay by Michael Piller. Story by Rick Berman, Michael Piller. Directed by David Carson. S1E1/2, 3 January 1993.

"Explorers." Teleplay by René Echevarria. Story by Hilary J. Bader. Directed by Cliff Bole. S3E22, 8 May 1995.

"Extreme Measures." Written by Bradley Thompson, David Weddle. Directed by Steve Posey. S7E23, 19 May 1999.

"Ferengi Love Songs." Written by Ira Steven Behr, Hans Beimler. Directed by Rene Auberjonois. S5E20, 21 April 1997.

"For the Cause." Teleplay by Ronald D. Moore. Story by Mark Gehred-O'Connell. Directed by James L. Conway. S4E22, 6 May 1996.

"For the Uniform." Written by Peter Allan Fields. Directed by Victor Lobl. S5E13, 3 February 1997.

"The Forsaken." Teleplay by Don Carlos Dunaway, Michael Piller. Story by Jim Trombetta. Directed by Les Landau. S1E17, 23 May 1993.

"Heart of Stone." Written by Ira Steven Behr, Robert Hewitt Wolfe. Directed by Alexander Singer. S3E14, 6 February 1995.

"Homefront." Written by Ira Steven Behr, Robert Hewitt Wolfe. Directed by David Livingston. S4E11, 1 January 1996.

"The Homecoming." Teleplay by Ira Steven Behr. Story by Jeri Taylor, Ira Steven Behr. Directed by Winrich Kolbe. S2E1, 26 September 1993.

"Improbable Cause." Teleplay by René Echevarria. Story by Robert Lederman, David R. Long. Directed by Avery Brooks. S3E20, 24 April 1995.

"In the Pale Moonlight." Teleplay by Michael Taylor. Story by Peter Allan Fields. Directed by Victor Lobl. S6E19, 15 April 1998.

"Inquisition." Written by Bradley Thompson, David Weddle. Directed by Michael Dorn. S6E18, 8 April 1998.

"The Jem'Hadar." Written by Ira Steven Behr. Directed by Kim Friedman. S2E26, 12 June 1994.

"Little Green Men." Teleplay by Ira Steven Behr, Robert Hewitt Wolfe. Story by Toni Marberry, Jack Trevino. Directed by James L. Conway. S4E8, 13 November 1995.

"A Man Alone." Teleplay by Michael Piller. Story by Gerald Sanford, Michael Piller. Directed by Paul Lynch. S1E4, 17 January 1993.

"The Maquis." Part 1: Teleplay by James Crocker. Story by Rick Berman, Michael Piller, Jeri Taylor, James Crocker. Directed by David Livingston. Part 2: Teleplay by Ira Steven Behr. Story by Rick Berman, Michael Piller, Jeri Taylor, Ira Steven Behr. Directed by Corey Allen. S2E20/21, 24 April 1994/1 May 1994.

"Necessary Evil." Written by Peter Allan Fields. Directed by James L. Conway. S2E8, 14 November 1993.

"Paradise Lost." Teleplay by Ira Steven Behr, Hans Beimler. Story by Ronald D. Moore. Directed by Reza Badiyi. S4E12, 8 January 1996.

"Profit and Lace." Written by Ira Steven Behr, Hans Beimler. Directed by Alexander Siddig. S6E23, 13 May 1998.

"Profit and Loss." Written by Flip Kobler, Cindy Marcus. Directed by Robert Wiemer. S2E18, 20 March 1994.

"Prophet Motive." Written by Ira Steven Behr, Robert Hewitt Wolfe. Directed by Rene Auberjonois. S3E16, 20 February 1995.

"Rapture." Teleplay by Hans Beimler. Story by L. J. Strom. Directed by Jonathan West. S5E10, 30 December 1996.

"Rules of Acquisition." Teleplay by Ira Steven Behr. Story by Hilary J. Bader. Directed by David Livingston. S2E7, 7 November 1993.

"Sacrifice of Angels." Written by Ira Steven Behr, Hans Beimler. Directed by Allan Kroeker. S6E6, 3 November 1997.

"Sanctuary." Teleplay by Frederick Rappaport. Story by Gabe Essoe, Kelley Miles. Directed by Les Landau. S2E10, 28 November 1993.

"The Search." Part 1: Teleplay by Ronald D. Moore. Directed by Kim Friedman. Part 2: Teleplay by Ira Steven Behr. Directed by Jonathan Frakes. Story by Ira Steven Behr, Robert Hewitt Wolfe. S3E1/2, 26 September 1994/3 October 1994.

"Second Skin." Written by Robert Hewitt Wolfe. Directed by Les Landau. S3E5, 24 October 1994.

"The Siege." Written by Michael Piller. Directed by Winrich Kolbe. S2E3, 10 October 1993.

"Statistical Probabilities." Teleplay by René Echevarria. Story by Pam Pietroforte. Directed by Anson Williams. S6E9, 22 November 1997.

"Strange Bedfellows." Written by Ronald D. Moore. Directed by Rene Auberjonois. S7E19, 21 April 1999.

"The Sword of Kahless." Teleplay by Hans Beimler. Story by Richard Danus. Directed by LeVar Burton. S4E9, 20 November 1995.

"Take Me Out to the Holosuite." Written by Ronald D. Moore. Directed by Chip Chalmers. S7E4, 21 October 1998.

"Tears of the Prophets." Written by Ira Steven Behr, Hans Beimler. Directed by Allan Kroeker. S6E26, 17 June 1998.

"A Time to Stand." Written by Ira Steven Behr, Hans Beimler. Directed by Allan Kroeker. S6E1, 29 September 1997.

"The Way of the Warrior." Written by Ira Steven Behr, Robert Hewitt Wolfe. Directed by James L. Conway. S4E1, 2 October 1995.

"To the Death." Written by Ira Steven Behr, Robert Hewitt Wolfe. Directed by LeVar Burton. S4E23, 13 May 1996.

"Treachery, Faith and the Great River." Teleplay by David Weddle, Bradley Thompson. Story by Philip Kim. Directed by Steve Posey. S7E6, 4 November 1998.

"Trials and Tribble-ations." Teleplay by Ronald D. Moore, René Echevarria. Story by Ira Steven Behr, Hans Beimler, Robert Hewitt Wolfe. Directed by Jonathan West. S5E6, 4 November 1996.

"Tribunal." Written by Bill Dial. Directed by Avery Brooks. S2E25, 5 June 1994.

"Valiant." Written by Ronald D. Moore. Directed by Mike Vejar. S6E22, 6 May 1998.

"What You Leave Behind." Written by Ira Steven Behr, Hans Beimler. Directed by Allan Kroeker. S7E25/26, 2 June 1999.

## Star Trek: Voyager
(1995–2001)

"Author, Author." Teleplay by Phyllis Strong, Mike Sussman. Story by Brannon Braga. Directed by David Livingston. S7E20, 18 April 2001.

"Basics." Written by Michael Piller. Directed by Winrich Kolbe. S2E26/S3E1, 20 May 1996/4 September 1996.

"Blood Fever." Written by Lisa Klink. Directed by Andrew J. Robinson. S3E16, 5 February 1997.

"Caretaker." Teleplay by Michael Piller, Jeri Taylor. Story by Rick Berman, Michael Piller, Jeri Taylor. Directed by Winrich Kolbe. S1E1/02, 16 January 1995.

"Collective." Teleplay by Michael Taylor. Story by Andrew Shepard Price, Mark Gaberman. Directed by Allison Liddi. S6E16, 16 February 2000.

"Dark Frontier." Written by Brannon Braga, Joe Menosky. Part 1: Directed by Cliff Bole. Part 2: Directed by Terry Windell. S5E15/16, 17 February 1999.

"Death Wish." Teleplay by Michael Piller. Story by Shawn Piller. Directed by James L. Conway. S2E18, 19 February 1996.

"Drive." Written by Michael Taylor. Directed by Winrich Kolbe. S7E3, 18 October 2000.

"Endgame." Teleplay by Kenneth Biller, Robert Doherty. Story by Rick Berman, Kenneth Biller, Brannon Braga. Directed by Allan Kroeker. S7E25/26, 23 May 2001.

"Equinox." Teleplay by Brannon Braga, Joe Menosky. Story by Rick Berman, Brannon Braga, Joe Menosky. Directed by David Livingston. S5E26/S6E1, 26 May 1999/22 September 1999.

"Future's End." Written by Brannon Braga, Joe Menosky. Part 1: Directed by David Livingston. Part 2: Directed by Cliff Bole. S3E8/9, 6 November 1996/13 November 1996.

"The Gift." Written by Joe Menosky. Directed by Anson Williams. S4E2, 10 September 1997.

"Good Shepherd." Teleplay by Dianna Gitto, Joe Menosky. Story by Dianna Gitto. Directed by Winrich Kolbe. S6E20, 15 March 2000.

"Human Error." Teleplay by Brannon Braga, André Bormanis. Story by André Bormanis, Kenneth Biller. Directed by Allan Kroeker. S7E18, 7 March 2001.

"Hunters." Written by Jeri Taylor. Directed by David Livingston. S4E15, 11 February 1998.

"Imperfection." Teleplay by Carleton Eastlake, Robert Doherty. Story by André Bormanis. Directed by David Livingston. S7E2, 11 October 2000.

"Infinite Regress." Teleplay by Robert Doherty. Story by Robert Doherty, Jimmy Diggs. Directed by David Livingston. S5E7, 25 November 1998.

"Inside Man." Written by Robert Doherty. Directed by Allan Kroeker. S7E6, 8 November 2000.

"The Killing Game." Written by Brannon Braga, Joe Menosky. Directed by David Livingston. S4E18/19, 4 March 1998.

"Learning Curve." Written by Ronald Wilkerson, Jean Louise Matthias. Directed by David Livingston. S1E16, 22 May 1995.

"Life Line." Teleplay by Robert Doherty, Raf Green, Brannon Braga. Story by John Bruno, Robert Picardo. Directed by Terry Windell. S6E24, 10 May 2000.

"Message in a Bottle." Teleplay by Lisa Klink. Story by Rick Williams. Directed by Nancy Malone. S4E14, 21 January 1998.

"Parallax." Teleplay by Brannon Braga. Story by Jim Trombetta. Directed by Kim Friedman. S1E3, 23 January 1995.

"Pathfinder." Teleplay by David Zabel, Kenneth Biller. Story by David Zabel. Directed by Mike Vejar. S6E10, 1 December 1999.

"Prey." Written by Brannon Braga. Directed by Allan Eastman. S4E16, 18 February 1998.

"The Raven." Teleplay by Bryan Fuller, Harry Doc Kloor. Story by Bryan Fuller. Directed by LeVar Burton. S4E6, 8 October 1997.

"Renaissance Man." Teleplay by Phyllis Strong, Mike Sussman. Story by Andrew Price, Mark Gaberman. Directed by Mike Vejar. S7E24, 16 May 2001.

"Scorpion." Written by Brannon Braga, Joe Menosky. Part 1: Directed by David Livingston. Part 2: Directed by Winrich Kolbe. S3E26/S4E1, 21 May 1997/3 September 1997.

"State of Flux." Teleplay by Chris Abbott. Story by Paul Robert Coyle. Directed by Robert Scheerer. S1E11, 10 April 1995.

"Survival Instinct." Written by Ronald D. Moore. Directed by Terry Windell. S6E2, 29 September 1999.

"Tinker, Tenor, Doctor, Spy." Teleplay by Joe Menosky. Story by Bill Vallely. Directed by John Bruno. S6E4, 13 October 1999.

"Unimatrix Zero." Teleplay by Brannon Braga, Joe Menosky. Part 1: Story by Mike Sussman. Directed by Allan Kroeker. Part 2: Story by Mike Sussman, Brannon Braga, Joe Menosky. Directed by Mike Vejar. S6E26/S7E1, 24 May 2000/4 October 2000.

"Unity." Written by Kenneth Biller. Directed by Robert Duncan McNeill. S3E17, 12 February 1997.

"The Void." Teleplay by Raf Green, James Kahn. Story by Raf Green, Kenneth Biller. Directed by Mike Vejar. S7E15, 14 February 2001.

## *Star Trek: Enterprise* (2001–2005)

"Acquisition." Teleplay by Maria Jacquemetton, Andre Jacquemetton. Story by Rick Berman, Brannon Braga. Directed by James Whitmore, Jr. S1E19, 27 March 2002.

"The Aenar." Teleplay by André Bormanis. Story by Manny Coto. Directed by Mike Vejar. S4E14, 11 February 2005.

"The Augments." Written by Mike Sussman. Directed by LeVar Burton. S4E6, 12 November 2004.

"Babel One." Written by Mike Sussman, André Bormanis. Directed by David Straiton. S4E12, 28 January 2005.

"Borderland." Written by Ken LaZebnik. Directed by David Livingston. S4E4, 29 October 2004.

"Broken Bow." Written by Rick Berman, Brannon Braga. Directed by James L. Conway. S1E1/2, 26 September 2001.

"Cease Fire." Written by Chris Black. Directed by David Straiton. S2E15, 12 February 2003.

"Cold Station 12." Written by Alan Brennert. Directed by Mike Vejar. S4E5, 5 November 2004.

"Dear Doctor." Written by Maria Jacquemetton, Andre Jacquemetton. Directed by James A. Contner. S1E13, 23 January 2002.

"Demons." Written by Manny Coto. Directed by LeVar Burton. S4E20, 6 May 2005.

"The Expanse." Written by Rick Berman, Brannon Braga. Directed by Allan Kroeker. S2E26, 21 May 2003.

"The Forge." Written by Judith Reeves-Stevens, Garfield Reeves-Stevens. Directed by Michael Grossman. S4E7, 19 November 2004.

"In a Mirror, Darkly." Part 1: Written by Mike Sussman. Directed by James L. Conway. Part 2: Teleplay by Mike Sussman. Story by Manny Coto. Directed by Marvin V. Rush. S4E18/19, 22 April 2005/29 April 2005.

"Judgment." Teleplay by David A. Goodman. Story by Taylor Elmore, David A. Goodman. Directed by James L. Conway. S2E19, 9 April 2003.

"Minefield." Written by John Shiban. Directed by James A. Contner. S2E3, 2 October 2002.

"Regeneration." Written by Mike Sussman, Phyllis Strong. Directed by David Livingston. S2E23, 7 May 2003.

"Terra Prime." Teleplay by Judith Reeves-Stevens, Garfield Reeves-Stevens, Manny Coto. Story by Judith Reeves-Stevens, Garfield Reeves-Stevens, André Bormanis. Directed by Marvin V. Rush. S4E21, 13 May 2005.

"These Are the Voyages…" Written by Rick Berman, Brannon Braga. Directed by Allan Kroeker. S4E22, 13 May 2005.

"United." Teleplay by Judith Reeves-Stevens, Garfield Reeves-Stevens. Story by Manny Coto. Directed by David Livingston. S4E13, 4 February 2005.

## *Star Trek: Discovery* (2017–)

"Battle at the Binary Stars." Teleplay by Gretchen J. Berg, Aaron Harberts. Story by Bryan Fuller. Directed by Adam Kane. S1E2, 24 September 2017.

"The Butcher's Knife Cares Not for the Lamb's Cry." Written by Jesse Alexander, Aron Eli Coleite. Directed by Olatunde Osunsanmi. S1E4, 8 October 2017.

"Choose Your Pain." Teleplay by Kemp Powers. Story by Gretchen J. Berg, Aaron Harberts, Kemp Powers. Directed by Lee Rose. S1E5, 15 October 2017.

"Context Is for Kings." Teleplay by Gretchen J. Berg, Aaron Harberts, Craig Sweeny. Story by Bryan Fuller, Gretchen J. Berg, Aaron Harberts. Directed by Akiva Goldsman. S1E3, 1 October 2017.

"Despite Yourself." Written by Sean Cochran. Directed by Jonathan Frakes. S1E10, 7 January 2018.

"Die Trying." Teleplay by Sean Cochran. Story by James Duff, Sean Cochran. Directed by Maja Vrvilo. S3E5, 12 November 2020.

"Lethe." Written by Joe Menosky, Ted Sullivan. Directed by Doug Aarniokoski. S1E6, 22 October 2017.

"An Obol for Charon." Teleplay by Alan McElroy, Andrew Colville. Story by Jordon Nardino, Gretchen J. Berg, Aaron Harberts. Directed by Lee Rose. S2E4, 7 February 2019.

"People of Earth." Written by Bo Yeon Kim, Erika Lippoldt. Directed by Jonathan Frakes. S3E3, 29 October 2020.

"Perpetual Infinity." Written by Alan McElroy, Brandon Schultz. Directed by Maja Vrvilo. S2E11, 28 March 2019.

"Project Daedalus." Written by Michelle Paradise. Directed by Jonathan Frakes. S2E9, 14 March 2019.

"The Sanctuary." Written by Kenneth Lin, Brandon Schultz. Directed by Jonathan Frakes. S3E8, 3 December 2020.

"Si Vis Pacem, Para Bellum." Written by Kirsten Beyer. Directed by John S. Scott. S1E8, 5 November 2017.

"Such Sweet Sorrow." Part 1 & 2: Written by Michelle Paradise, Jenny Lumet, Alex Kurtzman. Directed by Olatunde Osunsanmi. S2E13/14, 11 April 2019/18 April 2019.

"That Hope Is You Part 1." Written by Michelle Paradise, Jenny Lumet, Alex Kurtzman. Directed by Olatunde Osunsanmi. S3E1, 15 October 2020.

"That Hope Is You Part 2." Written by Michelle Paradise. Directed by Olatunde Osunsanmi. S3E13, 7 January 2021.

"Through the Valley of Shadows." Written by Bo Yeon Kim, Erika Lippoldt. Directed by Doug Aarniokoski. S2E12, 4 April 2019.

"Vaulting Ambition." Written by Jordon Nardino. Directed by Hanelle M. Culpepper. S1E12, 21 January 2018.

"The Vulcan Hello." Teleplay by Bryan Fuller, Akiva Goldsman. Story by Bryan Fuller, Alex Kurtzman. Directed by David Semel. S1E1, 24 September 2017.

"The War Without, The War Within." Written by Lisa Randolph. Directed by David Solomon. S1E14, 4 February 2018.

"Will You Take My Hand?." Teleplay by Gretchen J. Berg, Aaron Harberts. Story by Akiva Goldsman, Gretchen J. Berg, Aaron Harberts. Directed by Akiva Goldsman. S1E15, 11 February 2018.

## Star Trek: Short Treks (2018–)

"Calypso." Teleplay by Michael Chabon. Story by Sean Cochran, Michael Chabon. Directed by Olatunde Osunsanmi. S1E2, 8 November 2018.

"Children of Mars." Written by Kirsten Beyer, Alex Kurtzman, Jenny Lumet. Directed by Mark Pellington. S2E6, 9 January 2020.

## Star Trek: Picard (2020–)

"Absolute Candor." Written by Michael Chabon. Directed by Jonathan Frakes. S1E4, 13 February 2020.

"Et in Arcadia Ego." Part 1: Teleplay by Michael Chabon, Ayelet Waldman. Story by Michael Chabon, Ayelet Waldman, Akiva Goldsman. Part 2: Teleplay by Michael Chabon. Story by Michael Chabon, Akiva Goldsman. Directed by Akiva Goldsman. S1E9/10, 19 March 2020/26 March 2020.

"The Impossible Box." Written by Nick Zayas. Directed by Maja Vrvilo. S1E6, 27 February 2020.

"Maps and Legends." Written by Michael Chabon, Akiva Goldsman. Directed by Hanelle M. Culpepper. S1E2, 30 January 2020.

"Nepenthe." Written by Samantha Humphrey, Michael Chabon. Directed by Doug Aarniokoski. S1E7, 5 March 2020.

"Remembrance." Teleplay by Akiva Goldsman, James Duff. Story by Akiva Goldsman, Michael Chabon, Kirsten Beyer, Alex Kurtman, James Duff. Directed by Hanelle M. Culpepper. S1E1, 23 January 2020.

"Stardust City Rag." Written by Kirsten Beyer. Directed by Jonathan Frakes. S1E5, 20 February 2020.

## Star Trek: Lower Decks (2020–)

"No Small Parts." Written by Mike McMahan. Directed by Barry J. Kelly. S1E10, 8 October 2020.

## Feature Films

*Star Trek*. Written by Roberto Orci, Alex Kurtzman. Directed by J.J. Abrams. 8 May 2009.

*Star Trek: First Contact*. Screenplay by Brannon Braga, Ronald D. Moore. Story by Rick Berman, Brannon Braga, Ronald D. Moore. Directed by Jonathan Frakes. 22 November 1996.

*Star Trek: Generations*. Screenplay by Ronald D. Moore, Brannon Braga. Story by Rick Berman, Ronald D. Moore, Brannon Braga. Directed by David Carson. 18 November 1994.

*Star Trek: Insurrection*. Screenplay by Michael Piller. Story by Rick Berman, Michael Piller. Directed by Jonathan Frakes. 11 December 1998.

*Star Trek: The Motion Picture*. Screenplay by Harold Livingston. Story by Alan Dean Foster. Directed by Robert Wise. 7 December 1979.

*Star Trek: Nemesis*. Screenplay by John Logan. Story by John Logan, Rick Berman, Brent Spiner. Directed by Stuart Baird. 13 December 2002.

*Star Trek II: The Wrath of Khan*. Screenplay by Jack B. Sowards. Story by Harve Bennett, Jack B. Sowards. Directed by Nicholas Meyer. 4 June 1982.

*Star Trek III: The Search for Spock*. Written by Harve Bennett. Directed by Leonard Nimoy. 1 June 1984.

*Star Trek IV: The Voyage Home*. Screenplay by Steve Meerson, Peter Krikes, Harve Bennett, Nicholas Meyer. Story by Leonard Nimoy, Harve Bennett. Directed by Leonard Nimoy. 26 November 1986.

*Star Trek V: The Final Frontier*. Screenplay by David Loughery. Story by William Shatner, Harve Bennett, David Loughery. Directed by William Shatner. 9 June 1989.

*Star Trek VI: The Undiscovered Country*. Screenplay by Nicholas Meyer, Denny Martin Flinn. Story by Leonard Nimoy, Lawrence Konner, Mark Rosenthal. Directed by Nicolas Meyer. 6 December 1991.

*Star Trek Beyond*. Written by Simon Pegg, Doug Jung. Directed by Justin Lin. 22 July 2016.

*Star Trek Into Darkness*. Written by Roberto Orci, Alex Kurtzman, Damon Lindelof. Directed by J. J. Abrams. 16 May 2013.

# Index

"Absolute Candor" (*PIC* episode) 155
"Accession" (*DS9* episode) 80
"Acquisition" (*ENT* episode) 93
"The Adversary" (*DS9* episode) 115
"The Aenar" (*ENT* episode) 94
Alpha Quadrant 74, 85, 87, 114–8, 120–21, 125, 142, 147, 162, 169*n*1
"Amok Time" (*TOS* episode) 126
android 2, 50–2, 54, 153–6, 159, 166*n*15, 169*n*12
"Angel One" (*TNG* episode) 81, 90
anti-utopia 7, 125
"Apocalypse Rising" (*DS9* episode) 115
"The Apple" (*TOS* episode) 47, 82, 84, 126, 161
Archer, Jonathan 81, 93–4, 172*n*4
"The Arsenal of Freedom" (*TNG* episode) 90
artificial intelligence 50, 53, 150–1, 163, 174*n*10
artificial lifeform 31, 50–1, 55, 128, 130, 153–6, 163, 166*n*15, 170*n*12
"The Ascent" (*DS9* episode) 76
assimilation (Borg) 71, 111, 121, 127–8, 133–6, 138–9, 149, 155, 163, 172*n*4, 172*n*8, 173*n*16
"The Augments" (*ENT* episode) 169*n*12
"Author, Author" (*Voyager* episode) 53, 78, 81, 166*n*17, 166–7*n*18

B-4 (character) 154, 156
"Babel" (*DS9* episode) 169*n*8
"Babel One" (*ENT* episode) 94
Bacon, Francis 12, 24–8, 35–6, 38–9, 41, 67, 73
Bajor (planet) 62, 64, 75, 79, 105–6, 109, 112, 116, 118, 152, 169*n*8, 171*n*29
Bajorans 64–5, 76, 84, 105, 108–10, 112, 142, 161, 171*n*29, 173*n*7
"Balance of Terror" (*TOS* episode) 87, 94, 96, 170*n*19
Barclay, Reginald 54, 70–1, 122, 169*n*23
Bashir, Julien 76, 91, 112, 170*n*14, 171*n*24, 173*n*7
"Basics" (*Voyager* episode) 120
"Battle at the Binary Stars" (*DIS* episode) 145–6
"Battle Lines" (*DS9* episode) 75

"The Begotten" (*DS9* episode) 129
"Behind the Lines" (*DS9* episode) 78
Behr, Ira Steven 101, 108, 111–2
Berman, Rick 101–2, 109, 119, 141
"The Best of Both Worlds" (*TNG* episode) 74, 130–3, 135–136, 163, 170*n*21, 172*n*8, 173*n*14
Beta Quadrant 74
"The Big Goodbye" (*TNG* episode) 53
"Birthright" (*TNG* episode) 171*n*24
"Blaze of Glory" (*DS9* episode) 168*n*16, 171*n*30, 172*n*38
Bloch, Ernst 30
"Blood Fever" (*Voyager* episode) 172*n*2
"Body Parts" (*DS9* episode) 88
"Booby Trap" (*TNG* episode) 169*n*8
"Borderland" (*ENT* episode) 169*n*12
Borg (species) 7, 71, 74, 85–6, 88, 93, 111, 119–21, 123, 125–40, 142, 154–5, 162–3, 167*n*20, 168*n*13, 170*n*21, 172*n*4, 172*n*5, 172*n*7, 172*n*8, 172*n*9, 172*n*10, 173*n*12, 173*n*14, 173*n*15, 173*n*16, 173*n*17, 173*n*19, 173*n*20, 173*n*21, 174*n*15
Borg Queen 86, 88, 128–30, 132, 137–9, 167*n*20, 173*n*15
Braga, Brannon 119
bridge 43, 60, 129, 145, 160, 168*n*6
"Broken Bow" (*ENT* episode) 6, 94
"Broken Link" (*DS9* episode) 115, 172*n*37
"Brothers" (*TNG* episode) 52
Burnham, Michael 144–50, 152, 163
"The Butcher's Knife Cares Not for the Lamb's Cry" (*DIS* episode) 146
"By Inferno's Light" (*DS9* episode) 115–6

"Call to Arms" (*DS9* episode) 114, 116
"Calypso" (*ST* episode) 174*n*8
Campanella, Tommaso 12, 19–26, 28, 35, 38, 67, 73, 165*n*5, 165*n*6
"Captain's Holiday" (*TNG* episode) 170*n*18
Cardassia (planet) 109, 115–6, 118, 171*n*34
Cardassian Union 86, 105, 107, 124, 171*n*35
Cardassians 43, 50, 62, 64, 66, 74–5, 84–7, 105–11, 114–20, 124–5, 142, 162, 171*n*35, 172*n*38, 173*n*7

191

# Index

"Caretaker" (*Voyager* episode) 62, 76, 119–20, 171*n*24
"Cause and Effect" (*TNG* episode) 76
"Cease Fire" (*ENT* episode) 93
"Chain of Command" (*TNG* episode) 87, 106–7, 109, 169*n*3
Chakotay 68–9, 119–20, 138
Changelings 114–5, 125, 171*n*31
"The Changing Face of Evil" (*DS9* episode) 117–8
"Charlie X" (*TOS* episode) 62
Charter of the United Federation of Planets 74, 80–1
"The Child" (*TNG* episode) 61
"Children of Mars" (*ST* episode) 153
China 97–8, 104, 113–4
"Choose Your Pain" (*DIS* episode) 146, 149
"The Circle" (*DS9* episode) 110
City of the Sun 12, 19–24, 27–8, 35, 67, 73, 129, 160
"The Cloud Minders" (*TOS* episode) 89
Cochrane, Zefram 46, 147
"Cold Station 12" (*ENT* episode) 169*n*12
Cold War 7, 92, 94, 96–7, 99, 104, 121, 123
"Collective" (*Voyager* episode) 128–129, 168*n*13, 172*n*8
"Coming of Age" (*TNG* episode) 78
"The Conscience of the King" (*TOS* episode) 89
"Context Is for Kings" (*DIS* episode) 144, 146
"Conundrum" (*TNG* episode) 70
"Court Martial" (*TOS* episode) 76
"Crossover" (*DS9* episode) 112, 173*n*7
Crusher, Beverly 92, 161
Crusher, Wesley 82, 129, 169*n*10
cyborg 128, 130–1, 172*n*6

"Dark Frontier" (*Voyager* episode) 128–30, 132, 134, 172*n*4, 173*n*16
"Dark Page" (*TNG* episode) 61
Data (character) 3, 50–2, 54–5, 59, 61, 129, 134, 142, 151, 153–6, 159, 167*n*19, 167*n*20, 169*n*8, 169*n*12
"Datalore" (*TNG* episode) 51
"Data's Day" (*TNG* episode) 59, 61, 129
Dax, Jadzia 161, 174*n*13
"Dear Doctor" (*ENT* episode) 81
"Death Wish" (*Voyager* episode) 87
*Deep Space Nine* (space station) 58, 62–7, 69, 109–10, 112, 114–6, 120, 129, 167*n*21, 171*n*31, 173*n*7
"The Defector" (*TNG* episode) 75, 102
"Defiant" (*DS9* episode) 87
USS *Defiant* 62, 114, 167*n*21, 173*n*6
Delta Quadrant 69, 74, 80, 85, 88, 119–22, 172*n*4
"Demons" (*ENT* episode) 94, 169*n*4
"Descent" (*TNG* episode) 52, 134, 166*n*13, 174*n*15
"Despite Yourself" (*DIS* episode) 147

"The Die Is Cast" (*DS9* episode) 114
"Die Trying" (*DIS* episode) 151–2, 174*n*14
diplomacy 24, 58, 107, 124, 145
"Disaster" (*TNG* episode) 61, 129
USS *Discovery* 144–7, 149–52, 173*n*8
The Doctor 135, 166*n*17, 166*n*18
The Doctor (character) 135, 166*n*18
"Doctor Bashir, I Presume" (*DS9* episode) 76, 91
Dominion 74, 78, 85–6, 88, 113–8, 124–7, 146, 162, 171*n*32, 172*n*38, 172*n*43
Dominion War 78, 113, 117, 124, 162
"Dramatis Personae" (*DS9* episode) 112
"Drive" (*Voyager* episode) 129
"The Drumhead" (*TNG* episode) 69, 81
"Duet" (*DS9* episode) 109
dystopia 12–13, 53, 85, 127, 139–40, 163

Earth 6, 33–35, 37, 41–4, 46, 58, 74, 90–1, 93–4, 96, 98, 105–6, 110, 112, 115–7, 129–30, 142, 148, 151, 159, 161, 165*n*7, 165*n*3, 170*n*17, 171*n*36, 172*n*4, 173*n*16, 174*n*10
economy 14–6, 18–9, 21, 23, 25, 37, 77, 88–9, 97, 122, 160, 165*n*7
"Elementary, Dear Data" (*TNG* episode) 54
Emergency Medical Holographic Program *see* The Doctor
"Emissary" (*DS9* episode) 109, 112, 168*n*4, 171*n*24
"Encounter at Farpoint" (*TNG* episode) 59, 169*n*8, 171*n*24
"Endgame" (*Voyager* episode) 122, 129, 163–4, 168*n*13, 173*n*19
"The Enemy" (*TNG* episode) 170*n*22
"Ensign Ro" (*TNG* episode) 61, 76, 84, 105
USS *Enterprise* 5–6, 47–9, 58, 61, 75, 82, 89–90, 96–7, 100, 126, 143, 150–1, 161, 167*n*4
USS *Enterprise*-D 6, 41–5, 49–51, 53, 55, 59–62, 65–7, 70–2, 76, 79, 82–3, 85, 89–93, 100–4, 106–8, 119, 122, 127, 129–31, 133, 142, 153, 160, 168*n*4, 168*n*9, 168*n*12, 169*n*23, 169*n*10, 169*n*11, 170*n*15
USS *Enterprise*-E 79, 168*n*4, 173*n*15
"The Enterprise Incident" (*TOS* episode) 78
USS *Enterprise NX-01* 81, 94, 167*n*4, 168*n*12
"Equinox" (*Voyager* episode) 79, 84, 120, 122
"Errand of Mercy" (*TOS* episode) 96
"Et in Arcadia Ego" (*PIC* episode) 3, 155–6, 174*n*17
"Ethics" (*TNG* episode) 92
European Union 95, 169*n*5
"The Expanse" (*ENT* episode) 94
"Explorers" (*DS9* episode) 78
"Extreme Measures" (*DS9* episode) 75

"Face of the Enemy" (*TNG* episode) 87
"Family" (*TNG* episode) 69, 129
Federation Cabinet 75
Federation Council 75, 84, 86, 90, 103–4, 123, 148, 162–3

# Index

Federation president 75, 86, 123, 162, 171*n*36
Federation Supreme Court 76, 86
Ferengi 64–5, 74, 78, 85–8, 93, 113, 152, 162, 168*n*19, 170*n*17, 174*n*14
Ferengi Alliance 86–8
"Ferengi Love Songs" (*DS9* episode) 88
"First Contact" (*TNG* episode) 45
"The First Duty" (*TNG* episode) 69, 78, 169*n*2
"A Fistful of Datas" (*TNG* episode) 55
"For the Cause" (*DS9* episode) 78, 111, 171*n*30, 171*n*35
"For the Uniform" (*DS9* episode) 167*n*21, 171*n*30
"Force of Nature" (*TNG* episode) 75, 90
"The Forge" (*ENT* episode) 61, 93, 165*n*2
"The Forsaken" (*DS9* episode) 167*n*21
"Frame of Mind" (*TNG* episode) 61
"Friday's Child" (*TOS* episode) 96
"Future's End" (*Voyager* episode) 169*n*8

"Gambit" (*TNG* episode) 87
Gamma Quadrant 62, 74, 85, 88, 109, 112–3, 171*n*29, 171*n*32
Georgiou, Philippa 145–8
"The Gift" (*Voyager* episode) 135–6
"Good Shepherd" (*Voyager* episode) 69
Grand Nagus 86, 88
Guinan 51, 128, 133, 154

"Heart of Glory" (*TNG* episode) 100
"Heart of Stone" (*DS9* episode) 78, 168*n*19
"Hero Worship" (*TNG* episode) 61
"The High Ground" (*TNG* episode) 92
Hirogen 121
"Hollow Pursuits" (*TNG* episode) 54, 70
holodeck 44, 52–5, 60, 62, 65, 70–2, 151, 167*n*21, 167*n*24, 167*n*26
"The Homecoming" (*DS9* episode) 109
"Homefront" (*DS9* episode) 75, 115, 168*n*19
"The Host" (*TNG* episode) 61, 79
Hugh (Borg drone) 133–135, 155–156, 173*n*21, 174*n*15
"Human Error" (*Voyager* episode) 169*n*22
"Hunters" (*Voyager* episode) 121
Huxley, Aldous 29–30, 53, 70

"I Borg" (*TNG* episode) 133–5, 174*n*15
"The Icarus Factor" (*TNG* episode) 168*n*8
"Imperfection" (*Voyager* episode) 76
"The Impossible Box" (*PIC* episode) 155, 173*n*14
"Improbable Cause" (*DS9* episode) 114
"In a Mirror, Darkly" (*ENT* episode) 147, 173*n*6
"In the Pale Moonlight" (*DS9* episode) 116
"Infinite Regress" (*Voyager* episode) 129
"Inquisition" (*DS9* episode) 75, 78
"Inside Man" (*Voyager* episode) 171*n*24

Janeway, Kathryn 68–9, 71, 76, 79–80, 84, 120–2, 135–6, 139, 144, 161–2, 171*n*24, 173*n*19
Jem'Hadar 86, 88, 113
"The Jem'Hadar" (*DS9* episode) 113
"Journey to Babel" (*TOS* episode) 74, 95, 170*n*18
"Journey's End" (*TNG* episode) 75, 107, 120
"Judgment" (*ENT* episode) 93
Jurati, Agnes 153–4, 156
"Justice" (*TNG* episode) 82

Kazon 120–1
Khan (character) 90–1, 131, 143, 169*n*12
Khitomer Accords 79, 97, 115, 169*n*9, 170*n*23
Khitomer Massacre 100, 103, 170*n*22
"The Killing Game" (*Voyager* episode) 121
Kim, Harry 164
Kira, Nerys 144, 161, 173*n*7
Kirk, James T. 1, 42, 47, 49, 75–7, 82–5, 89–90, 96–7, 100, 126, 142–3, 145, 157, 161, 166*n*14
Klingon Empire 85–7, 94, 103–4, 115–6, 124, 135–6, 143, 170*n*23
Klingon-Federation War 104, 123, 145
Klingon High Council 85–86, 103, 148, 170*n*23
Klingons 50, 65–6, 74, 85–7, 92–8, 100–4, 112, 114–9, 123–5, 135–6, 143–50, 161–2, 165*n*2, 169*n*9, 170*n*19, 170*n*20, 170*n*22, 170*n*23, 171*n*35, 172*n*37, 173*n*3, 173*n*7
Kurtzman, Alex 6, 143

LaForge, Geordi 54–5, 76, 91, 131, 134, 173*n*21
"The Last Outpost" (*TNG* episode) 170*n*17
latinum, gold-pressed 77
"Learning Curve" (*Voyager* episode) 69–70
"Lethe" (*DIS* episode) 148
"Life Line" (*Voyager* episode) 166*n*17, 171*n*24
"Little Green Men" (*DS9* episode) 170*n*17
Locutus (Borg) 133, 135–136
Lore 51–2, 134, 151
"Lower Decks" (*TNG* episode) 61, 68–9, 107

Maddox, Bruce 51, 153–5
main engineering 60, 127, 173*n*15
"A Man Alone" (*DS9* episode) 65–66
"Manhunt" (*TNG* episode) 95
"Maps and Legends" (*PIC* episode) 154–5
Maquis 69–70, 78, 81, 84, 108, 110–2, 116, 119–20, 149, 162–3, 171*n*30, 171*n*35, 172*n*38
"The Maquis" (*DS9* episode) 81, 110, 112
"The Masterpiece Society" (*TNG* episode) 85, 91
"The Measure of a Man" (*TNG* episode) 2, 51, 76–7, 153–4, 166*n*18
"Message in a Bottle" (*Voyager* episode) 120, 171*n*33
"Minefield" (*ENT* episode) 93
"Mirror, Mirror" (*TOS* episode) 147
Mirror Universe 147–9, 173*n*6, 173*n*7

# Index

Moore, Ronald D. 102, 109, 119
More, Thomas 11–2, 14–26, 28, 35, 37–8, 67, 70–1, 73, 77, 87, 124, 160, 165n3

"The Naked Now" (*TNG* episode) 167n19
"Necessary Evil" (*DS9* episode) 109
"Nepenthe" (*PIC* episode) 174n17
neutral zone 96, 100–2
"The Neutral Zone" (*TNG* episode) 41, 100–1, 160, 163, 169n6
New Atlantis 12, 24–5, 28, 35–6, 39, 41, 67, 73, 160
new technology 7, 31, 33, 38–9, 41, 89–90, 151, 158–9
"No Small Parts" (*LD* episode) 174n17
"The Nth Degree" (*TNG* episode) 61

O'Brien, Miles 69, 129
"An Obol for Charon" (*DIS* episode) 150, 167n21
Obsidian Order 86–7, 114
Odo 88, 171n31
"The Omega Glory" (*TOS* episode) 76
"11001001" (*TNG* episode) 168n8
Orwell, George 29–30, 38, 48

"Paradise Lost" (*DS9* episode) 75, 115
"Parallax" (*Voyager* episode) 78
"Parallels" (*TNG* episode) 141–2
Paris, Tom 76, 129, 168n13, 169n22, 169n8
"Pathfinder" (*Voyager* episode) 122, 169n23, 171n24
"The Pegasus" (*TNG* episode) 78, 104, 171n25
"People of Earth" (*DIS* episode) 151
"Perpetual Infinity" (*DIS* episode) 144, 150
phaser 46, 48, 127
photon torpedo 46
Picard, Jean-Luc 1, 41–4, 46, 50–3, 55, 59, 61, 68, 70, 75–7, 79, 81–5, 91, 101–8, 111, 129–31, 133–4, 142, 152–6, 160, 162–3, 167n23, 169n20, 169n5, 169n6, 171n24, 172n8, 173n14, 173n17, 173n3, 174n15, 174n17
Pike, Christopher 6, 143, 150, 167n21
Piller, Michael 101–2, 109, 119
"Preemptive Strike" (*TNG* episode) 108
"Prey" (*Voyager* episode) 71
"The Price" (*TNG* episode) 76, 168n8
Prime Directive 81–5, 97, 110, 159, 169n10, 169n11
"A Private Little War" (*TOS* episode) 96–7, 161
"Profit and Lace" (*DS9* episode) 88
"Profit and Loss" (*DS9* episode) 171n34
"Project Daedalus" (*DIS* episode) 150
"Prophet Motive" (*DS9* episode) 88

Q (character) 127, 172n5
"Q Who" (*TNG* episode) 127–30, 172n4, 172n7
Qo'nos (planet) 85
Quark 65, 88, 170n17, 171n24

"Rapture" (*DS9* episode) 75
"The Raven" (*Voyager* episode) 172n4
"Redemption" (*TNG* episode) 103
"Regeneration" (*ENT* episode) 93, 142, 172n4, 173n16
"Remembrance" (*PIC* episode) 153–4
"Renaissance Man" (*Voyager* episode) 61
replicator 43, 47, 61–2, 65, 159, 167n24
"The Return of the Archons" (*TOS* episode) 47, 84, 126, 161
"Reunion" (*TNG* episode) 103
"Rightful Heir" (*TNG* episode) 85
Riker, William 68, 70, 142, 156, 172n7, 172n11, 174n17
Roddenberry, Gene 5, 41–2, 45–6, 58–9, 77, 95, 97, 99–102, 104, 112, 146, 161, 163, 165n2, 168n6, 172n37
Romulan Senate 86–7
Romulan Star Empire 86, 96, 100, 115–6, 124, 153–4
Romulans 50, 66, 74–5, 78, 85–7, 93–8, 100–4, 114–8, 124–5, 142, 151–5, 161–3, 170n19, 170n22, 170n23, 172n41
Romulus (planet) 79, 87, 104, 142–3
"Rules of Acquisition" (*DS9* episode) 88, 113

"Sacrifice of Angels" (*DS9* episode) 116
"Samaritan Snare" (*TNG* episode) 50, 131
"The Sanctuary" (*DIS* episode) 152
"Sanctuary" (*DS9* episode) 65
Sarek (character) 95, 144, 171n23
"Sarek" (*TNG* episode) 95, 171n23
Saru (character) 149
"Schisms" (*TNG* episode) 61
"Scorpion" (*Voyager* episode) 68, 120–1, 132, 134, 172n8, 172n9
"The Search" (*DS9* episode) 88, 114, 125, 172n43
"Second Skin" (*DS9* episode) 171n34
Section 31 78, 86, 143, 150, 162
Seven of Nine 68, 71, 121, 129, 132, 134–7, 155–6, 172n4, 172n8, 172n9, 173n20
shapeshifters *see* Changelings
Shelley, Mary 29, 31–2
"Si Vis Pacem, Para Bellum" (*DIS* episode) 147
sickbay 60, 62, 83
"The Siege" (*DS9* episode) 110
"Sins of the Father" (*TNG* episode) 103, 168n12
Sisko, Benjamin 75, 80, 110–2, 115–6, 129
Solow, Herbert F. 5, 41, 96, 166n5
Soviet Union 44, 96–9, 102, 104, 123, 171n25
"Space Seed" (*TOS* episode) 90, 143
spaceship 7, 34, 41–3, 45–6, 52, 55, 57–8, 62–4, 66–70, 72, 129, 146, 159–60, 166n4, 166n5, 167n3
Species 8472 121
Spock 82, 85, 89–90, 100, 104, 125–6, 132, 143–5, 150–1, 172n3, 173n1, 174n9, 174n11

## Index

spore drive  146–7, 173*n*4, 174*n*9
Stamets, Paul  146, 149, 152, 173*n*4
*Star Trek* (2009 film)  6, 141–2, 153
*Star Trek: First Contact*  6, 8–9, 44, 46, 75, 77, 93, 128–32, 142, 163, 167*n*20, 167*n*23, 168*n*4, 168*n*7, 173*n*15
*Star Trek: Generations*  6, 9, 52, 58, 129–30, 153, 168*n*4, 173*n*3
*Star Trek: Insurrection*  6, 9, 44–5, 61, 75, 79, 81, 83–4, 157, 162–3, 165*ch*2*n*3, 171*n*24, 173*n*11
*Star Trek: The Motion Picture*  5, 8, 174*n*10
*Star Trek: Nemesis*  6, 9, 79, 87, 141–2, 152–4, 172*n*41, 173*n*11
*Star Trek II: The Wrath of Khan*  5, 8, 91, 131–2, 143, 169*n*12, 174*n*14
*Star Trek III: The Search for Spock*  5, 8, 167*n*4
*Star Trek IV: The Voyage Home*  5, 8, 58, 75, 77
*Star Trek V: The Final Frontier*  5, 8
*Star Trek VI: The Undiscovered Country*  6, 9, 75, 79, 85, 92, 97, 168*n*12, 169*n*9, 170*n*20, 170*n*23
*Star Trek Beyond*  6, 143
*Star Trek Into Darkness*  6, 142–3, 169*n*12
"Stardust City Rag" (*PIC* episode)  155
Starfleet  7, 43, 45–6, 49–51, 58–62, 64–7, 68–70, 75–81, 84, 86, 93, 100–4, 106, 108–12, 114–20, 122–3, 126, 127, 138, 142–3, 146–51, 153–4, 162–3, 169*n*22, 169*n*7, 169*n*10, 171*n*30
Starfleet Academy  69, 78, 169*n*8
"Starship Mine" (*TNG* episode)  170*n*15
"State of Flux" (*Voyager* episode)  120
"Statistical Probabilities" (*DS9* episode)  170*n*14
"Strange Bedfellows" (*DS9* episode)  117–118
"Such Sweet Sorrow" (*DIS* episode)  150–1
"Survival Instinct" (*Voyager* episode)  134–5
"Suspicions" (*TNG* episode)  61
Suvin, Darko  30, 37
"The Sword of Kahless" (*DS9* episode)  112
"Symbiosis" (*TNG* episode)  81

"Take Me Out to the Holosuite" (*DS9* episode)  169*n*2
Tal Shiar  86–7, 114, 155
"Tapestry" (*TNG* episode)  169*n*20
"A Taste of Armageddon" (*TOS* episode)  48, 75
Taylor, Jeri  109, 119
"Tears of the Prophets" (*DS9* episode)  117
technology  7, 29–34, 36–9, 41–56, 58, 60–2, 81, 83, 87, 89–91, 103–4, 114, 117, 120–2, 128, 131–3, 135, 139, 146–7, 151–2, 154, 158–9, 161, 163, 165*n*7, 166*n*5, 166*n*7, 166*n*14, 167*n*24, 169*n*8, 169*n*11, 173*n*14, 174*n*12
Temporal Cold War  93
Ten Forward  60–2, 68, 70, 153
"Terra Prime" (*ENT* episode)  78, 94
Terran Empire  147, 173*n*7

terrorism  78, 81, 84, 92–4, 105, 107–9, 112, 123, 143, 149, 170*n*15
"That Hope Is You Part 1" (*DIS* episode)  151
"That Hope Is You Part 2" (*DIS* episode)  152
"These Are the Voyages…" (*ENT* episode)  74, 94, 171*n*25
"Through the Valley of Shadows" (DIS episode)  150
"A Time to Stand" (*DS9* episode)  116
"Tin Man" (*TNG* episode)  169*n*8
"Tinker, Tenor, Doctor, Spy" (*Voyager* episode)  81
"To the Death" (*DS9* episode)  88
Torres, B'Elanna  119, 129, 161, 168*n*13, 169*n*22
transporter  43–4, 47–9, 60–1, 146, 159, 166*n*5, 173*n*14
"Treachery, Faith and the Great River" (*DS9* episode)  88
Treaty of Organia  96
"Trials and Tribble-ations" (*DS9* episode)  96
"Tribunal" (*DS9* episode)  78, 87
Troi, Deanna  156, 161, 169*n*23, 171*n*24, 172*n*39, 172*n*11, 174*n*17
"The Trouble with Tribbles" (*TOS* episode)  96, 169*n*3
turbolift  60
Tuvok  70, 119, 125

"The Ultimate Computer" (*TOS* episode)  49, 151
"Unification" (*TNG* episode)  87, 104, 174*n*11
"Unimatrix Zero" (*Voyager* episode)  129, 136–8, 139
"United" (*ENT* episode)  94
United Earth  74, 76, 93–5, 151, 169*n*5
United Federation of Planets  7, 45–6, 48, 58, 62–4, 67–8, 74–87, 90–1, 93–8, 100–24, 126–7, 136, 139, 142–3, 145–9, 151–8, 161–4, 165*ch*1*n*3, 165*ch*1*n*4, 169*n*2, 169*n*9, 169*n*11, 170*n*20, 170*n*21, 170*n*23, 170*n*25, 171*n*30, 171*n*32, 171*n*35, 171*n*36, 171*n*37, 172*n*41, 172*n*4
United States of America  44–5, 76, 89, 94–6, 102, 106–7, 109, 112, 117, 119–20, 123, 149, 161, 165*n*8, 171*n*25, 171*n*28
"Unity" (*Voyager* episode)  129, 138–9
"Unnatural Selection" (*TNG* episode)  91
"Up the Long Ladder" (*TNG* episode)  50, 91, 169*n*5
Utopia (novel)  11–23, 27–8, 35, 37–9, 67, 71, 73, 77, 87, 124, 129, 158, 160, 165*ch*1*n*4

"Valiant" (*DS9* episode)  69, 168*n*19
"Vaulting Ambition" (*DIS* episode)  148
Verne, Jules  31, 33, 37–8, 44, 57
"The Void" (*Voyager* episode)  80, 122
Vorta  86, 88
USS *Voyager*  58, 62, 67–71, 79–80, 84, 119–22, 134–5, 136, 139, 166*n*17, 166*n*18, 167*n*22, 168*n*13, 169*n*23, 172*n*9, 174*n*14

# Index

Vulcan (planet)  74, 94–5, 104, 126, 142, 152
"The Vulcan Hello" (*DIS* episode)  145
Vulcans  46, 85, 87, 93–5, 100, 104, 112, 119, 125–6, 132, 144–5, 147, 151–2, 159, 162, 165*ch*1*n*2, 171*n*23

"The War Without, the War Within" (*DIS* episode)  148–9
warp drive  37, 43, 45–8, 81, 83, 90, 151–2, 158, 174*n*12
"The Way of the Warrior" (*DS9* episode)  115
"We'll Always Have Paris" (*TNG* episode)  168*n*8
Wells, H.G.  31–5, 38, 52, 74
"What You Leave Behind" (*DS9* episode)  118

"When the Bough Breaks" (*TNG* episode)  61
"Where No One Has Gone Before" (*TNG* episode)  74
"Who Watches the Watchers" (*TNG* episode)  45, 83
"Will You Take My Hand?" (*DIS* episode)  149
Worf  55, 58, 61, 92, 100–1, 103, 122, 135–6, 141, 170*n*20, 170*n*22, 173*n*11
wormhole  62, 109, 112–3, 115–6, 150–1, 168*n*14, 171*n*29
"The Wounded" (*TNG* episode)  87, 105

"Yesterday's Enterprise" (*TNG* episode)  168*n*4, 170*n*23

www.ingramcontent.com/pod-product-compliance
Lightning Source LLC
Chambersburg PA
CBHW032045300426
44117CB00009B/1192